Blood fr

RECONSIDERATIONS IN
SOUTHERN AFRICAN HISTORY

Richard Elphick and Jeffrey Butler, Editors

Blood from Your Children

The Colonial Origins
of Generational Conflict
in South Africa

Benedict Carton

University Press of Virginia

Charlottesville and London

The University Press of Virginia
© 2000 by the Rector and Visitors of the University of Virginia
All rights reserved
Printed in the United States of America
First published in 2000

The paper used in this publication meets the minimum requirements of the American
National Standard for Information Sciences—Permanence of Paper for Printed Library
Materials, ANSI Z39.48-1984.

Library of Congress Cataloging-in-Publication Data

Carton, Benedict.
    Blood from your children : the colonial origins of generational
conflict in South Africa / Benedict Carton.
        p.   cm. — (Reconsiderations in southern African history)
    Includes bibliographical references (p.) and index.
    ISBN 0-8139-1931-2 (alk. paper). —ISBN 0-8139-1932-0 (pbk. :
alk. paper)
    1. Zulu Rebellion, 1906. 2. Conflict of generations—South
Africa. I. Title. II. Series.
DT1921.C37 2000
968.04´9—dc21   99-33683
                                                                    CIP

To Sipho Mchunu and Felix Nzama, and in memory of my father, Norman Carton

Contents

Maps

Preface

Ten years ago I went to Africa for the first time to, among other places, northern Namibia and southern Angola. I volunteered to monitor the South African military withdrawal from a bush war, reporting political violence along the remote border region for the Namibian Council of Churches. The first all-race ballot supervised by the United Nations was six months ahead. It was the twilight of cold war rivalries and apartheid, the epochal forces that stirred my political awakening. I wanted to be where the struggle was unfolding.

I naively assumed that I could cope with the specter of bloodshed, and I drew strength from the local Africans who took me in. Few could speak English, so I communicated through my interpreter, who spoke Oshiwambo, the language of the area. Many had survived the terror inflicted by South African counterinsurgency units hunting members of the Southwest African People's Organization (SWAPO), the national independence movement of Namibia. What I heard changed my view of resistance and the toll it exacted on families, dividing revolutionary children from more quiescent parents and guerilla daughters from traditional fathers. Liberation demanded more than exorcising colonial oppression; it challenged fundamental loyalties that lay beneath ideology.

My initial stay in Natal and KwaZulu, South Africa, came after my stint as a violence monitor. There I witnessed a civil conflict among isiZulu-speaking Africans over how to combat white subjugation. Supporters of the Zulu nationalist organization, Inkatha, marked as their enemy the United Democratic Front (UDF), the antiapartheid vanguard active before the unbanning of the African National Congress (ANC) in 1990. Undercurrents of generational betrayal led to retaliatory attacks; "comrades," young UDF activists seeking a nonracial democratic future, repudiated Inkatha's call for political restraint, ethnic chauvinism, and the rule of elder Zulu patriarchs. This factionalism erupted into an internecine feuding that nearly derailed the 1994 elections and Nelson Mandela's triumph.

Still unable to reach Africans in their own language, I learned isiZulu during my graduate studies at Yale University and in extended stays in South Africa. While visiting Natal and rural KwaZulu in 1991, the name *Bhambatha* emerged repeatedly in intriguing contexts. Bhambatha was the chief noted for inciting the 1906 head tax rebellion against the British Natal Colony. Certain UDF "comrades" evoked Bhambatha as a hero of the last bold opposition to white rule before the surge inaugurated by the students' Soweto uprising in 1976. Some Inkatha defenders saw Bhambatha as a proto-nationalist who tried to restore Zulu luster but who had gone too far in provoking his unruly warriors and in defying the call of Zulu royalty to surrender. Older, apolitical Africans in the Thukela basin, the core area of the 1906 head tax revolt and the frontier between historic Natal and Zulu-land, presented still another perspective of the rebel leader. Bhambatha had harnessed the *impi yamakhanda,* the young men's "war of the heads" against patriarchal power. A durable strand joined these accounts: Bhambatha and the 1906 rebellion as a symbol of youths' attempts to confront domination and win greater autonomy.

Roughly two generations after the official demise of colonialism in Africa, we are still witnessing its fading legacy. The defiance of children fills part of the vacuum. Boy soldiers in the west and central regions of the continent now wage anarchic war, severing hands in Sierra Leone, immolating villagers in Angola, and enslaving neighbors in Sudan. Many unemployed youths in South Africa, once praised for sacrificing education to overturn apartheid, have become robbers and killers. Media reports depict such disaffected young people as careening in a world without kinship, prey to criminals who thrive on mayhem. Those characterizations fail to probe more deeply than the immediate past to uncover what compels Africa's young men and women to avenge their alienation. *Blood from Your Children* provides one historical explanation for this phenomenon.

A Zulu expression says we become wiser through our relationships with other people, and writing a book echoes the spirit of that sentiment.

I received generous support for my work from the following sources: The H. F. Guggenheim Foundation, Andrew W. Mellon Foundation, and Fulbright-Hays Fellowship. Funds obtained through Yale University include the John Addison Porter Prize, Arthur and Mary Wright Prize, and stipends from the Smith Richardson Foundation, MacArthur Foundation, John F. Enders Fellowship, and Orville H. Schell Jr. Center for International Human Rights.

I am indebted to a diverse community of isiZulu-speaking people. My language instructors at Yale University, Sandra Sanneh and Ziba Jiyane, taught me isiZulu grammar and speech; my hosts in the Thukela valley, Sipho Mchunu and Felix Nzama and their families, cajoled me into using their "ukuhlonipha" dialect and muffling my New York inflection. They also imparted customs and surrounded me with protective kin. The homesteads of Nxumalo, Cube, Gasa, Cele, and Chief Dhlomo, and others elsewhere in KwaZulu and Natal bestowed the gifts of their hospitality and historical memory.

Numerous scholars in South Africa were magnanimous with their time and expertise. The Department of Historical Studies at the University of Natal, Pietermaritzburg, was my host in 1992 and 1993. Robert Morrell, Bill Guest, John Laband, Iain Edwards, and Ruth Edgecombe encouraged me to ferret out the generational theme. Jeff Guy was a wellspring of Zulu history. Phil Bonner, Paul la Hausse, and Charles van Onselen offered timely and critical appraisals of my preliminary conclusions.

My research focused on primary evidence in South African archives. I thank the Director of the Natal Archives in Pietermaritzburg, Judith Hawley, and her staff for meeting every request. Nisha Gokool provided unwavering assistance, as did Patrick Dlamini, Pius Mabi, Sipho Sibisi, and Wilson Xaba. My appreciation also extends to archivists and librarians at these holdings: National Archives, Natal Museum, Natal Society Library, Killie Campbell Library, KwaMuhle Local History Museum, and William Cullen Library.

Several scholars helped shape the book in important ways. Series editors Jeffrey Butler and Richard Elphick shepherded me from youth to historian. John Wright, Bill Freund, Luise White, Thomas McClendon, and Dauril Alden exposed my inaccuracies and proposed alternative, finer analyses. Early on, Robert Harms, Leonard Thompson, Howard Lamar, Diana Wylie, and members of the Yale University Southern African Research Program provided invaluable direction. Richard Holway, editor of history and social sciences at the University Press of Virginia, and his colleagues granted essential support.

My editor, Jeannette Hopkins, gave me vision I thought I never had. She urged me to move beyond my distress as I cut up the old manuscript, literally with scissors, and reconfigured pieces into a more lucid whole. Together we found themes that took the new manuscript on a passage I could not have plotted alone. En route, Jeannette was mentor and taskmaster, insisting that I allow historical actors to speak for themselves.

Various readers, but especially Jane Curran, my copyeditor, Wynne Cougill, Andrew Davis, and Robert Hodgins, untangled complicated phrases and quickened sluggish prose. Virginia Reynolds, Holly Ennis, and Christian Heltne drew the maps. Cara Pretorius put together a superb index.

I have relished my sojourns in South Africa because they have bound me closer to people devoted to the culture and history of their country. I acknowledge only some here: Fiona Rankin-Smith and Angus Gibson, Robert Hodgins and Jan Neethling, Steve Kotze, Gavin Whitelaw and Jan Sprackett, Clive van den Berg, the families Govindasamy, Maggs, Kentridge, Shongwe, Bavuma, Strauss, Findlay, and Brouckaert. The dedication of family and friends in America sustained my enthusiasm during this long process. I expressly thank my mother, Betsy, and brother, Jake; also Rob Snyder and Louisa Hall, Wilhelm Joseph, Patrick and Jo Heller, Julie Horowitz, George Gollub, Viv Walt, Tony Marx, Eric Allina, Dodie McDow, Rukhsana Siddiqui, Patri Collins, Peter Alegi, and Branly Cadet. My colleagues at George Mason University in the Departments of History and Art History, and in African American Studies, provided crucial support in the book's last stage. I am particularly grateful to the following: Jack and Jane Censer, Jeffrey Stewart, Gilbert Morris, Susie Smith, Larry Levine, Roy Rosenzweig, Greg Brown, Jeff Horn, Brian Platt, Tobie Meyer-Fong, Marion Deshmukh, Steve Diner, Phyllis Slade-Martin, Rex Wade, and Rosie Zagarri. The spirit of my grandfather Isaac Davis Hall and of the human rights pioneer Marshall Perlin, men who told me history with integrity is the best story, hovered over the final manuscript. My wife, Louise Marie Vis, did far more than endure the monopolizing effects of the book. She contributed forceful insights, along with her love.

Note on Orthography and Translation

MANY OF THE SAME terms and names are spelled differently in this book. I use recent orthography for most Afrikaans and isiZulu words. When quoting sources (with antiquated orthography), I did not change original text. For example, I write Bhambatha, *ukulobola,* Thukela, Nquthu, Nkandla, and Kranskop; these words often appear in colonial records as Bambata, lobola, Tugela, Nqutu, Nkandhla, and Krantzkop.

The parentheses within quotations are part of the primary text. I use square brackets when editing or translating cited evidence.

Blood from Your Children

Introduction

BLOOD FROM YOUR CHILDREN is a tale of betrayal and revenge, of the diminishing authority of elders and the surging power of youths, in an isiZulu-speaking African society. In late-nineteenth-century South Africa, rivalries between African and colonial patriarchal systems kindled conflicts between African elders and youths and between older African husbands and their young wives. This book explores the ensuing generational strife as it intensified during thirty years of encroaching colonialism up to 1910, when four British colonies of southern Africa joined under white rule to form the Union of South Africa.[1]

From 1843 to 1879 the rugged landscape of thorns, ridges, and forests in the lower and middle Thukela basin—the region of this study—served as a frontier zone between two patriarchal political powers, the Zulu kingdom to the north and the British colonial possession, Natal, to the south. The Thukela River was an official boundary between Natal and Zululand, but Africans saw the river as a fictive and porous border, one readily forded for purposes of farming, herding, and trading. During the final decade of the nineteenth century, the white Natal government extended a minimal administration over the Zulu kingdom, which British imperial forces had conquered in 1879. Only a scattering of colonial courts and plots owned by missionary orders and white settlers dotted the divisions, or districts, of the lower and middle Thukela basin. In the rest of Natal to the south, clusters of British immigrants had carved out vast holdings, and government magistrates exerted tighter jurisdiction over African affairs (map 1).[2]

At the turn of the twentieth century, as environmental disasters were crippling agricultural production, Natal colonists compelled Africans to give up more and more land, labor, and taxes. Slipping farther into poverty, the great majority of African subsistence producers, *amabhinca,* strained to uphold homestead practices like polygyny, through which a husband supported multiple wives. Even the rare commercially successful farmers of the small African Christian community, *amakholwa,* saw their progress slowed. The wages young African men earned as migrant workers on South Africa's commercial farms and mines enabled their families to buy supplies for only the barest existence.

Colony of Natal 1905
Magisterial Divisions
Natal (Proper) and Zululand

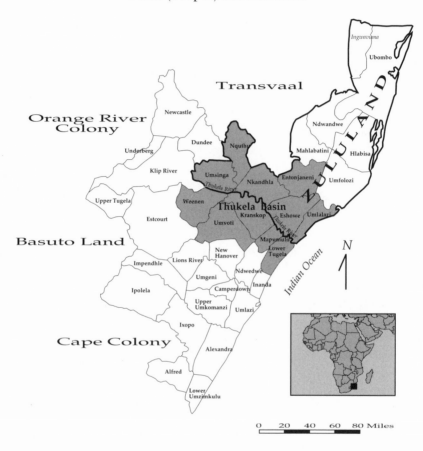

In 1905 the Natal legislature passed a poll tax effective the next year on unmarried men eighteen years and older; the law applied equally to whites, Asians—most of them from India—and Africans. Those liable for the poll tax were part of the first generation of African youths to come of age with expanding access to wage employment, redress of grievances in colonial courts, and refuge in Christian missions. When summoned in early 1906 to pay the tax, many young African men vehemently refused. In the lower and middle Thukela basin, poll tax disturbances ignited a revolt that smol-dered fitfully until 1908. These rebels fought to protect gains earned while straddling two worlds, the African homestead and settler society. African sons confronted both a Natal government that took their wealth and their own male elders, many of whom detested white rule yet appeared to acquiesce in its creeping disruption of family life.

White settlers named that insurrection "Bhambatha's rebellion," after the chief who was said to have sparked it. To many rebels, however, the outbreak was instead the "war of the heads," *impi yamakhanda,* an expression of their rage against the poll or "head" tax and the prevailing exemplars of patriarchy, for it was upon the heads of the unmarried young men, not the fathers who urged compliance with the new law, that the colonial government had imposed this latest onerous responsibility. *Blood from Your Children* tells the story of the "war of the heads," using it as a lens through which to view a dimension of social change largely overlooked in African historiography: the generational and related gender struggles that reconfigured domestic power relationships.[3]

Homestead crises were not new in a society where a small number of homestead heads shielded their power from rivals, but the mounting family turmoil in the decade before 1906 exposed patriarchs' inability to contain assertive young men and women. Although scholars have emphasized the rigid control of African wives and youths within precolonial society and their subordination under white rule, this book focuses on the competition between African and colonial patriarchies that both narrowed and broadened life prospects for young Africans.[4]

One feud between a father and son from the Mondisa clan displays the shifting power relationships between African generations. The setting was a chief's residence in Nkandla, a magisterial division in the middle Thukela basin. The dispute pitted a young man, Gudhla, against his father, Chief Matshana kaMondisa, a polygynous homestead head, *umnumzane.* Matshana was both the custodian of his own kinship network of wives, children, and relations and the political ruler of the Sithole chiefdom, a territory of homesteads. On the eve of the "war of the heads" in 1905, father and son argued their differences before a white colonial magistrate. Gudhla said that adversity had spoiled his relationship with his father; he had been desperate to find food for his mother during a decade when the rains were scarce and the earth brittle, and when crops were consumed every second year by locusts. The harsh droughts and the worst insect infestation in living memory had propelled him to leave his family to toil for white settlers. His wages bought provisions and livestock that helped replenish his homestead herd after the virulent rinderpest epidemic of 1896 and 1897 ravaged cattle across southern Africa. With his savings, Gudhla paid the tax on his mother's hut. But in his father Matshana's eyes, Gudhla was wantonly disrespectful in calling the neighboring male elders *abafokazana,* "persons of no account" or "weaklings."[5]

Gudhla was walking a dangerous line by flaunting his freedom to acquire and be recognized for his own wealth and breaching a code of generational deference. Older people were typically seen as possessing wisdom or other special attributes, and youths like Gudhla who disgraced their elders could incur the scorn of public criticism and the fury of ancestral spirits as well.[6] Patriarchs could try to curb willful behavior by invoking divine retribution; they mediated between the temporal and spiritual worlds, communing with departed ancestors on behalf of the living.

Matshana rebuked his son, but to no avail, and in 1905 he informed the Nkandla magistrate that Gudhla deserved to be disowned. Matshana, "too old" to travel to the colonial magistrate, sent messengers to the courthouse to plead that the complaint be adjudicated in his own homestead. Since Matshana was known for his loyalty to the colonial government, the magistrate acceded to his request; at the chief's residence about one hundred people gathered to hear the case, among them Matshana's nearly twenty advisers, fifty followers, and his family members.

Matshana spoke first to "the Government's Magistrate . . . so that [he could not] be disputed afterwards"; then he addressed his son: "Your mother was never placed in any position in my kraal [homestead], you only hold the rank of any of my ordinary sons, and even if you had behaved yourself, you would have not been entitled to consideration." He charged that Gudhla had "dared to interfere with my daughters [by] incit[ing] them to run away to the Mission Station" in an effort "to thwart and upset my arrangements for the marriage of my daughters, and ma[k]e them treat me with contempt."[7] The runaway daughters meant a loss of labor and *ukulobola,* the bridewealth cattle the young women would bring into Matshana's homestead at their marriage.[8]

Matshana's position and identity, symbolized by his revered headring, had been called into question by his son Gudhla's recalcitrance. The headring was a token of Matshana's status as *ikhehla,* a member of a broad group of male elders, *amadoda,* who were obliged to promote the well-being of their homestead. Gudhla's behavior, his father said, had poisoned the Mondisa homestead and threatened to disturb his followers in the Sithole chiefdom. If a chief could not govern his own family, how could he command his followers?

Gudhla replied that he was no errant child. Indeed, he blamed his father for neglecting the reciprocal obligations that justified the obedience of young men and women to their elders. When Gudhla had wed for the first time he had not relied on his father, as had been customary, to sponsor his marriage. Instead, with his own wages he had purchased his bridewealth cattle to offer to his new wife's homestead. His father weakened his own authority, Gudhla implied, by failing to procure enough food or collect enough hut tax money for the entire homestead. As for the flight of his sisters, Gudhla would accept no blame. In the face of patriarchal reproach, Gudhla flashed the unruly temperament of the *abasha,* the "younger generation [who said] old people gave into white people."[9] Since the late 1890s the *abasha* had increasingly inspired gang fights, raucous beer parties, and worse—so went the protests of fathers—blatant sexual escapades.

Matshana urged a halt to the hearing: "It is useless to talk on this subject any more." The Nkandla magistrate agreed and approved Matshana's request to exile his son.[10] Colonial officials, as expected, had sanctioned the rule of male elders. The chief's legal victory turned out to be illusory; within a year, Matshana "was obliged to sleep in hiding away from his kraal," fearful of losing his own life since young men from the emerging anti–poll tax movement prowled the bush around his homestead. He felt especially vulnerable because no fewer than five of his sons had joined the rebel bands raiding the homesteads of *amambuka,* those African patriarchs perceived as traitors for their loyalty to the colonial government.[11]

The Gudhla-Matshana schism defines the nucleus of *Blood from Your Children.* This book begins by outlining the climactic processes from the late 1700s to mid-1800s that transformed African political patriarchy in and around the Thukela basin. Drawing on the comparatively abundant primary documents generated during white rule, this narrative then concentrates on the late-nineteenth-century collisions between African and colonial patriarchal systems and their ripple effects on homestead power relationships. By the 1905 court case escalating African generational conflict had led to the episode in which a son's defiance enmeshed the women of his father's homestead, who were also seeking security and greater autonomy. Pulled into the judicial fray were Gudhla's mother, whom he said he supported financially; his wife, whom he boasted he had married without requiring his father's bridewealth cattle; and his runaway sisters, who had escaped on the eve of their arranged marriages, undeterred by fear of their father's wrath. Sons and daughters, children and parents, husbands and wives, vied—or cooperated—with one another in pursuit of power.

Bonds between generations shaped gender relations and vice versa; colonial intervention further tangled these familial alliances. The mutually reinforcing relationships of generation and gender effectively maintained patriarchal authority but also weakened it. White officials like the Nkandla magistrate had a stake in checking domestic unrest and, where possible, bolstered African patriarchs who were responsible for raising homestead taxes and for mustering youths to labor for colonists.

Roughly three decades ago, scholars began to interpret evidence of such local turbulences as a sign of gathering opposition to European subjugation, harbingers of a clash between Africans wedded to precapitalist relations and colonists bent on imposing capitalist relations by military conquest, taxation, and wage labor. Contemporary historians like William Beinart, Colin Bundy, and Jeff Peires demythologized notions of steady and united African resistance. Their work showed that indigenous societies in the eastern Cape coped with colonialism by alternating between forms of accommodation and confrontation.[12] As for Bhambatha's rebellion, it has been portrayed as the culminating battle between Africans protecting their imperiled traditions and white settlers attempting to turn African labor into a commodity, a process some scholars call "proletarianization."

To Shula Marks in her landmark 1970 book, *Reluctant Rebellion,* the origins of the 1906 revolt can be traced to the excessive colonial demands for land, labor, and taxes from homesteads and to magistrates' encroachment on African authority. In a 1986 essay, "Class, Ideology and the Bambatha Rebellion," Marks modified her earlier findings to demonstrate that poll tax insurgents also evoked martial symbols of the Zulu kingdom to galvanize popular support for restoring a historical rampart against the trespasses of capitalism. Persistent white settler aggression, she writes, inspired Africans' subversive "consciousness" but also doomed the 1906 outbreak. A populace staggered by colonial meddling—thus, irresolute about joining an imminent confrontation—failed to heed Bhambatha's cry for a sweeping revolt.[13]

John Lambert, in *Betrayed Trust,* reexamines the late-nineteenth-century colonial incursions that undermined both the homestead economy and the authority of chiefs and homestead heads. He pinpoints "the processes of alienation, impoverishment, and proletarianization" as inciting Bhambatha's uprising. Like Marks, Lambert concentrates on hostile encounters between Africans and whites over the control of production and labor, and the accumulation and distribution of resources.[14] These intricate analyses of the political economy of colonial Natal, however, do not venture extensively into homestead entanglements. *Blood from Your Children* seeks to understand the dynamics of family life in an African society stumbling into the "war of the heads" and counters the scholarly perspective that poll tax rebels had disavowed proletarianization for the glory of rehabilitating the Zulu kingdom. My narrative shows that young men in the lower and middle Thukela basin revolted to defend progressive strategies for their own social advancement. For many rebels, this meant embracing, not renouncing, proletarianization.

Some scholars now raise critical questions about the extent to which capitalism upset the so-called balance of African societies. They urge caution in using sources—like the early-twentieth-century anthropological studies of southern Africa on which Marks herself relied in *Reluctant Rebellion*—that portray timeless traditional customs on the eve of colonial invasion. Current academic cautions cite the "faulty" methodology of early anthropologists such as A. T. Bryant, who compressed "Zulu" culture, temporally and spatially, into a static tableau of untroubled patriarchy.[15]

Displacing outdated ethnographic standards are more theoretical works of anthropology, such as those of Claude Meillassoux, who in the late 1970s and early 1980s outlined a precapitalist African household structured by gender and generational divisions. Meillassoux's archetype of gerontocracy centered on a group of ruling male elders who benefited from the labor of youths and wives—juniors—and who regulated the fertility of women by delaying the marriage of young men. Historians John Wright and Jeff Guy integrated Meillassoux's methodology into their own analyses of homestead relations within the Zulu kingdom, demonstrating that homestead heads formed a local elite with powers to regulate bridewealth exchanges and extract labor from women and youths. By contrast, the anthropological research of W. D. Hammond-Tooke highlighted the capacity of homestead juniors to acquire resources by laboring for various African patriarchs who did not always act in concert.[16] Although Meillassoux's model reduces women and youths to ancillary agents of social change, his ideas stimulated other scholars to consider why homestead juniors themselves conformed to patriarchal expectations.

Since the mid-1980s historical accounts of rural family life in southern Africa have emphasized changing gender status and roles. In 1993 Elizabeth Eldredge, for example, questioned the monolithic nature of African patriarchy. She asserted that women's social position in relation to men's cannot be understood simply as gender inequality since the pursuit of family security was the principal consideration of African wives and mothers. Nevertheless, the pivotal conceptual category in any analysis of women and patriarchy—that is, generation—has been underresearched. Although some studies, like that of William Beinart's on migrant youth subculture in the eastern Cape and Peter Delius's on youth politics in the northern Transvaal, had delineated a generational dimension, only now are historians accenting this neglected concept. Thomas McClendon, for example, is documenting a plethora of antagonisms between African elders and youths in twentieth-century Natal courts.[17]

For the first half of the twentieth century, two eyewitness accounts written by white participants in the 1906 revolt provided the basic story line of Bhambatha's rebellion. Both describe plucky colonial soldiers marching into rebel country and routing hordes of African warriors. The first account was Captain W. Bosman's 1907 book, *The Natal Rebellion of 1906*. The second, *A History of the Zulu Rebellion,* written six years later by James Stuart, a colonial official fluent in isiZulu, was far more nuanced. Stuart was sympathetic to African patriarchs who protested the Natal Colony's failure to bolster homestead elders' dwindling status. He solicited many views not only from African chiefs but also from captured poll tax rebels.[18]

   Blood from Your Children relies on the ethnography I constructed from the archival materials of the late nineteenth and early twentieth centuries and from the contemporary testimony of isiZulu-speaking Africans. Crucial among the primary sources is the correspondence of the Natal government, especially that of officials of the Department of Native Affairs who became alarmed at the challenges from young Africans. Emergency telegrams, for example, reveal in flashes, as other sources rarely show, recurring violence in outlying districts. Records demonstrate that magistrates, stung by the realization that so much disorder was occurring on their watch, consulted with homestead patriarchs for suggestions of reform. These historical documents are, of course, encumbered by bias, particularly by the tendency of colonial transcribers to mute the voices of Africans themselves. In keeping with native customary law, homestead women and children were treated as wards of the male guardians who spoke for them.

   However, the African perspectives that survive on paper, including rare statements of women and youths, provide far more evidence of power relationships than the accounts of anthropologists who described indigenous society as an unchanging relic in the modern world. In the magisterial divisions abutting the Thukela River, colonial officials noted homestead disputes involving bridewealth cattle, succession, and vendettas. These reports relied on local information gathered by local Africans and communicated in some version of isiZulu and English.

The pool of evidence can be significantly enlarged, too, by reports in newspapers, by photographic images of homestead life and of events during the "war of the heads," and by accounts in missionary letters and private papers of colonists concerned with "native affairs." In testimony before periodic native affairs commissions of the Natal government, African fathers, dismayed by the erosion of respect for rank and age, recall a rosy past in which their status was secure; their lamentations tend to confirm a suspicion among colonial officials that "tribal" supports were crumbling as youths' disrespect grew. The most illustrative such material is the legal record of Thukela basin divisions, where, from the 1880s to the 1890s, magistrates and isiZulu-speaking court interpreters detailed accounts of simmering discord within homesteads and chiefdoms. This documentation is replete with spousal statements from divorce proceedings, rulings from "faction fights," and judgments from cases dealing with violations of sexual mores that African patriarchs claimed were once widely honored. Another source that vividly reflects the intensifying generational struggles is the docket of treason trials, in which elders testifying for the Crown prosecution revealed how their unruly sons inflamed the poll tax protests.[19]

The ethnography in *The James Stuart Archive,* a four-volume set of interviews with African men in the late nineteenth and early twentieth centuries, offers more than a thousand pages of testimony on varying interpretations of the customs, rituals, and regional history of Natal and Zululand. Stuart sought out Zulu sages as informants and meticulously inscribed their responses in isiZulu and in English. His career in the Natal colonial administration, as a magistrate and, in 1909, as the assistant secretary for native affairs, did not keep him from venting criticisms of white rule.[20] Further ethnographic data are available on audiotapes and in typed transcripts from an oral history project by university students who two decades ago interviewed aged Africans about their memories of life at the time of the 1906 revolt.

The field interviews I myself conducted, between 1990 and 1997 during extended stays in the lower and middle Thukela basin and elsewhere in Natal and KwaZulu, demonstrated continuities of past cultural expressions of homestead authority. The persons with whom I spoke were almost all commoners I selected because of their (and their forebears') long residence in a particular magisterial division. Their oral testimony brought archival records to life in subtle and substantial ways.

The Natal government itself had restricted African testimony in the late 1800s and early 1900s to declarations of elder men, and in writing down their responses, colonial officials probably paraphrased and distorted what was actually said. In researching *Blood from Your Children,* I have had to rely, nonetheless, on such documentation published by whites for accounts of homestead relationships. African patriarchs, shorn of their privileges, were often deliberately circumspect when speaking before whites; at native affairs commissions, most African witnesses, virtually all men of senior rank, answered questions with a variety of respectful, abbreviated, and evasive responses. Fear of punishment for expressing criticism doubtless outweighed candor about the troubles they encountered in trying to balance colonial demands against obligations to their youths and women. Moreover, Africans appearing in courts had to give testimony in an adversarial atmosphere, where, as defendants, they were required to abide by European judicial procedures. Thus, court appearances were formal and intimidating occasions for Africans unaccustomed to meeting colonial officials and lacking fluency in English.

Yet not all Africans called to an official public assembly were intimidated into concealing the wrongs committed against them. Elders who aired grievances spoke wistfully of a gilded age when youths and young wives were deferential. Their accounts, peppered with accusations against white settlers and unruly juniors alike, focused on an array of hostile forces. They complained of juniors' increased mobility as well as of environmental disasters that, when combined with colonial exactions, imposed a pernicious pattern of hardship.

Such glimpses of African domestic life in written documents, photographs, and recorded oral testimony capture the vitality in homestead power relationships. When these threads of history are woven into the analytical fabric of competing patriarchy, the resulting narrative can approximate a forceful, if not definitive, story of rising generational turmoil. *Blood from Your Children* explores how Africans' personal frailties, strengths, and jealousies turned allegiances, rooted in blood and obligation, into bitter rivalries that threw a society into fundamental social change.

CHAPTER ONE

Competing African and Colonial Political Patriarchies

The Thukela Setting

IN ISIZULU THE WORD *uThukela* means the "river that flows with alarming suddenness." The Thukela starts as no more than a brook in the Drakensberg range one hundred miles west of the Indian Ocean. As its waters drop from the mountains, tributaries join the flow and quicken its currents. A strong channel forms in the Drakensberg foothills, becomes a sprawling basin, and coils along the valley floor to the sea. Steady downpours swell the Thukela into a muddy torrent that can swiftly inundate lowlands and drown people and livestock. But floods are infrequent because rain is rare, except in a thin strip of undulating subtropical shoreline, where year-round humid air maintains lush vegetation and enriches the fertile soil.[1]

Away from the coast, tropical foliage gives way to a brown mottle. Thirty miles inland the elevation rises to two thousand feet, and on a clear day the Indian Ocean appears as a black arcing sliver on the eastern horizon. Higher elevations capture moisture from rising winds that turn the climate temperate. Woods and thicket, clustering in the damp hollows, create a shadowy background for spellbinding folklore about "short, luminous figures," *imikhovu,* who haunted the tangles, and with "feet and hands . . . no bigger than those of children" bellowed "as if their tongues had been cut out."[2]

In the interior basin lowlands close to the Thukela banks, the environment is hot and brittle most of the year. Thorn trees cast shade, yet the sharp needles jutting from their limbs can easily puncture the flesh of those who seek relief from the sun. From October to February, the spring and summer months, rare cloudbursts break the heat but also pelt the baked earth, with the runoff from storms creating deep gullies. Scrub roots grip the thin topsoil, drinking up minerals and depriving other flora of nutrients. Knolls provide some arable ground, but by the late nineteenth century poor fertility had limited the cycle for sowing corn and sorghum to once a year. Few other plants thrive in "Thorn Country"; one of them, sweetveldt, is a nutritious grass favored by grazing livestock during the dry winter.[3]

Africans in the lower and middle Thukela basin seemed to prefer any other available climate to arid "Thorn Country." In the late nineteenth century, colonial officials estimated that seventy thousand Africans lived in the wetter shoreline divisions of northern Natal, Lower Tugela and Mapumulo, and another forty thousand resided just across the border in Zululand's Eshowe and Umlalazi divisions. By contrast, the sparse data on hinterland Africans suggest a population density of forty per square mile, about half the density of divisions along the coast. Census numbers for Africans in the middle basin are so indefinite that we have no accurate estimate of the total hinterland population.[4]

The far more precise census figures for the sparse white population indicate that in the 1880s twice as many whites lived inland as at the shore. During this decade, the Afrikaner and British settlers in the middle Thukela basin began steadily appropriating land from Africans. Most of the whites bred livestock and cultivated gardens, occasionally producing surplus staples for sale at local markets. The settlers who raised sheep and cattle preferred labor tenancy on their farms. They also rented productive land and residential sites to African patriarchs and their families in exchange for the periodic service of their sons. White absentee landlords frequently leased tracts to homestead heads, who paid their fees by selling part of their grain harvest.[5]

Two thousand or so colonists settled in the tropical belt near the mouth of the Thukela River, where the climate was favorable for growing sugar. A few white sugar planters in the Natal Colony's Lower Tugela division may have dreamed of expanding their holdings into grand plantations, but they had neither the experience nor the capital to do so; instead they supplemented their incomes by renting plots to African tenant farmers. White Christian missionaries also maintained three stations along the coast, two established by the American Board Missions of Massachusetts and one by Norwegians, who together supported several hundred Christian Africans known as the *amakholwa,* the "believers."[6]

African Homestead Life

Colonial-period photographs and official records show that from the 1880s onward, thousands of African homesteads or *imizi* dotted the plains, plateaus, and ridges along the Thukela River. Within each homestead compound, Africans generally lived in thatch, wood, and mud huts around a central cattle enclosure. Each hut, or *indlu,* usually sheltered a wife and her children, a household within a homestead of hut households. Some homestead heads—known singly as *umnumzana* and in colonial records referred to as the "kraal head"—had an *indlu* of their own, and sometimes their adolescent sons had their own group *indlu.* Wealthier patriarchs with more spouses and more children tended to have the largest compounds. Colonial officials in the late nineteenth century offhandedly assessed the size of a homestead as averaging between seven and twelve people, but such numerical estimates were misleading. Homestead composition fluctuated, for example, as daughters married into other homesteads, sons took wives while still living with their own patriarch, youths departed from home to work for white settlers, and disputes, some requiring colonial mediation, split families.[7]

Thus, a patriarch achieved prominence in a hierarchical domestic setting where familial relationships changed many times within an individual's lifetime. Senior authority ebbed and flowed as youths climbed in generational standing, gradually as they matured, or abruptly through marriage or colonial favor. Men appointed and paid by the Natal government to report African transgressions to magistrates enjoyed benefits of elder status, a path to upward social mobility for young men of humble means.

A homestead's social core evolved gradually, with a patriarch and his married brothers, if they lived with him, likely exercising authority over wives and youths for a prolonged period of time. A homestead's social periphery, in contrast to the nucleus, was far more dynamic and reflected a wider array of identities, including young male and female siblings, female and male cousins, aunts and uncles, and unrelated dependents such as herd boys from poorer homesteads who offered their services to patriarchs rich in cattle. Recent brides and husbands with only one wife were usually considered neither youths nor elders but were on the top rung of junior status. As youths rose in status, only a limited number of males made the leap to homestead head, and only a few females rose to first or chief wife. With the prospect that seniority was beyond the reach of many Africans, domestic relationships could be strained, particularly when certain junior males and females were first to reach a loftier standing.

Brothers and sisters within a polygynous homestead conformed to their own hierarchy of authority and privileges, in which the allocation of work and food was based largely on age. The ranking young man and the homestead head's designated heir, the *inkosana,* was ordinarily the oldest son, a youth who might have been no more than a week older than brothers from his father's other wives; he would probably direct his male siblings' daily tasks and claim the choice portions of a slaughtered goat or cow. The heir could also draw on the labor of unmarried females within his homestead, who had their own pecking order comparable to that of the unmarried males.[8] With sons and daughters so close in age, cooperation among siblings could flare into overt competition and aggravate social tensions. As wage laborers and Christians, youths acquired knowledge that also emboldened them at home to violate codes of generational respect. Outside this domestic world were larger, fluid political entities ruled by chiefs who exerted continual pressure on relationships within and between homesteads.

Marshaling Youths to Serve Patriarchy

A century before, in the late 1700s, African homesteads in the middle and lower Thukela basin had endured the dislocating effects of rivalries among African chiefs—the region's political "fathers"—who sought to extend their rule by forcibly incorporating vulnerable neighbors. With scant primary sources, scholars can only surmise that these conflicts intensified as several ascending African political patriarchies, known as "paramountcies," competed for control of the labor and material birthright of homestead youths. Historians disagree over the precipitating causes of the ensuing wars between militarized paramountcies, one of which was an emerging Zulu chiefdom.

At the end of the eighteenth century, powerful chiefs in the Thukela basin and elsewhere in southeast Africa appeared to spark a process of political centralization, enlisting homestead heads to band their sons into common labor and fighting corps to serve the needs of a cluster of homesteads within a larger territory, known as a chiefdom. The broad consensus among historians is that after European traders established Delagoa Bay as an Indian Ocean ivory trading post in the mid-1700s, chiefs deployed youth groups to hunt elephants and haul tusks from the hinterland to the coast. For some maturing boys, the search for ivory developed into a crucial phase in the achievement of manhood.[9]

Certain oral traditions suggest that cattle became a valuable trading commodity, if not more lucrative than ivory, because by the turn of the nineteenth century hunters had killed off so many elephants. The most dominant political patriarchs—the paramount chiefs—then converted youth hunting bands into armed regiments, or *amabutho,* to subdue rivals and to seize their livestock and pastures. It is likely that single young men had to procure cattle and other valuable articles from their homestead heads to advance in social standing. As the chiefdoms weakened filial obligations, plundered livestock was another source of wealth for unmarried male soldiers. With a growing trade in cattle and with armed campaigns capturing more and more herds, livestock supplanted other kinds of bridewealth as the chosen offering of *ukulobola*.[10]

The *amabutho* system provided another path for young men to gain in rank as husbands and a means to create their own homesteads, thus undermining the capacity of African patriarchs to keep adult sons laboring for their elders. The paramount chiefs who dispatched their *amabutho* on raids threatened those patriarchs who sought only to preserve their sovereignty. Rather than confront the stronger invaders, some defensive chiefs moved their followers southward from long-held territories just north of the Thukela River to lands flanking the river, turning the basin into an area of flight and instability.[11]

Historians are tentative in their explanations of how chiefs who marshaled young male fighters evolved into regional power brokers and stoked upheavals known as the *mfecane,* the violent "crushing" or "scattering" of southern African people. Until recently, the fabled Shaka, the leader of a marginal chiefdom who rose to prominence through combat and diplomacy, has been depicted both as the catalyst of the *mfecane* and the despotic founder of a martial nineteenth-century Zulu empire.[12] In fact, the assertion that his warriors annihilated or dispersed the inhabitants of Natal on the eve of colonial settlement was long used by whites professing to save South Africa from tribal anarchy. As apartheid was collapsing in the 1980s, scholars began to reconsider Shaka's legacy. Harrowing details of the *mfecane* have been traced to dubious sources, tales of early-nineteenth-century white traders and missionaries who demonized the Zulu (primarily after Shaka's reign) to boost their own wealth or prestige, or both.[13] Although a few past authors have portrayed Shaka more subtly, alternatively as menacing and magnanimous, bullying his adversaries into submission and cajoling remnants of chiefdoms to enter his fold, even this small minority of writers seldom raised, much less answered, an essential question: Why would an ambitious chief eliminate his enemies' followers if political dominance hinged on a leader's capacity to harness the allegiance, labor, and tribute of ever greater numbers of loyal supporters?

Neither Shaka's prowess nor Zulu activities alone illuminate the complex-

ity of the *mfecane*. Instead, a far-reaching scholarly reexamination is underway to explore the tangle of political alliances, widespread commercial links,
and regional antagonisms of other paramount African chiefs and their subjects. Historians of frontier societies on the periphery of Shaka's influence
have challenged the concept of Zulu belligerence by asserting that Europeans hunting for elephant tusks, hides, and slaves and the expanding Cape
settlement forced African chiefs and their followers to flee their territories.
Shaka's so-called merciless tactics could have been the defensive maneuvers
of a political patriarch who saw his influence endangered by livestock raiders,
land-hungry competitors, and rival chiefs.[14]

Such new considerations have shifted the *mfecane* debate, once primarily
centered on two historical explanations. The first speculated that the Zulu
chiefdom assumed power when the population in southeast Africa, before
Shaka's ascendance, reached a critical density, with resultant territorial conflicts between chiefdoms. The second postulated that drought and destructive agricultural practices wore out the land and caused crop failure, with the
search for food and competition over land provoking more extensive wars
among paramount African chiefs.[15]

Current interpretations are considering demographic and environmental
factors, while emphasizing the rivalries spawned by alliances among African
chiefdoms, European hunters and settlers, and international merchants,
some of whom traded in slaves on the Cape frontier and the Indian Ocean
coast. The largest body of available historical documents, including European shipping logs and diaries and colonial correspondence (the lion's share
generated by the Portuguese in Delagoa Bay), may support such a multiple
perspective.[16]

Ascendant Zulu Patriarchy and White Interlopers

The upheavals in southeast Africa attracted Europeans eager to tap into the
spoils of raiding. A few British traders approached Zulu territory from the
south, exploring a small area one hundred miles south of the mouth of the
Thukela River. The British expelled the Dutch government from the Cape
Colony in 1806 and converted the Table Bay way station into a naval post
on the vital sea route to India. In the mid-1820s British merchants Francis
Farewell and Henry Fynn had founded a coastal trading preserve in Port
Natal—the present-day site of the city of Durban. Hoping to exploit the
Delagoa Bay trade in ivory, animal skins, corn, and possibly African slaves
destined for Brazil, Farewell and Fynn arranged to become Zulu clients, not

only to stay in Port Natal, but also to set up their own homesteads. Indeed, there is fragmentary evidence that they embraced the responsibilities of African homestead heads, taking multiple local wives of their own and offering cattle tribute to Zulu dignitaries who could have siphoned off this livestock to young men enlisted in *amabutho*. Shaka watched the British newcomers warily. According to one oral tradition, the Zulu king's suspicion had provoked his somber prophesy: "No ordinary man will inherit those cattle; [the] day I die the country will be overrun by locusts; it will be ruled by white men."[17]

Throughout the kingdom's consolidation, Zulu leaders encountered opposition from allies who balked at interference in their local affairs and from adversarial paramountcies such as the Ngwane in the west and the Chunu to the south. In the second decade of the nineteenth century, Zulu power relied on an amalgam of client chiefdoms offering loyalty to Shaka as king. The royal house, by and large, recognized Thukela basin chiefs' sovereignty over their own followers but expected, in return, to receive material tribute and assumed that unmarried men and women would surrender their labor intermittently to the king. Shaka also abolished the earlier ceremonial circumcision of teenage boys, a custom that might have been declining, and replaced it with the ritual of drafting young men and a scattering of young women into single-sex regiments with a mix of military and labor functions. Each regiment was to serve the Zulu kingdom, sometimes for as long as two decades; the males acted principally as the king's stockkeepers and soldiers, the females as cultivators of his fields. When regiments were disbanded, the male *amabutho* veterans received bridewealth from the royal house to create their own households, but only after the king, like a homestead head governing his own children, determined that their service to him was at an end.[18]

While the *amabutho,* which harnessed both the kingdom's martial strength and its productive capacity, achieved notoriety for the fear they aroused, the men's and women's regiments operated primarily as labor brigades for the king. Historians who study gender relations during the early Zulu kingdom argue that greater burdens were placed on women who had worked in and around homesteads. Although females close to the royal house enjoyed some privileges of power, such as having attendants of their own, most women, especially young women, were required to produce food both for their own families and for relations away in the regiments. Scholars have only begun to assess how women in the Zulu kingdom might have rationalized their own low social status in such a manifestly patriarchal society.[19]

In the Zulu heartland rigid codes of conduct were imposed on youths and elders alike. For example, to ignore the requirement that males drop face down when in sight of the bathing "maidens" of the king could lead to death. Yet the royal house ultimately preferred nurturing patronage within a hierarchy, rewarding loyal chiefs with cattle captured in raids. The most privileged of all chiefs were the *amantungwa* nobility in the heartland north of the Thukela basin or those linked to Zulu ancestry. In the next tier down was a ruling echelon of regional chiefs, who were nominally attached to the royal house and charged with mustering young men and women to serve the king. Not related by kinship to the first-level aristocracy, this middle-tier nobility nonetheless enjoyed some of the privileges of *amantungwa* status. On the lowest of the three levels were the *amalala* chiefs and commoners living outside the heartland in the Thukela basin and lands southwest of this region—already by the first decade of 1800 considered a repository for dissidents—and along the coast south of the mouth of the Thukela River. According to Dinya, the son of an *amantungwa* homestead head, the Zulu aristocracy disdained the *amalala* "because they sp[oke] with their tongues lying down (lala) [and] because they sle[pt] (lala) with their fingers up their anuses." Shaka barred such *amalala* young men from his inner circle of regiments, relegating them to the status of herders in remote cattle posts.[20]

Under the leadership of the royal house, homestead elders doubtless suffered some loss of control over youths in their own families. The Zulu king usurped a central role of homestead heads in the arrangements of marriages, dangling future *ukulobola* cattle before youths who were commandeered into his regiments and permitting some male *amabutho* members to wed lovers in female *amabutho*. Shaka insisted that some homestead heads present their daughters to him as tribute; isolated in the *isigodlo*, a secluded quarter within the royal enclosure, these "maidens" were for the king's own pleasure or presented as wives to prominent *amantungwa* patriarchs in return for bridewealth. Thus, the kingdom opened channels of opportunity for male youths and restricted them for young females given over to Shaka as tribute.[21]

Yet to a large extent the royal house honored the authority of homestead heads and the entrenched hierarchical principles of customary respect. With young men destined for years of bachelorhood in the regiments, older patriarchs had fewer competing suitors when seeking out more wives for themselves and thus could build up their homesteads with the most desirable form of human wealth, more sons and daughters. Indeed, the conventions of the Zulu kingdom itself depended on rituals that chiefs and ordinary

homestead patriarchs had long employed to maintain the obedience of followers, wives, and children. The king's "first-fruits" ritual, the *umkhosi,* a
spectacular annual celebration that promoted the sanctity of Zulu rule,
mirrored a similar ceremony conducted by chiefs at harvest time. Shaka's
expectations for receiving homage, labor, and tribute appeared to follow
existing social patterns in which the younger, largely unmarried generation
owed services to the older, married generation.[22]

At the same time, however, Shaka was apparently tormented by the con-
spiracies of a wealthy patriarchal household, where dependent children and
relatives coveted sources of power and tribute. Plagued especially by generational tensions, Shaka sought to avoid struggles for succession and concentrated his power by removing potential rivals. Many of the eyewitness
accounts of Shaka's murderous behavior are exaggerated, but several stories
maintain that he killed all the sons of the women who bore his children,
eliminating possible male heirs and thus averting the strife that could arise
when the eldest sons of a homestead head competed to inherit their father's
mantle. However, Shaka's strategy did not erase threats to his position; in
1824 an assassination plan was hatched against him from inside his own
court. Shaka survived and sought to stabilize his house; in 1827 he tried to
enforce widespread mourning for the death of his mother Nandi and massacred those who supposedly showed insufficient sorrow for her passing, a
likely pretense for eradicating political opponents. Shaka's tactics were in
vain. In 1828 another assassin, this time the king's own servant, stabbed him
to death. The king's brothers, Dingana and Mhlangana, were part of the
plot. The cycle of murder was not over; Dingana killed Mhlangana and
seized power for himself, filling the vacuum of succession.[23]

There were deep generational overtones in one of Dingana's first decisions as Zulu king. He reduced the length of military service, breaking up
some of Shaka's male *amabutho* and furnishing bridewealth cattle so that
they could marry brides from a women's regiment demobilized in order that
its members could become wives. Ndukwana, a Zulu oral historian, recalled
in 1900 the maxim that might have explained Dingana's acts: "A new king
cannot rule with the previous king's regiments." This relinquishing of control probably alerted dissidents in the kingdom that African patriarchs might
now assert more independence once again. But it was only a brief respite.
In the early 1830s Dingana followed Shaka's example by seeking to consol-
idate his regal position, forming his own *amabutho* and preparing his young
male soldiers for campaigns to raid cattle and subdue chiefdoms that were
rejecting his authority.[24]

The shake-up in power occasioned by Shaka's death and Dingana's renewed military operations led to the flight of subjects from the Zulu kingdom. Some of these dissidents went to live with European merchants in Port Natal who were at the time pressing Britain to annex their settlement in order to protect it from possible Zulu aggression. Dingana, seeing the merchants and refugees as threats to his own plan to acquire trade goods and muskets through Port Natal, sought intelligence about the wider world of white people from an English missionary named Allen Gardiner, an adviser to the Zulu court, convinced him otherwise. Gardiner was a pioneer in the first wave of missionaries, virtually all men, who established field stations throughout southeast Africa. The Christian evangelists who followed from Britain, the United States, Germany, and Norway were soon to turn Natal and Zululand into the most thickly populated missionary region on the African continent.[25] In the next decades the missionaries tried to wrest patriarchal authority from homestead heads by proselytizing their wives and youths.

White Rivals for Control of African Patriarchy

After the trickle of white traders and missionaries into Natal there came a stream, when hundreds of *voortrekkers*—the descendants of the first Dutch burghers and frontiersmen in the Cape Colony—crossed the Drakensberg Mountains in 1837 and 1838 and pushed into the western Thukela basin. The *voortrekkers* had left the Cape to escape an inhospitable colonial patriarchy, the stricter governance that had followed the British occupation in 1806. These Dutch-speaking emigrants sought to reconstruct the frontier patriarchy they had under the weak Dutch colonial government, when for 150 years their forebears lived in patriarchal households, imported slaves to work on their farms, and increasingly forbade intimate contact between whites and people of African and Asian descent. The British government, responding to London-based humanitarian pressure, halted the slave trade in British ships in 1807 and freed Cape Colony slaves in 1838.

The *voortrekkers* who moved into the western Thukela basin encountered Africans who had just survived nearly two decades of instability, following the extension of Zulu dominance in the region, the fragmentation of the once powerful Hlubi chiefdom, and the consolidation of the Ngwane, an adversarial chiefdom of the Zulu. In a region of political flux, the *voortrekkers* sought to turn an extensive territory near the Thukela River into a staging area for a white-dominated society. Asserting rights to establish private farms, they ignored the landholding customs of basin peoples who held territory communally under the custodianship of patriarchs.[26]

A *voortrekker* delegation, in an effort to hold onto an expanse of land that lay close to Dingana's sphere of influence, went to negotiate with the Zulu royal house. The king killed them soon thereafter and in early 1838 dispatched regiments to destroy the hinterland white encampments and Port Natal. Zulu fighters on the coast drove away the settler inhabitants, some into the sea and onto a ship docked offshore. In the interior Thukela basin, however, the *voortrekkers* repulsed a contingent of Dingana's army. Reinforced by five hundred men and several cannons, they had prepared for a showdown at the Ncome River in the western Thukela basin. They circled the wagons (into a *laager*) and then cut down a charging Zulu force many times their number. The *voortrekkers* were convinced that God had sanctified both their victory at the "Battle of Blood River" and their design for a new republic of Natalia.[27]

The Zulu defeat at Ncome River spurred Dingana to withdraw his forces in 1839 to the heartland above the Thukela basin and to march his army northward to attack the nascent Swazi kingdom. From the Thukela region of the Zulu kingdom, he summoned additional regiments, commanded by his brother Mpande, but his call went unanswered. Dingana's army was vanquished by a hastily organized Swazi force. After these two losses, Mpande, a minor prince in the royal house who had built up a large following, fled across the Thukela River, luring perhaps as many as several tens of thousands of subjects away from Dingana into Natal. Zulu oral tradition commemorates that exodus as "the breaking of the rope that held the nation together." The *voortrekkers,* though initially suspicious that the rupture in the Zulu kingdom was a subterfuge, soon accepted Mpande as an ally who sought to escape from Dingana's retribution. They forged a military alliance with the Zulu refugees, and the two forces attacked the Zulu heartland in 1840. The invading armies pursued the remnants of Dingana's forces, and Mpande's own regiments sealed his brother's fate, driving Dingana into the northeast borderlands of the Zulu kingdom, where he was killed by African political adversaries.[28]

Mpande assumed the royal mantle, but at a price. The *voortrekker* fighters, expecting to be compensated, compelled Mpande to surrender more than thirty thousand cattle—the reward Zulu young men in the regiments received for military service—and rights to an extensive region flanking the kingdom. The *voortrekkers,* with little regard for the reciprocal obligations that governed African patriarchy, confiscated the territory south of the Thukela, an area known by then simply as Natal. As with Shaka earlier, the sibling rivalries within the royal Zulu patriarchy weakened the cohesion of forces that could have resisted colonial intrusion, at least for a time. From 1840 to 1843, thousands of Africans who had settled north of the Thukela River after incorporation into Shaka's fold returned to their ancestral lands in Natal. Their arrival coincided with spreading conflict among Africans over land, especially near the border of the Cape Colony and the Republic of Natalia. By then Africans outnumbered the nearly six thousand white settlers by perhaps fifty thousand or more. Meanwhile, seventy-five miles south of the Thukela River and fifty miles inland from the sea, the *voortrekkers* established a capital of their own in Pietermaritzburg. To British colonial authorities, the African clashes over pasture and territory just south of Pietermaritzburg threatened their hold over the unstable frontier in the northeastern Cape, and in 1843 they issued a proclamation annexing Natal for the Crown. With insufficient resources to fight the imperial takeover, the *voortrekkers* gave in. After two years their new homeland had become a "district" of the Cape Colony controlled by a small British colonial administration stationed in Pietermaritzburg. The majority of the Dutch settlers left and headed for pastures west of the Drakensberg range; those who stayed behind secured from Mpande in 1847 a territory called Klip River in the western reaches of the Zulu kingdom (map 2).[29]

Grafting Colonialism onto African Patriarchy in Natal

In 1846 a British administration, headed by a lieutenant governor and assisted by a colonial secretary and "diplomatic agent to the native tribes," began roughing out boundaries around pockets of land to be held by Africans or by colonists. The British allowed white settlers to buy and sell land, but indigenous people were to live on communal holdings in "locations" or reserves, most of them in the outlying areas of Natal. The Pietermaritzburg government established a "commission for locating natives" to impose formal limits on indigenous settlement, and until the end of the decade this commission created reserves for Africans but proposed no plans for forced removals. Preferring not to move from their long-established plots, few homesteads actually settled in these new locations (map 3).[30]

The British "diplomatic agent to the native tribes," Theophilus Shepstone, promoted "traditional supports of law and order," and with a tiny bureaucracy and virtually no financial backing from London, he could not consider dislodging chiefdoms from their sites. Shrewdly aware of how patriarchy functioned among Africans, Shepstone cajoled chiefs into accept-

Natal, Zulu Kingdom and Klip River: 1845–1879

ing him as vital interlocutor between them and the Natal government. The future "great father of whites" or "Somsewu," as Africans in Natal and Zululand would call Shepstone, made British rule appear dependent on cooperation between colonial officials, principally white magistrates in the Department of Native Affairs, and homestead patriarchs. The Natal chiefs, the elite Africans whom he perceived as "strong leaders" and who professed loyalty to whites, were expected to accede to a major new policy: unsurveyed expanses of land, populated by homesteads but shunned by whites because of poor arability and remoteness from settler towns, would become

Natal African Locations: 1850s

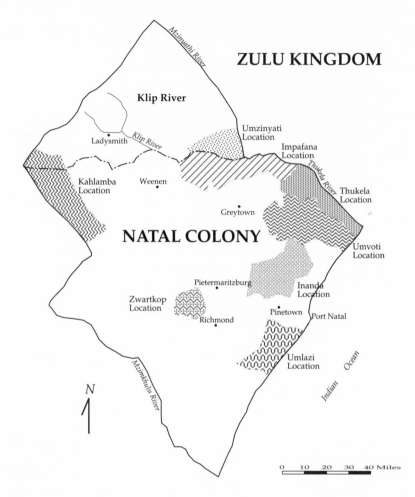

Crown land and would be partitioned into divisions. Except for parcels set aside (starting in the 1850s) as foreign-based Christian mission stations, most Natal land occupied by Africans would be owned by the Crown.[31]

With a boundary structure in place, the Natal government policies crafted by British officials required the collection of local revenue and implementation by magistrates as well as African patriarchs. In 1848 a hut tax was imposed on every homestead within each district according to the number of households in a domestic compound, essentially the number of wives and their huts. However, in raising revenue from Africans, the government recognized that a homestead head was to be solely responsible for paying the assessment for his entire family.

Shepstone wove indigenous customs and British legal procedures together into a fabric called "native customary law." He had observed the social hierarchies within homesteads, the Natal "native laws" reinforcing women and youths as wards of their homestead head. Shepstone and the colonial magistrates who implemented his system ensured that this hierarchical, patriarchal arrangement continued to function in their own courts.

In 1850 a select number of magistrates became "Administrators of Native Law," the final arbiters in most criminal cases involving Africans. African chiefs also became virtual civil servants, that is, as long as they deferred to white officials. Chiefs were to retain jurisdiction over civil cases and some minor criminal cases but ultimately were to be regarded as "mere hereditary deputies" with "prerogatives . . . transferred to the Crown." The "Shepstone system," with its flexible legal arm—"native customary law"—was the foundation of Natal "native policy" for decades to come.[32]

In his visits to chiefdoms to hear the opinions of African patriarchs, Shepstone adapted indigenous political rituals and held open-air meetings with male elders in imitation of the *ibandla,* the chief's council. This personal style, a mixture of prudent chief and colonial protector, seemed to impress some African patriarchs. A Thukela basin headman described Shepstone's "wont to hold frequent intercourse with the Chiefs and Headmen. He took his seat under a tree and invited any man to state grievances or make remarks on any matter which concerned him. . . . This system suited us exactly."[33]

White Political Patriarchs of Natal African Society

In the first decade of British rule in Natal, Shepstone enlisted chiefs to resolve a dilemma over African political rights. With between one-third and one-half of Africans lacking political leadership, according to Shepstone's estimate, in the middle and southern part of Natal, "the diplomatic agent to the tribes" tried to assign scattered bands of Africans to Natal's chiefs. These refugees had moved south across the Thukela River from their ancestral lands to escape the aggression of expanding and migrating chiefdoms such as the Ngwane, Chunu, and Zulu. When Shepstone found no hereditary leader among an African group, he often installed a man he considered capable of becoming a chief, usually a pliable, ambitious commoner.

Yet whether chiefs were hereditary or appointed by the colonial government, Shepstone forbade them to assemble young men into regiments, lest these armed bodies threaten the whites of Natal. In 1848 he began enforcing *isibhalo,* a policy that compelled chiefs to muster African labor brigades for colonial public works. He also effectively annulled the chiefs' custom of raising tribute by requiring permission to do so from the Natal governor, who rarely granted this right. Grafting what he believed was a Zulu legacy of centralized kingship onto the Africans of Natal, Shepstone envisioned the native administration as the reigning political authority, led by the "Supreme Chief," the governor.

In 1852 a Natal commission of inquiry investigated "the past and present state of" African affairs in Natal, revealing a schism between settlers and leading government officials. The disagreement, at its heart, concerned contrasting visions of colonial patriarchy. White witnesses before the commission rebuked Shepstone for vesting African male authorities with political responsibilities and complained that the reserve system bolstered the homestead economy and encouraged homestead heads to ignore colonial labor needs. Customary laws were a primary target, particularly the rights of parents to maneuver their youths into marriages and to conduct bridewealth cattle exchanges, a vexatious issue because the white settlers viewed *ukulobola* as an immoral "sale" of daughters. Colonial farmers advocated laws designed to undermine homestead heads' control over youths and to compel African sons and daughters to work on the settlers' farms. The colonial government feared that deeper official incursions into homestead life would alienate Natal Africans, perhaps driving them into an alliance with the Zulu kingdom.[34]

Contrary to the fears of white authorities, during the 1840s and 1850s the Zulu king Mpande did not seek to challenge Natal's dominion. Rather, he appeared to be concerned with shoring up his own political base in the kingdom's heartland by bestowing cattle on regional chiefs and marrying off his daughters to powerful supporters. The Zulu state still summoned youths for "little *umkhosi*" celebrations, a festival that preceded by one month the principal *umkhosi.* The king assembled the "younger warriors," inviting their attendants (the boys who carried a soldier's provisions), and gave them a taste of royal privilege. Mtshayankomo, the son of Mpande's leading court praiser, told of one "little *umkhosi*" in which bands of revelers were sent to "foreign parts" to capture a "fighting bull, pitch black in colour, a big, old one, that would rip out people's innards." The bull, a symbol of Zulu masculinity, was driven to the king's enclosure, where "its tendons [were] slashed [lest] it overc[o]me all the warriors." The bull was then slaughtered and roasted over a huge fire. The "young boys, who had not reached puberty, the carriers of mats and blankets," lavishly feasted on "[s]trips of meat as long as one's arm."[35] While the details of tracking and disabling this bull might be embellished, Mpande probably understood, like his dethroned brothers before him, that he had to win the allegiance of youths, his main line of defense against invasion. The rite honoring the contributions of mere boys may have been designed to augment the king's fatherly influence, possibly in response to a patriarchal colonial administration to the south that purported to govern through appointed African chiefs.

The Zulu royal house continued to marry off female regiments to foster the loyalty of male regiments who were eager to secure bridewealth from the dwindling royal herds, find wives, and start their own homesteads. But after Mpande snapped "the rope that held the nation together" in his feud with Dingana, youths who did not want to serve Zulu patriarchy could more easily flee across the Thukela River to an autonomous region. In 1900 a homestead head in Mpande's reign remembered that the king would "authorize girls to put on the topknot (kehla) and then [match] them [as wives] to a regiment or regiments of men. [Yet after the] girls were [told to join the] older men, . . . many would elope to Natal with their sweethearts (younger men), from whence they could not be recovered." The African refugee communities in the colony provided sanctuary for such young couples; the homestead head pointed out that the "way to Natal [was] opened up by Mpande."[36]

Within his own family, Mpande, unlike Shaka, raised sons to carry on the Zulu line, thus making himself especially vulnerable to the intrigue that had already riven the Zulu kingdom's founders and caused the deaths of both kings and heirs. As Mpande's sons matured, they began to jostle for succession. In 1856, two of them, Cetshwayo and Mbuyazi, quarreled over succession. Cetshwayo, with a large personal following known as the uSuthu, had the clout to defeat his brother Mbuyazi. Although the primary evidence is muddled, King Mpande seemed to favor Mbuyazi and is thought to have urged him to raise an army to fight his brother. Mbuyazi amassed his forces in the southeastern Thukela basin, where he came under attack just as summer rains swelled the Thukela to flood stage. With retreat across the channel virtually impossible, Mbuyazi and thousands of his supporters were trapped and then massacred by Cetshwayo's army at the battle of Ndondakusuka.[37]

Nearly a century and a half later, accounts of the slaughter are still vividly recounted. In 1992 Malombo Dube, an elderly man whose ancestors lived near the battle site, recounted his great-grandfather's tale in an interview with me. Mbuyazi's followers attempted to escape by swimming across the river, but almost all were drowned, their corpses damming a sharp bend in the Thukela. Dube pointed from his homestead to a curved section of the river: "That is *emathanjeni,* the 'place of the bones.'"[38]

Some stragglers from Mbuyazi's contingent slipped into Natal, their presence raising the possibility for Mpande that the Natal Colony would intervene to stop the bloodshed and chaos in the area. Since consolidating his kingdom after the death of his brother Dingana, Mpande himself had kept white authorities from meddling in Zulu affairs by using missionaries to mediate with officials in Pietermaritzburg, but he could do little to forestall disorder. In the late 1850s the *voortrekkers,* now known as Boers, had begun herding their cattle from farms adjoining the western Zulu kingdom into the northern Thukela basin, and the war-weary Zulu had had to accommodate their expansion. In 1861 Cetshwayo, who had been slowly taking over diplomatic functions from his father Mpande, ceded a parcel of the northwest kingdom to the Boers in return for recognition of his right as successor. Alarmed by the land transfer to Britain's Dutch-speaking colonial rivals in the Transvaal, Shepstone acknowledged Cetshwayo as heir, exacting a promise that he would not ally with the Boers.[39]

African patriarchy within the Zulu kingdom had experienced the first wave of colonial invasions that would increase in frequency and intensity beginning in the 1860s, as white settlers south of the Thukela clamored for greater access to the labor and land of African youths in both Natal and Zululand. Some of the Africans, who since the 1840s had left Zululand for Natal, sought employment with colonists, but the labor shortages were not substantially eased. Natal settlers continued to complain that the Zulu kingdom locked its youths into regimental service, and that within their own colony Shepstone's provision of communal land impoverished the labor market since most able-bodied Natal Africans—particularly the young— were obliged by homestead heads to stay in homesteads on reserve land. The government persisted in its land reserve system, unwilling to appease the white farmers whose erratic harvests could not compare to the more reliable homestead supplies of staples that fed the population of Natal. The settler population was still too small to convince the colonial government to change its strategies.[40]

By the early 1850s five thousand British and Irish immigrants had landed in Natal. Their sponsor was a settler, Joseph Byrne, who hoped to encourage more whites to plant cash crops such as sugar in the vicinity of Pietermaritzburg and along the southern coast of Natal. In 1856 Britain declared Natal a colony of the Crown with its own representative government, severing its dependency on the Cape administration. During the next decade, the Natal Colony felt more secure about protecting its borders; it stepped up the promotion of white immigration, advertising assisted passage for a fresh start from Great Britain and generous land grants to newcomers at a time of depression in the European industrial economy. The colonial population rose in the early 1860s to nearly 14,000, still less than a tenth of Natal's Africans, estimated then at 156,000 and growing rapidly. Yet despite land grants, the new European immigrants turned away from agriculture to other ventures, such as buying goods at Durban harbor to sell to colonists in the hinterland who had to import their manufactured goods from Britain. The raw materials produced locally were exported back to be finished in the mother country. Commercial hamlets with typical English countryside names such as Richmond and York connected to each other by rough wagon trails, soon dotted the map north and west of Pietermaritzburg.[41]

A depression that wrecked the colonial economy in the latter half of the 1860s caused insolvent settlers to sell their land to speculators. By 1870 the speculators owned 25 percent of the acreage set aside for whites in Natal. They became absentee landlords and allowed African homesteads to rent plots. In the 1870s white farmers began to produce steadier yields, despite shortages of local farm labor. The Natal government tried to remedy the shortages by recruiting indentured men and women from India to grow sugar cane on settler-owned coastal plantations. In the drier interior, colonial farmers were now meeting subsistence requirements and occasionally producing a surplus for sale in nearby markets. They had learned to attract African youths to work for wages by negotiating with their homestead head to release them temporarily from daily tasks, often paying the African patriarch for services of his young men. Class divisions among colonists became more apparent as companies bought up plots designated for whites in order to rent to Africans, mainly in the Natal Midlands. One such enterprise, the Natal Land and Colonisation Company, leased acreage to African homestead heads while it waited for land values to rise. In 1864 the colonial government turned over the African reserves, then almost 15 percent of the 2.2 million acres in the colony, to the Natal Native Trust, a government body that safeguarded African rights to hold "tribal" or communal title (not individual title) to their land. One quarter of the trust territory was now abutting the Thukela River.[42]

With land at their disposal, chiefs in northern Natal were able to uphold their customary authority far better than their counterparts in magisterial divisions to the south, where whites had been able to appropriate more territory and Africans were crowded into reserves. The Natal Native Trust provided some security to African homesteads by barring the sale of reserve land to whites, much to the disappointment of "up-country" settlers near the Thukela, who were not persuaded by the fact that the system of communal landholdings paid dividends to their colonial government. Natal officials, under Shepstone's stewardship, had a stake in safeguarding the material foundations of homestead life. The 1848 hut tax, for example, had become a remarkably efficient way for the colonial patriarchy to collect revenue, with polygynous homestead heads effectively supporting an insolvent colony.[43]

After diamonds were discovered just north of the Orange River and the Cape Colony in the late 1860s, hundreds of young African men from Natal converged on the diggings near Kimberley, receiving pay for mine labor exceeding any they had previously earned. Homestead heads could now meet colonial tax and rent requirements from the wages of their migrant sons. Government fees for migrants' passes to travel through Natal generated further income for the colony. In the early 1870s African taxes, fees, and customs charges collected from Africans contributed 75 percent of the Natal government's expenditures, with the principal share of taxes going to upgrade postal delivery, roads, and defense for white settlers. Yet the colony invested little to build infrastructure for Natal Africans. White officials in native administration reined in their costs by relying on homestead heads to safeguard order locally, a hallmark of the "Shepstone system." Customary law was flexible enough to give African chiefs leeway in certain rulings but rigid enough to circumscribe their overall jurisdiction. Although most criminal cases involving Africans came before a resident magistrate, as did civil disputes between Africans and colonists, the majority of homestead dwellers appearing in court were male elders who were recognized by the Natal government as the sole authority over wives, children, and dependents.[44]

The statutes protecting African patriarchy in Natal gradually came under increasing scrutiny from colonists, especially as mining stimulated economic growth. Diamonds led to a surge in European immigration that, in turn, helped establish industrial development in South Africa. Emboldened by the new prospects for wealth and eager to marshal the labor of African youths, Natal colonists sought to weaken the powers of Natal chiefs and homestead heads in the early 1870s, challenging what they perceived as a dangerous competing patriarchy, the Zulu kingdom.[45]

Colonial Conquest and Emerging African Generational Struggles

In Natal homestead heads became accustomed to their sons working in the mines and on commercial farms, but in Zululand many male elders, especially the patriarchs in Cetshwayo's royal house, had rejected itinerant wage labor to avoid draining the Zulu military of young men. When diamond discoveries attracted so many whites to Kimberley, only four hundred miles to the west of the Zulu kingdom, prominent Zulu chiefs felt threatened and began to lose confidence in Cetshwayo's ability to keep colonial intervention at bay, particularly with the governments of Natal, the Transvaal Republic, and Portuguese East Africa all impinging on Zulu borders. Cetshwayo, anticipating this peril, fortified his army—including female regiments—with weapons acquired from European traders near Delagoa Bay. Some of these "guns were . . . evidently got from the Portuguese," a soldier of Cetshwayo's recalled in 1912, and were distributed to "sections of girl regiments. . . . These girls were the king's bodyguard, and went about with him from kraal to kraal."[46]

In 1873, a year after his father Mpande's natural death, Cetshwayo asserted his royal mandate over the kingdom by calling Shepstone to witness his "coronation" in acknowledgment of Zulu sovereignty north of the Thukela River. The secretary for native affairs interpreted the invitation as an opportunity to exert his patriarchal influence (not to mention the Crown's) over Zulu affairs. During the so-called coronation, Shepstone collected intelligence on the Zulu army, according to an alleged eyewitness, Mtshayankomo, whose account is marred by a jumbled chronology. Using the isiZulu name for Shepstone, Mtshayankomo said that "Somsewu" asked a Zulu regiment commander named Masiphula, "'Could you too show what you do among yourselves when you pretend to fight.' . . . Standing where we were, we [rattled] our raised shields. The horses [of Shepstone's delegation] took fright; some leaped over the kraal fence, throwing off their riders; others jumped onto the huts. Somsewu was startled, for he had seen that we did not carry assegais [spears] and had expected us to dance." Shepstone "exclaimed, 'Hau! Are you playing tricks on me? My child, are you trying to frighten me? What is this, Masipula? . . . I too shall bring up my young men.'"[47] Although Cetshwayo's coronation ceremony seemed to have alienated the "great white father," no white troops arrived immediately in the Zulu kingdom. Over the next five years, however, a series of crises would push the new king to the threshold of war.

In 1876 Cetshwayo confronted a challenge from young women in the Thukela basin of Zululand. Ndukwana, a Zulu oral historian, remembered in 1900 that "at the first mkosi [the festival of kingship] held by Cetshwayo, i.e. after Mpande's death," an eminent regiment of older men "was ordered to [take wives from a regiment] of girls known as the Ingcugce." But the "Ingcugce girls refused to marry . . . as directed"; they "were contemptuous" of their future husbands, for the "girls wanted to marry the younger men." Ndukwana said the "girls were then taken by force and married; others, to escape this, cut off their topknots," their crown of woven grass and animal hide symbolizing their readiness to honor the king's order to marry. Some defiant young women fled to their homesteads and reconstructed their own topknots. "When they went to show themselves with their new headrings," Cetshwayo commanded "an impi [a regiment of male soldiers] to kill the girls of the Ingcugce lot still remaining unmarried." A merciless expedition followed, Ndukwana recounted. "Any of these girls found in a kraal [homestead] were killed."[48]

As the hunt for the runaways took soldiers into the northern Thukela basin, Mtshayankomo, who was a member of the *inGobamakhosi* regiment dispatched by Cetshwayo, enlisted the help of the dissident women's own homestead heads. Zulu patriarchy was to be salvaged at the expense of their own daughters' lives. Mtshayankomo reported: "We Ngobamakosi were twelve companies (amaviyo) strong. We killed thirty-one girls. We found them hiding . . . with their men in forests. They were pointed out to us by their fathers."[49]

The security of the Zulu kingdom became more tenuous by the time nearby paramount chiefs succumbed to colonial intervention. The British had subjugated Xhosa regents in the eastern Cape during the 1850s and 1860s. The BaSotho king Moshoeshoe, seeking protection from Boer encroachment in 1868, requested that Great Britain annex his own mountain kingdom. Within Natal, the colonial government was punishing recalcitrant chiefs. In 1873 it crushed Langalibalele, a powerful independent Thukela basin chief who, in contravention of colonial laws, allowed the young men of his chiefdom to use their own wages earned in migrant labor to buy guns for their own regiments. The pressures spawned in Zululand by these white conquests in Natal and elsewhere contributed to the conflicts between Cetshwayo's elite army regiments along generational lines. Some young male soldiers wanted to win glory in a war against a colonial army, distressed that their reward for years of service to the Zulu army—the stores of bridewealth cattle—might one day be surrendered by their elder patriarchs as a way to appease colonial demands. Some of the more seasoned, older Zulu soldiers advocated a more defensive approach. In a microcosm of this rivalry, in 1878 a regiment of older men, *uThulwana,* attacked the *inGobamakhosi,* a regiment of young men. One bystander to the battle watched the *uThulwana* "stab [the *inGobamakhosi*] until the sun went down." Another Zulu eyewitness claimed that Cetshwayo was displeased that "the youths [in fighting] are covering us with blood [and so] ordered men . . . to kill the iNgobamakosi." But the king apparently withdrew his order when a headman close to him "reproved him, . . . 'It is the fault of the king who took the youths and pushed them onto the older men.'"[50]

The combination of internecine killing and colonial expansionism propelled a confrontation over the future of autonomous African patriarchy within the Zulu kingdom. After annexing the Boer Transvaal Republic in 1877 in an effort to build colonial support for a white-dominated confederation in southern Africa, Great Britain promised somewhat gratuitously to protect Natal from Cetshwayo's aggression and at the end of 1878 issued an ultimatum to the Zulu king to give up hundreds of cattle as tribute and disband his army. Some historians emphasize that white settlers, fearing an immediate Zulu attack, disapproved of this brinkmanship; other historians argue that colonial opinion was immaterial, as the hostile policies of imperialists were driving Cetshwayo headlong into war. With the Zulu king wavering, armed young men mobilized to strike the "English." The Zulu chief Ndhlovu recalled in 1902 that at this time of crisis "Cetshwayo [was taking] his advice from hot-headed young men" whose "bearing . . . toward their elders was extremely impudent."[51]

The imperial ultimatum expired on 11 January 1879. A British and colonial force of roughly seventeen thousand soldiers prepared to invade Zululand within a few hours of the deadline. White troops, presuming a quick victory and buttressed by thousands of armed Africans in the Natal Native Contingent, streamed into the kingdom from the west and south in several columns. At first they encountered only sporadic resistance, until one British detachment stationed field quarters on a plain in an area known as

Isandlwana. The main Zulu army, perhaps twenty thousand strong and armed with spears and rifles, was in the vicinity and quickly attacked, winning a spectacular victory.

The outcome intoxicated the Zulu military and induced the white invaders to devote greater resources to the war. The British complement dug into positions, and at the Rorke's Drift mission station a small column firing from behind barriers repulsed thousands of charging Zulu fighters, slaying hundreds without significant casualties of their own. In other operations during subsequent months colonial and imperial soldiers, reinforced by troops from overseas and with overwhelming firepower, defeated uSuthu supporters in the far corners of the kingdom, killing several thousand Zulu and dispersing many more thousands from the ranks of regiments to their homesteads. By 1880 the British had captured Cetshwayo, exiled him to the Cape, disbanded his regiments, and proposed a plan to dismantle the foundation of Zulu political patriarchy. The means to achieve glory on the battlefield was cut off for many male youths.

In the postwar settlement devised by Sir Garnet Wolseley, the new British high commissioner for southeastern Africa, Zululand was carved into thirteen territories, each under a chief sanctioned by the Crown, a version of Shepstone's Natal system of colonial rule through co-opted African patriarchs. The northern portion of the Thukela basin was to be a "frontier" buffer between the Natal Colony and the chiefdoms in Zululand that had fought for Cetshwayo. The British assigned the task of implementing the territorial design to Melmoth Osborn, the first resident commissioner in Zululand.[52]

John Dunn, a prominent white trader and former adviser to Zulu kings, and Hlubi Molife, an African headman and soldier in the Natal Native Contingent, were appointed chiefs, Dunn to rule over the coast to Nkandla district, Molife over most of the Nquthu district. Both, in turn, imposed a colonial model of African patriarchal order, replacing local headmen with African men of their choice from Natal and ejecting some resistant homestead residents from their ancestral lands. Melmoth Osborn vested the most power in two chiefs in northern Zululand known for their dislike of Cetshwayo: Hamu, a Zulu prince, and Zibhebhu, leader of the Mandlakazi chiefdom. There is a persistent view among historians, with a few notable exceptions, that Wolseley's settlement deliberately laid the ground for future internecine struggles in Zululand (map 4).[53]

Nonetheless, for colonial officials, southern Zululand—the northern half of the Thukela basin—had become the testing site for a new and more

Wolseley's 1879 Settlement

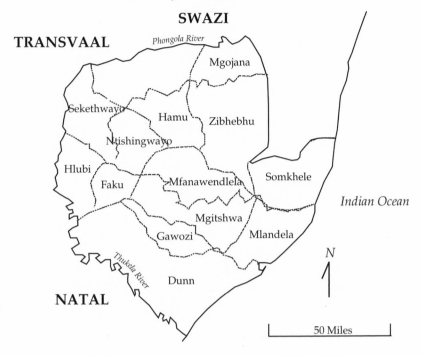

restrictive government within the defeated kingdom. Zulu patriarchs, like their elder Natal African counterparts across the Thukela River, were suffering the humiliation of eroding authority. Although the lure of labor migrancy at first had bolstered homesteads, it had begun to loosen African filial obligations, releasing existing tensions between elders and youths. In the final two decades of the nineteenth century, African patriarchs in the middle and lower Thukela basin would confront the painful consequences of colonial conquest. In the words of Zulu chief Ndhlovu, the "youths had come to defy the nation."[54]

CHAPTER TWO

African Patriarchs: "Made of Copper" Who "Should Be of Gold"

In Homestead Hierarchy No Youth Is "the Equal of a Man"

AN AFRICAN BOY could abide his lowly duty, cracking the switch that was "cut for him by his elder brother" to drive cattle to pastures above the Thukela River. But the meat of the cattle he tended was a luxury he probably seldom tasted. Boys, like their young brothers and the females of the homestead, subsisted instead on corn porridge and *amasi,* a curdled milk; these were the principal dishes from the foods raised on land provided by the patriarch. Adult men (*amadoda*) rarely engaged in farming—except to clear ground, fashion tools, dig storage pits for grain, or plough. They primarily reared livestock and slaughtered and dressed the meat and skins. Male elders' wives and daughters performed household chores, with the younger, unmarried women handling the heavy work such as planting crops and hauling water for cooking. Some colonial officials in the late nineteenth century noted a disparity in homestead labor obligations. African women were too industrious, they complained, while African men loafed and avoided the employment offered by white settlers.[1]

In the 1880s, Thukela basin homesteads showed remarkable resilience in times when drought parched the landscape, or when livestock disease decimated the cattle herds, or when land shortages forced a search for arable ground. A narrow range of crops—corn, potatoes, and sorghum—anchored the local agriculture economy. Some homestead heads branched out, purchasing ploughs to increase harvests and wagons to transport surplus crops to settler hamlets, particularly near Durban. In the late 1800s, as the mining fields of Kimberley and the Witwatersrand burgeoned into industrial centers, it was homestead grain from Natal that helped to feed African and white urban dwellers who could not grow food for themselves.[2]

Most Africans conserved their own resources to survive recurrent bad seasons, supplementing homestead food reserves by foraging wild green edibles and, if they were male, by hunting game. In periods of scarcity, as in periods of plenty, a patriarch depended on the work of women and children in his homestead. White farmers with no similar extended kinship networks found it difficult to recruit laborers and thus sought the cooperation of homestead heads, usually offering them cash for the labor of their youths.

The colonial government also depended on the agricultural surplus of African homesteads to supply its own local markets, for white farmers were at best only erratically productive; instead of planting extensive fields of staples, as the Africans did, colonists concentrated on profitable exports. The export goods—wattle trees, wool, tea, and tobacco—were vulnerable to severe weather, insect infestation, and, most critically, labor shortages. Occasionally young men entered into their own labor contracts with settlers. Colonial landowners also fitted workers into a paternalistic framework, placing in charge a male custodian, the African or white overseer, but they did not assume the obligations of homestead heads to support their African laborers over the long term.[3]

An African homestead head had other labor options that white farmers did not have; he could recruit workers from outside his own homestead. If he was prosperous—that is, if he possessed a large herd, used ploughs to expand his harvests, or exercised political power—he could draw on the labor of youths with no ties to himself. For example, if he wished to move his herd, he could allocate cattle to boys in faraway valleys, who would lead the cows to prime grazing and thereby earn a calf or two, milk and leather, and perhaps status as nominal "children" of their patron. Even a poor homestead head with few cattle and a small domestic labor force could attract neighborhood helpers to weed his fields or thatch a hut roof by an offer of beer. Within family settings, unmarried men, *izinsizwa,* had rights to command the labor of younger boys and girls, usually their siblings; sons and daughters without spouses depended on their own domestic circle for support.[4]

In the Thukela basin, a small ruling African elite, a chief and his headmen, exercised rights to extract wealth from homestead heads and their families, the vast majority of them commoners with limited powers to command resources outside their kinship network. Chiefdoms varied in size and scale; the larger ones were usually divided into districts, which in turn were segmented into neighborhoods, with a chief ruling over extensive areas through *izinduna,* his headmen or political representatives. In matters of governance, a chief could elicit valuable advice from a group of select male elders, the *ibandla.*[5]

Chiefdoms, like homesteads, grew, split, and reconfigured over time. A chief's power could be subverted in myriad ways. For example, a colonial decree could depose him, a local feud could fester over his succession, and his followers could leave him for another chief. With no individual owner-ship over communal reserve land, a chief ensured obedience through recip-rocal obligations. Followers offered to *ukukhonza* their chief, to pay him homage and tribute in cattle, grain, beer, and labor. Homestead inhabitants, particularly young women and young men, served their chief in various capacities, the females weeding his gardens and the males herding his live-stock and protecting (in groups) the chiefdom from external threat. When the Natal government compelled Africans to labor for settler society, such as through the *isibhalo* system that enlisted young African men to build roads and other public works projects, a chief was expected to resist such unpopular colonial pressures. Beyond combating a common adversary, chiefs fostered community allegiance by organizing festivals at times of harvest, adjudicating disputes, and allotting land. In 1900, one African patri-arch described the ideal process: "Applicants wishing to build kraals [home-steads] would go to the [chief] who would, if he felt so disposed, indicate the spot to be built on, i.e. within his recognized boundaries. . . . A com-moner, when a spot is pointed out . . . himself understands that he is pre-sented with a kraal site, grazing ground and garden[s]."[6]

Homestead male elders, for their part, earned the loyalty of women and youths by upholding rituals that invoked obedience. In the 1890s, 1920s, and 1990s, African patriarchs from the Thukela basin testified to bolstering their position by projecting their *isibuko sikababa,* the masculine aura sur-rounding them. This *isibuko sikababa* was the metaphorical "lens" through which their sons could visualize their past forefathers and thus learn to "mirror" or copy proper patriarchal bearing. Today, some elder men in the middle Thukela basin impart this convention of honoring their paternal ancestors, although they have modified *isibuko sikababa* into *isithombe si-kababa,* the image (like a photograph) of the patriarch's lineage. During public ceremonies, a son who sang the praises of his family could recount tales about his homestead head's *isibuko sikababa.*[7] In *ukuhlonipha,* a practice of deference, male and female youths and married women avoided male eld-ers. One homestead head, Ndukwana, set the tone of a figurative encounter:

"Going along a path—meeting one another—it was recognized that [a male] youth (insizwa) must make way for a mature man (indoda) [and if] he failed to do so, the latter would go to the men of the place of the mnumzane [the youth's homestead head], who would fine the boy, asking how he came to regard himself as the equal of a man."[8] This description is compelling in what it conveys about expectations of respect, yet many encounters between *insizwa* and *indoda* might not have followed Ndukwana's script of stylized gestures.

Elder men could inspire awe by invoking the specter of ancestral spirits, the *amadlozi*. In initiating sacred celebrations, patriarchs made supreme appeals, ladling beer onto the ground, the shell of the spirits' subterranean region, to beseech *amadlozi* to keep the revelers from calamity. In the early 1900s, some homestead heads told colonial officials of consulting the divine realm in dreams during mourning observances and ritual sacrifices and when seeking sanction for selecting an heir apparent. Most fathers hoped to proclaim their male successor, usually the first son, before old age incapacitated them. A patriarch could thus minimize dissension over who would assume the mantle among the eldest boys who were quite close in age and from different mothers of unequal rank.[9]

The guidance of the patriarch, which relied on the support of homestead members like his senior wife, was decisive in suppressing family squabbles. He was the custodian of homestead property—cattle, goats, sheep, weapons, farming implements, even wages earned by sons outside the homestead. He contributed livestock to a common familial herd and to each hut in his own homestead, and he parceled out land and tools. He could transfer property from one hut household to another, an arrangement especially pivotal in marriage placing, but he usually had to take account of family members who were seeking to protect or enlarge their own share of domestic resources. If a son from a homestead hut with a meager herd required *ukulobola* to win a bride, his father could borrow a few head of cattle from another hut within his homestead, usually after consulting the wife of that hut. Such negotiations could create domestic tensions if promises of compensation were delayed or broken. Some unmarried wage-earning male migrants were able to mingle cattle that they bought with the livestock of their own hut household. It is likely that these young men drew on the support of their mothers, who would have coordinated production in hut households, and their younger male siblings, who would have herded not only for the homestead head but also for their older brothers.[10]

The historical record is silent as to how many cattle young men could acquire before arousing their homestead head's reaction. A patriarch retained the right to confiscate cattle from dependents in order to redistribute familial resources. Despite young men's capacity to accumulate their own nominal wealth, as long as they were living with their homestead head their autonomy was substantially circumscribed. Most unmarried males labored for their patriarch, in anticipation of receiving bridewealth that would allow them to take a wife and jump in rank as married men. With his homestead head's permission, a young man usually could secure *ukulobola* cattle from his own homestead's store and ensure his bride "welfare."

Taking additional wives became increasingly possible for married men as they matured since by that time they might themselves have received *ukulobola* for the marriage of their own daughters. Polygynists, consequently, tried to amass more cattle than young men. Older men usually had produced more daughters and were in a commanding position to be on the receiving end in the marriage market. Indeed, many fathers pressed for a large bridewealth, despite colonial laws that curtailed such customs, in order to make it impossible for a young suitor to meet the *ukulobola* requirement, thereby giving preference to the older polygynist suitor. By granting a first option to husbands with multiple wives and accumulated cattle, homestead heads could uphold their own elite position; more wives meant more children, a large progeny of laborers, and also more marriageable daughters, who in turn would bring in more bridewealth cattle. It was a cycle that benefited those who had the most. Even *amakholwa* patriarchs who wanted to break away from homestead rituals and embrace such elements of colonial society as private property and Christianity defied missionaries by observing the *ukulobola* custom. The patriarchs "saw commercial advantage in marrying off their daughters."[11]

The practice of polygyny distressed missionaries, officials, and settlers in Natal, many of whom believed that homestead heads were forcing their daughters into unwanted unions with aged men who ignored the biblical injunction of monogamy. In 1869 the colonial government imposed a comprehensive marriage law on Africans, decreeing that women could not be married against their will and that homestead heads could not set *ukulobola* beyond the capacity of unmarried grooms to pay; white resident magistrates would penalize transgressors of the marriage law. Bridewealth was to be fixed on a sliding scale: ten head of cattle for most ordinary men or "commoners," fifteen for headmen, twenty for appointed chiefs, and an unlimited number for hereditary chiefs. *Ukulobola* was to be delivered at once, making illegal the practice whereby a homestead head could slowly release— "trickle"— their sons' bridewealth to extend their dependence on him.[12]

The middle Thukela basin: Mountains, June 1906 (top) (C3534/47); homestead with cattle enclosure, c. 1900 (bottom) (C4731). Photographs courtesy of the Natal Archives, Pietermaritzburg.

Men's activities: Male elders, *amadoda*, preparing skins, c. 1900 (top) (C763); two
young men giving snuff to "headringed" male elders, c. 1900 (bottom) (C714).
Photographs courtesy of the Natal Archives, Pietermaritzburg.

Young men's martial life: With fighting sticks, shields, and ornamental beads, c. 1900 (top) (C167/1); in staged faction fight, c. 1900 (bottom) (C4741). Photographs courtesy of the Natal Archives, Pietermaritzburg.

Women's domestic world: A bride-to-be, c. 1900 (opposite page, top) (C748); unmarried women standing and married women sitting, c. 1900 (opposite page, bottom) (C757); mother grinding corn, c. 1900 (above) (C4730). Photographs courtesy of the Natal Archives, Pietermaritzburg.

Nor, of course, did young male labor migrants have to rely solely on their father for bridewealth since they had wages of their own that could be applied toward the purchase of cattle. Umnini, a headman from the Thukela basin, complained in 1882 that since "young men . . . can pay for their own wives," they could make their intentions plain to sweethearts. Joko, an elder from Umnini's Umvoti district, reported that "[g]irls and boys get married directly when they are of marriageable age, [the] young men in accordance with the privileges they enjoy" as wage earners.[13]

Bolstering the White Minority Weakens African Chiefs

The Natal government's maneuvers to circumvent African marriage practices undercut a chief's ability to resolve local disputes over the delivery of *ukulobola* cattle. Furthermore, the three-tier colonial system of land tenure (the communal reserves, Crown land, and private farms) reduced the ability of Natal chiefs to allocate new gardens and pastures to followers; resident magistrates, too, arbitrarily divided chiefdoms by natural geographic location, ignoring traditional boundaries. The secretary for native affairs argued that chiefs "have neither the means nor the power to . . . control tribes the members of which are dispersed over a number of magistracies and miles away from them."[14]

Colonial impositions merely compounded the possibility of political fragmentation, already apparent in struggles for succession, where a chief
became vulnerable due "to the internal conflicts in regard to [his] inheritance." A chiefdom, in effect, "exist[ed] for the purpose of giving birth and
developing communities, that, in time, bec[a]me more and more independent of and even antagonistic to the parent body." To shore up what
Natal authorities perceived as increasingly ineffective indigenous leadership,
throughout the 1880s white officials persistently tightened the administration of chieftaincy, which they saw as reflecting, writ large, the power of the
homestead head. Whenever a chief ruled more than several thousand followers at any one time, the Department of Native Affairs found ways to
shrink his influence. Seeking to keep chiefs beholden to white authority, the
government, for example, required them to forfeit to resident magistrates
all fines they had collected. Chiefs were also to be versions of colonial civil
servants in return for a small cash salary. They recruited young men from
homesteads for *isibhalo,* government public works, and, beginning in 1885,
required these youths to obtain a pass from a white magistrate before leaving for work outside Natal.[15]

The resident magistrates, drawn mostly from among settler farmers, dealt
with a mix of cases concerning whites and Africans. Administrators of native
law, who adjudicated criminal cases involving Africans, were few and far
between in the colony. It was rare for a white magistrate to converse fluently
with Africans in their own language; many government officials spoke halt-
ing isiZulu and showed only a rudimentary grasp of homestead customs.
The Natal Colony paid small salaries to magistrates, staffing their courts
generally with one white clerk who could serve as interpreter and prosecutor, an African *induna* or headman, and a few policemen. In the presence of
this loose network of colonial authority, some chiefs with the largest chiefdoms on the Natal side of the Thukela basin mustered their young men into
labor and fighting bands and fined unruly followers, contrary to government laws that forbade them from doing so.[16] Thus, chiefdoms experienced
colonialism unevenly as a consequence of inconsistent and weak policies and
erratic government practices. From the colonial capital of Pietermaritzburg
northward, white officials tended to have less control over local African
affairs than their counterparts in southern Natal.

After the collapse of the Zulu kingdom, chiefdoms just north of the
Thukela River began to encounter more intrusive white rule only in the final
two decades of the nineteenth century. The Anglo-Zulu war ended in 1880
with a peace settlement that in practice deposed any chief who resisted the
dictates of the Crown (including King Cetshwayo, who was banished to

Cape Town). The government could appoint in his place an African patriarch loyal to the Natal Colony. In the northern Thukela basin local rulers sympathetic to the Zulu royal house lost power. Colonial interference fomented popular discontent against the new leaders appointed by white officials. The 1880 accord failed to bring reconciliation; instead, it stoked rivalries among chiefs that resulted in bloodshed between the *uSuthu,* Cetshwayo's adherents, and the procolonial Zulu faction, led by Chief Zibhebhu of the Mandlakazi. Although in 1883 Great Britain returned the Zulu king it had banished, Cetshwayo's reappearance in Zululand actually incited the *uSuthu* to challenge the procolonial Mandlakazi faction (map 5).[17]

The following year, Cetshwayo died mysteriously during a civil war in which thousands of *uSuthu* fighters were slaughtered by the Mandlakazi-led army. His son, Dinuzulu, strengthened the *uSuthu* with white mercenaries, Boer commandos from the Transvaal; the augmented force beat back the Mandlakazi. But Dinuzulu's alliance with Afrikaners cost him 2,700,00 acres of prime Zulu grazing land, which the Boers claimed as

1883 Partition of Zululand

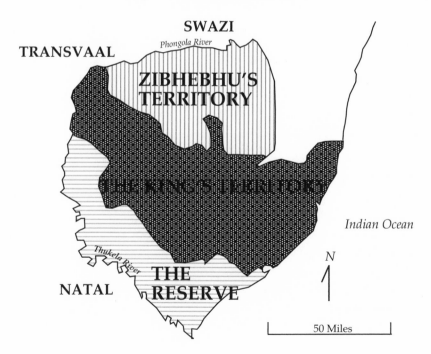

their "New Republic." As Dinuzulu mobilized regiments to stop further Afrikaner expansionism, the British intervened, at first recognizing the Boer territory but then seizing a portion of its western section, which it renamed "Proviso B" (map 6).[18]

By 1887, Britain had scaled back Afrikaner settlements and declared Zululand a British colony, putting in place a token officialdom within a territory that stretched from the Thukela River to a northern border made by the Mkhuze River. The Natal governor himself oversaw the duties of the resident commissioner of Zululand in Eshowe, and the resident commissioner, in turn, supervised local Zululand officials. Revenue for colonial operations

New Republic and Colony of Zululand with Proviso B 1887–1888

was raised from a hut tax, although most chiefs in Zululand, unlike their counterparts south of the Thukela River, could still collect their own tribute and fines from homesteads, mostly in livestock. Imperial authorities in Zululand introduced elements of "native customary law," permitting women to obtain legal divorces for the first time and fixing bridewealth on a sliding scale, as in Natal. Colonial magistrates also took over chiefs' criminal prosecutions, with civil jurisdiction left to the chiefs. In 1889 imperial officials in Natal convicted Dinuzulu of sedition, sentencing him to ten years on St. Helena Island in the Atlantic Ocean.[19]

Of the nearly 155,000 residents of Zululand, fewer than 1,000 were white at the time it became a British colony. The resident commissioner sought to balance the interests of the white community against the overwhelming African majority. Settler encroachment, he wrote, was a delicate "question [that] should be dealt with on a broad basis, consideration being given to the interests of the Europeans at large, and our obligation to the Zulu people, and not by individual favor." The imperial administration in Eshowe effectively co-opted African chiefs and headmen to implement, with minimal dislocation, a variation of Shepstone's indirect rule. The resident commissioner prided himself that in 1892 "no difficulty was experienced in the collection of the Hut-tax, which was punctually and readily paid by the natives." In his summation the next year he reported that "the Chiefs and people [continue to show] obedience to the Government."[20]

Responsible Government Constraining African Patriarchy

In the 1890s generational tensions within homesteads, particularly between young men and their elders, emerged in obvious ways as the various forms of colonial patriarchy became ascendant in the Thukela basin. The growth of colonial dominance was gradual because, despite grand settler designs for commercial agriculture, Natal government policies were devised to protect core elements of African patriarchy perceived to benefit the colony as a whole. Resident magistrates safeguarded some of the powers of Natal chiefs and African homestead heads as long as these patriarchs used their vested authority, upheld by "native customary law," to control youths and women within their own communities.

In 1893 the British government acceded to settler demands that the Natal Colony be granted "responsible" government, a form of self-government that gave virtual independence to the Natal parliament and administration. From the cautious perspective of the Colonial Office in London, responsible government had now become possible with Natal integrated into an imperial trade system through railways that provided transport for the mines near Kimberley and Johannesburg, for migrant labor, for agricultural exports, and for coal from fields in northern Natal. White farmers in Natal, for their part, hoped that this greater political responsibility would open up more land and stimulate more profit. They were impatient to get underway and pressured the government to let them plant sugar cane along Zululand's fertile shoreline and wattle trees on its inland slopes. The colonists in the southern Thukela basin who grew produce for local sale were eager to compete against the economically autonomous neighboring African homesteads that still held sway in the regional markets.[21]

Mercantile and coal-mining interests that had once shaped political debate now shared the attention of colonial and imperial officials with a bloc of farmers wielding considerable influence over newspapers whose own fortunes were tied to agriculture. The settlers, long discontented with imperial rule, increasingly urged the Natal government to introduce a more rigid governance of Africans by adding to the Native Code, the book of native customary law. Natal legislators and officials had been widening the scope of the Native Code since 1878 with laws that revoked certain rights of chiefs. For example, prosecutions of young men charged in gang or "faction fights" were taken away from the chiefs and handled by resident magistrates.

In 1891 a new Code of Native Law, which drew heavily from the old code, granted to the Natal governor "absolute power to appoint and dismiss chiefs," and to the resident magistrates the right to choose successors of chiefs and headmen. The code formalized the homestead head's legal rights as patriarch, declaring the women and children within his homestead "minors in the law," without power to "alienate property" or enter into labor contracts. Women, like children, could not hold property, and sons had to hand over their wages to their fathers. These sections of the 1891 code entrenched male domination and made certain violations of patriarchal authority a crime. A son could now be prosecuted for refusing to turn over his wages to his father, and a mother could face punishment if her husband objected to her giving some of her own hut property, such as farming implements, to their son.[22]

By 1893, when Natal became a self-governing colony with a cabinet responsible to an elected parliament, the Code of Native Law was a grab bag of 298 rules spread over twenty-six chapters. The Colonial Office retained the legal mandate to veto any bill involving Africans and Indians. However, in practice the Natal government became one subject to limited imperial control.

Under responsible government, as in the past, Africans were relegated to the bottom of the official white-dominated hierarchy. The governor of Natal was the constitutional head representing the Crown. Lawmaking and administration were controlled by a prime minister, cabinet members, and elected members of parliament. A bureaucracy of 44 white civil servants and hundreds of African chiefs, headmen, and "official witnesses" (the Africans whom resident magistrates chose to sanction all homestead marriages) administered native customary laws. The white secretary for native affairs and two colonial deputies—the undersecretary for native affairs in Pietermaritzburg, Natal, and the resident commissioner in Eshowe, Zululand—were in charge of the native administration. The next level of officialdom, principally white magistrates, were custodians of native policy and administration. The 31 resident magistrates in Natal reported to the undersecretary; in Zululand, eleven magistrates reported to the resident commissioner for native affairs. In the lower stratum were hereditary chiefs, and below them were the colonial administration's appointed chiefs. Of the 231 chiefs in Natal and 83 in Zululand, close to one-half were hereditary. The colonial administration could not function without the active assistance of chiefs.[23]

"Circumstances Have Changed, and Rulers Have Changed" in Zululand

In African homesteads and on settler lands south of the Thukela basin, white officials had now become the keepers of law and order and the final arbiters of politically charged local disputes. In 1895 Zondi chief Bhambatha in Kranskop division was required to visit his magistrate in order to persuade the government to "recognize" followers who had left his chiefdom to live on a rival Bomvu chief's land. But the Kranskop magistrate informed Bhambatha that he had no authority "on lands falling under the AmaBomvu," and if he hoped to "take up fresh ground" he could do so only "by special permission" of the colony. Even if Bhambatha could have shunted followers onto territory in another district, he could face rebuke from officials for removing "residence from one Magisterial Division to another . . . without the permission of the Magistrate." The government's efforts "to check the indiscriminate settlement of Natives of different tribes" curtailed the autonomy of chiefs; this demonstrated to youths just how quickly their political fathers could lose their actual power.[24]

In contrast, north of the Thukela River, hereditary rights to chieftaincy had generally remained valid, at least on paper, because imperial authorities

themselves insisted that the hereditary chiefs be shielded from the colonial
native administration. The resident commissioner advocated "that all chiefs
and head-men [in Zululand] should be informed that [the government] had
no power to make chiefs," declaring in 1894 that "Section 33 of the Laws and
Regulations [provided to] Chiefs . . . original jurisdiction . . . in all Civil
Cases between Natives of their Tribes respectively." Nonetheless, white officials scaled back the jurisdiction of chiefs in Zululand appointed by the
Natal Colony by assigning magistrates to handle their legal affairs. Two
years later, the resident commissioner explained to a deputation of chiefs
from southern Zululand that "circumstances have changed, and rulers have
changed; people are increasing in numbers: the land occupied by the Zulus
is very far less than it was, it is for the Government to give the people gardens and this it does as it sees right." By 1897, the responsible government
of Natal had extended its administration northward, when Great Britain
allowed it to annex Zululand. Although colonial rule was to be implemented gradually, officials, like the Zululand Crown prosecutor, for example, had become subject to the attorney general of Natal. Magistrates in
Zululand placed restrictions on the assembling of young men into armed
brigades "without permission of the Supreme Chief," that is, the governor
of the colony.[25]

Colonial officials still recognized that it was important to create the
appearance of a strong Zulu chieftaincy. This explains in part the return of
Dinuzulu from his St. Helena prison in 1898 "to be employed in native matters . . . [as] the Governor's representative." As a puppet of the government
with a salary nearly ten times the highest annual payment to a Natal chief,
Dinuzulu had to seek official permission before he could occupy his own
homestead in the Entonjaneni division, a hallowed area of graves of past
Zulu kings. The government did react when certain Natal settlers, primarily
commercial farmers, urged that the full Code of Native Law be imposed on
Zululand, and that the territory north of the Thukela be converted into large
white-owned properties. Zululand, almost all of it still Crown territory, was
to be sheltered temporarily under "the existing system of [communal] land
tenure . . . for five years . . . until a joint Imperial and Colonial Commission
. . . be appointed to delimit sufficient . . . reserves for Native locations."[26]

With Famine, Migrant Sons "Disappoint [Their] Dependent[s]"

In Natal proper—the territory south of the Thukela River—white farmers
had progressively appropriated agricultural land from Africans, for protect-

ing the territorial integrity of chiefs and homestead heads was no longer a priority of the colonial government. From the late 1870s to the early 1890s, when the African population doubled, homesteads were compelled to consume their harvests at the same time that the surpluses they stored or sold had dwindled to perilously low levels. As a consequence, African cultivators increasingly abandoned the delicate balance attained by nurturing, or fallowing, their fields and exploiting the land. In the coastal division of Lower Tugela arable ground devoted to corn crops rose from 5,500 acres in 1879 to about 13,000 acres in 1893. During the same time period, in the interior district of Umvoti the acreage used by homesteads went from 2,600 to 23,000, in Weenen it went from 5,500 to 34,000, and in Umsinga the increase was from 6,300 to 21,000 acres. Cattle and goat herds of Africans had multiplied dramatically as well, distressing pasture ecologies. Homestead farmers were exhausting their land, although in the short run they were able to feed their households.[27]

With an environmental crisis threatening rural Africans, more and more young men departed from their homesteads to work in the industrial centers of the Transvaal, some to stay for long periods of time. In the 1890s roughly 20 percent of the able-bodied Africans of Natal, primarily young men, were spending two-thirds of their working time outside their homesteads. The Weenen magistrate told his colleagues in Pietermaritzburg that "the stream of the able-bodied Native population from this Colony to Johannesburg to seek employment continues. . . . To the woeful disappointment of those dependent on them, the promise to remit, or bring back their earnings [is] in a great many cases forgotten." The Lower Tugela magistrate reported that men "with no property of any description" were leaving for the "Gold Fields, or other labour centers for years at a time, . . . neglecting to send any money [for] food, payment of hut tax or rent." In addition to weakening the homesteads they left behind, the young Africans found themselves seduced by city life around the mines.[28]

The homesteads' need for cash grew in the 1890s as a succession of natural calamities—locusts, drought, and cattle disease—drove African families into greater poverty. In late 1894 the largest swarm of locusts "in memory" descended upon Natal and Zululand. In two years the red hoppers stripped bare two-thirds of the corn and consumed half the sorghum. Homestead heads had to depend on the wages contributed to the common purse by their migrant sons to buy grain imported from the Transvaal and Basutoland. By 1896, the *Times of Natal* was reporting deteriorating living conditions, with "[s]warms of locusts [driving] native women and children . . .

about the country in a starving condition, begging for food." A magistrate in the northern Thukela basin who observed the "great scarcity of food" recommended that the government supply relief to homesteads. The secretary for native affairs complied but reminded the officials responsible for doling out provisions that they sold grain at "cost price" so "the young men . . . should be urged to work, in order to obtain the means for the purchase of food."[29]

Although locust attacks abated by mid-1896, drought soon browned and wrinkled the landscape. Rumors spread of a cattle scourge—the viral rinderpest. Homestead heads like Mr. J. Mapumulo wrote to the *Natal Mercury* in Durban: "we are on the eve of being robbed of . . . our earthly and dearest possession—our cattle." To unmarried young men and women dependent on bridewealth cattle to start their own families, rinderpest would bring the frustration of expectations. As the scourge traveled from east and central Africa southward to the Cape, it left herds rotting in pastures. When in late 1896 colonial officials heard reports of the first cattle with the disease near northern Natal, they encouraged settlers to corral their own livestock and adopt precautionary measures. Inoculation with bile serum from cows that had succumbed to rinderpest was the only known remedy.[30]

To slow the outbreak the government initiated a vaccination program, but Africans were wary of the claim that injecting bile from stricken cattle into wholesome cattle would work. The Mapumulo magistrate reported that "the natives . . . are mostly against inoculation and those who wish to have their cattle inoculated say they are afraid to have them done, as other natives say they are bringing the disease nearer to them." The Eshowe magistrate discovered similar resistance; by 1897 only 2,000 of the 28,000 cattle held by homestead heads in his jurisdiction had been vaccinated, and nearly all the untreated 26,000 were wiped out by year's end. In the Kranskop division only one in ten cows in African herds survived 1897.[31]

The epidemic also destroyed the cattle by-products integral to "nearly everything in [homestead] life" and crippled the ox-wagon transport network that brought produce and tools from coastal towns to the hinterland. Anglican missionary Charles Johnson in Nquthu declared that rinderpest spelled "ruin for the natives" and listed the consequences: "[T]hey till the land with oxen, they clothe themselves and their families in dressed cowskins, . . . 'Amasi' (sour milk) is their main article of food for at least 8 months of the year; and in this district the only fuel they have for cooking . . . is compressed sunbaked blocks of cow-dung." In just four years, as the series of natural catastrophes decimated crops and cattle and as homesteads were forced to drain their emergency stores of food, many Africans slid the short distance from subsistence to starvation. The security once afforded by extended kinship networks now offered little support. In 1898 the Weenen magistrate said "[n]atives are in actual *want*, . . . absolutely without food, or money with which to buy it." He had seen Africans "gathering . . . pig weed, and such wild edibles, for their sustenance." Thukela basin homesteads had rebounded from near collapse over the past half century, but now bad times lingered: cattle had a lengthy gestation period, and it took far longer to reach precrisis levels with herds than it did with crops. Moreover, cattle, unlike grain, were a source of wealth and prestige to patriarchs accustomed to upholding their authority by rewarding laboring young men.[32]

The effects of rinderpest further ripped the complex web of homestead privileges and rights, both diminishing the capacity of the young to achieve independence and increasing the dependence of elders upon them. In the words of homestead head Dhlozi from Mapumulo division, a "man who has no cattle is an umfokazana [a person of no account]. . . . Now [that] cattle are killed off we are nothing." A chief in the middle Thukela basin said in 1897 that "because of the losses of so many cattle from the disease, many natives will, for a long time to come, fail to comply with the custom regarding the giving of 'lobola.'" A homestead head who had to delay giving his sons bridewealth, without providing any tangible reward for their labor, had to call on them to work for wages to buy healthy cows. Elders' reliance on their sons grew daily as the material base of homesteads decreased, a relationship that became even more entrenched during the Anglo-Boer War from 1899 to 1902, when Britons and Boers fought for control over one quarter of the world's known reserves of gold and vast deposits of diamonds.[33]

At the start of the war, mining companies in the Transvaal, Cape, and Natal cut operations and severed the contracts of many African workers, sending some young men home to the Thukela basin. Recurrent droughts and locust swarms were again sowing destruction in northern Natal and southern Zululand, forcing African fathers in magisterial divisions like Kranskop to scrounge for money to buy grain. The unanticipated return of the labor migrants saddled homesteads with even greater food deficits. The search for a short-term strategy to bolster sagging production throughout the Anglo-Boer War became crucial for survival. When the white troops brought hostilities and chaos into the Thukela basin itself, homesteads ironically received a momentary reprieve from suffering, as British forces employed former labor migrants to track or fight Boer guerillas, rewarding them with wages and rations. Homestead heads could thereby satisfy minimum tax requirements and acquire bare necessities, but little else.[34]

The pro-British Natal government waged simultaneous, if different, battles, one against its arch enemy, the Afrikaner commandos who launched hit-and-run attacks on British convoys, and the other against the African homesteads in the colony. The Natal Legislature was now preoccupied with granting settler farmers advantages; new laws compelled African farm tenants to work white-owned land, and by 1900 most big private holdings in the Midlands and northern Natal had African tenants who sent youths to perform odd jobs for their white landlord in return for arable ground. Most tenants coped with rising rents for their gardens and pastures and constant worrying lest they be evicted at the owner's discretion. In 1901 the Identification Pass Law effectively locked the sons of these tenants into service on white farms by requiring African travelers to get an identity document containing their name and permanent residence; time and money difficulties associated with obtaining such documents discouraged many young men from leaving their place of service.[35]

When the Anglo-Boer War ended in May 1902, industries resumed production and commerce in Natal, and the Transvaal revived. The economic activity lured African young men once again from the Thukela basin to wage employment in Pietermaritzburg and Durban. The high incidence of itinerant labor was remarkable given the restrictive measures the colony took to preserve the labor pool for white farmers. The government required African men to apply for "Outward Passes" from their resident magistrates before leaving the colony, as well as for "Inward Passes" from Natal officials stationed in major towns such as Johannesburg for the privilege of crossing back over the border.[36] The financial benefit was considerable for elders and their dependents at home, but the exodus of youths was cruelly double-edged, as labor migrancy depleted magisterial divisions of their youngest men.

The overwhelming number of migrants were "males over the age of 15"; the second largest category, though considerably fewer, was of "males under 15." The third and fourth categories of labor migrants were "adult females" and "females under 15" years. Although more female adults than girls entered migrancy, women were a minority compared to the total of young men and boys. In 1903 the Nkandla magistrate counted 50 percent more women than men in his rural division; the following year the Mapumulo and Kranskop magistrates produced a similar estimate.[37]

"Cornered in One Spot"

Migrant wages were trickling back to rural fathers, but higher taxes coupled with price inflation in the postwar marketplace swallowed supplemental income. In 1903 the Natal Colony doubled the hut tax on Crown holdings in an effort to halt an influx of homesteads onto that land. Already in debt, homestead heads took out new loans to pay the mounting taxes, only to find themselves beholden to colonial moneylenders. White farmers in northern Natal and elsewhere burdened African tenants by raising rents on their farms. Rent arrears, in turn, provided the legal justification for settlers to evict homesteads from their land and replace them. These homeless Africans had few options other than to offer their services cheaply at another private farm. At the same time, the government eliminated African rights to purchase land in mission reserves and prohibited Africans from buying Crown land. The small number of commercially prosperous homestead heads who had either obtained farms through missionary trustees or clubbed together in the 1890s to purchase Crown land now diminished to a mere handful.[38]

Peace between the warring white powers had brought no tranquility to Africans in the Thukela basin. The Anglo-Boer War merely slowed the trend of colonists buying Crown land and reducing the acreage available to homesteads. From 1895 to 1905, homestead corn production dropped 75 percent and sorghum 80 percent, at a time when there were more people in need of food. Africans now comprised nine of ten people in Natal, with births having risen nearly a third in one decade. Homestead dwellers were streaming from barren reserves, described by one group of elders in 1906 as "islands" of "waste," to rent plots on Crown land and take up tenancy on white-owned farms. There was no real alternative for him or his sons, lamented one father in the coastal Mapumulo district. His survival hinged on the resources of whites: "[W]e are . . . unable to fly off into the sky and build in regions perchance to be found there. The ground is hard or we would have dug ourselves out of sight, for we would run away and hide ourselves, ... We are oppressed (cindezela'd), and shut in [by] the sea. Had not this been the case we would long ago have fled from this land, but you have come upon [us] cornered in one spot."[39] Land shortages must have brought despair to junior men and women with expectations that they would receive productive resources from their elders.

Some white settlers, meanwhile, were relishing unprecedented successes of their own. After decades of trial and error they had learned how to exploit their land and combat the vagaries of climate and pestilence. Only a handful of colonial farms in 1902 grew half the yearly corn in Natal and virtually all the exportable sugar, tea, tobacco, and wattle trees, four commodities that together accounted for almost a quarter of the annual market value of all crops. By contrast, thousands of Africans were planting half the corn on deteriorating land.

There were roughly four thousand settler farmers in Natal. By 1903 they had bought up even more Crown land, enlarging the area under their private title to eight million acres, two-thirds of the entire colony's land south of the Thukela River. In Natal's more than twelve million acres, the reserves covered one-sixth of the territory, the rest remaining primarily Crown land.[40]

At the close of the Anglo-Boer War, African homesteads north of the Thukela River were vulnerable to a new colonial encroachment. By 1904 settler farmers were awaiting the findings of a two-year joint imperial and colonial commission to "delimit" Zululand, that is, to allow whites to own extensive properties north of the Thukela River. Since 1902, the Zululand-Lands Delimitation Commission had toured the province, describing in its final report a region once perceived as verdant, "at least four-fifths . . . frightfully rugged, broken and barren or fever-stricken." "Those who are under the impression as many appear to be that [there existed] undulating plains, suitable for European occupation," it warned, "are sadly mistaken." The Delimitation Commission proposed no ambitious plan to remove Zulu homesteads, but, in anticipation of an outcry from colonial farmers and land speculators, it "threw open" for sugar cultivation a fertile crescent nearly seventy miles long from the Thukela River north to the Umlalazi River. The hinterland, "in many parts already overcrowded" with the children and youths born in the late-nineteenth-century population boom, was an area that "so many Europeans [wanted] for stock farming," but it remained in African hands. The commission was reluctant to displace the longtime residents and their large families from "a large portion of the Thorn Country" because an exodus of refugees would threaten the fragile ecologies of "the most densely populated" districts of the lower Thukela basin. As in Natal, there was a widespread fear among officials that Zululand's natural resources would be difficult to replenish.[41]

In Mapumulo division on the border of Zululand, the resident magistrate wrote in 1904 that crop failure and hunger had driven Africans to hunt out of season. After a tour of the bush, he pronounced the area desolate. "Two years ago, the Division . . . abounded in game [but] going over . . .

ground where it was at one time considered to be plentiful, would probably end in not a shot being fired throughout the day." The magistrate apparently did not consider the deleterious effect of drought and locusts on
grazing game. In southern Zululand land shortages pushed homestead
farmers in wooded divisions to "cut the bush nearest their homes" to clear
fields. The harsh drought of 1900 had persisted; by 1903, the Eshowe magistrate described how homesteads were compelled "to subsist almost entirely
on what they were able to buy, beg, and . . . steal." After locusts ate surviving crops and fresh outbreaks of livestock diseases killed cattle in the Mahlabathini, Entonjaneni, and Umlalazi divisions, starvation imperiled entire
chiefdoms.[42]

In this time of disaster the Natal Colony sent its conservator of forests to
survey Zululand for timber planting, the first venture resulting from the
Delimitation Commission's lifting of barriers against white settlement. In
1905 sugar planters crossed the Thukela northward, carrying leases from the
government for thousands of acres. The next year white settlers evicted
many homesteads from coastal divisions and cleared miles of ground for
cane. Zulu elders who were allowed to remain "objected to paying rentals"
for their long-held plots. Harvest time in the Thukela basin, ordinarily a
period for patriarchs to organize feasts to show their generosity, now
became a focus of their failure to safeguard homestead security. After
another poor growing season in 1905, one deputation of homestead heads
told a magistrate near Durban of "past dry and rainless years, coupled with
the fact that all arable land was taken up by Europeans."[43]

With their future on the land threatened, African youths increasingly
looked to the migrant nexus for the means to support their families and
their own hopes for prosperity. The homestead patriarchs visiting the resident magistrate in Durban attributed their own slim margin of subsistence
to the young men "going out to work," those who were "the wagons that
carried [and] the Gardens that fed." When famine threatened us," the elders
said, "we were saved by our sons. They earned the money [for] Government
Taxes and the landlords' rents (ever since our cattle died off with rinderpest
and robbed us of the only other means of acquiring money by the sale of
cattle), . . . it was their hard earned money that enabled us to buy rice, beans,
imported mealies [corn], and other overseas foodstuffs, we would not have
deigned to touch in former years, to keep ourselves, our wives and families
alive."[44] Homestead heads saw their authority severely diminished; their
sons stood to inherit a collapsing social structure with little promise of
enjoying customary privileges.

"The Ferocity of the Young Men" Aroused,
"They Sought Old Scores"

White settlers had, in taking the land, uprooted the spiritual foundation of homesteads—in the words of Eshowe chief Bagibele, "ploughing up the land [and] turning up [the] bones" of his ancestors. The loss of land and burial grounds symbolized the loss of ancestral place. Several years earlier the homestead head Ndukwana had lamented "how can we give praise, seeing that practically the whole land is in possession of various individuals who have purchased it with money?" The continuity of the interment sites and spirits associated with these sacred places had encouraged youths to serve the "principles that guided their fathers and forefathers." Young men who wanted one day to enjoy the privileges of elders understood that rituals heralding the succession of a new homestead head often took place around the departed patriarch's grave.[45] With the material and spiritual base of African patriarchy eroded by colonial intrusions and natural disasters, more and more young men were growing disenchanted, seeing the homesteads they would inherit drift into deep poverty and their homestead heads become impotent to arrest this grim slide. Unable to look forward to the prerogatives of power, sons became restless, their frustrations building for an outlet. The social mechanisms that normally checked their unruliness had depended on the ability of fathers to discipline from a position of strength; now in their weakened state, homestead heads could not curb young men from turning public gatherings like beer parties into riots.

When alcoholic beverages were consumed in public, homestead guests were expected to sip politely from a pot and then pass it around. A proper demeanor of respect was the general rule. At the turn of the century, youths were increasingly instigating drunken brawls and engaging in sexual adventuring during events in which patriarchs assumed that they could impose tight order and punish disruptive behavior. The homestead hierarchy had determined who could or could not drink. Men, young and old, and some aged women, particularly widows, were permitted to drink, but children and young women were precluded from attending beer assemblies and even from coming near the brew pot, although a homestead head would enlist the females in his homestead to ferment *amabele,* sorghum beer. At a drinking festival male youths were to abstain until married men had consumed first. Young men were admonished to stay sober enough to heed the homestead heads' commands. The older male host had the power to dissolve any "quarrels, wranglings and fightings" and to prevent male youths from flirting with young women, who, by law, should not even have been present.[46]

Rules of conduct at beer parties, of course, were broken; what was striking about the incidents involving alcohol and youths were the descriptions of the frequent turmoil. These reports must be scrutinized, for colonial officials and eyewitnesses might have exaggerated the furor. To dismiss this evidence, however, would be to turn a deaf ear to African patriarchs who themselves were loudly protesting the infringements on their position in the domestic hierarchy: magisterial interference that came with government lip service to African patriarchy, ruinous cattle losses from disease and resulting breakdowns of marriage arrangements, settler land appropriations, and social perils of labor migrancy. Homestead heads saw the domestic unruliness as a harbinger of their impotence, for each time the government authorities disciplined youths, the elders found their standing being diminished, either by their own children, white officials, or both.

In 1897 and 1898, American Board missionaries in Umvoti division reported a breakdown in the entrenched drinking decorum: "the prospect of losing . . . cattle by rinderpest . . . aroused the ferocity of the young men and they sought old scores for quarrels." Boys, "robbed . . . of their occupation of herding," found an outlet for their aggression in fights at weddings, where alcohol consumption and taunting between groups of young men turned a normally festive time into a fight. In response, the government passed a law in 1898 to assist homestead heads in dictating when "assemblies" could be held "for the purpose of feasting and beer drinking." Resident magistrates decreed that "the host [was to be legally] responsible for the good . . . order of his guests," and singled out youths as potentially the most troublesome, hence to be subject to the severest limitations. Young men could drink only when "specially invited to do so by a principal man." The law reinforced the customs that barred young women from the brew pot.[47]

These strictures notwithstanding, over the next decade aggressive youths were not dissuaded, and many unruly beer parties exposed elders to magisterial reprimands and fines. In 1907 homestead head Nkantolo said, "Formerly, boys would never venture to drink with men. But now they not only joined them, but went outside and courted married women." With the use of sugarcane and sweet potato in the home brewing process, alcoholic beverages had become more potent. One highly intoxicating liquor, *isishimeyane,* especially provoked young male drinkers into brawls.[48] The spectacle of young men squaring off frightened white authorities. Violence that scared whites alarmed homestead elders, for nothing brought down the wrath of the government on elders more than a public disturbance.

While drunken quarrels led to many of these outbursts, some fights among youths, typically called "faction fights" by colonists, had their origins in sober rivalries. Clashes could be triggered when young men armed with sticks arrived at a party in a procession and began to contest with groups from another locale for the affections of unmarried women. Indeed, the abolition of the Zulu age-regiment system, *amabutho,* by the British did not stop young men from continuing to gather into fighting bands, *amaviyo.* With homesteads and herds crowded together and resources limited in divisions like Umsinga, Umvoti, and Kranskop, skirmishes between these *amaviyo* arose from disputes over garden and grazing boundaries and water sources. Feuds between homesteads and between chieftaincies were common, and sniping between opposing cattle herders doubtless incited a number of melees. Factional conflicts could be sustained after the first clash by the desire for revenge, *ukuphindisela,* "to retaliate or take back," according to Thukela basin residents, who themselves battled within and between chiefdoms in "Thorn Country" for control over pasture and potentially new homestead sites.[49]

In Mapumulo criminal court, cases involving young men engaged in faction fights soared from 124 in 1896 to 631 in 1897. The Mapumulo magistrate warned "the natives of [his] intention to pass somewhat severe sentences [for] faction fighting . . . which is as a general rule confined to young men." After 1900 the rising number of such cases in other districts reflected young men's mounting contempt for their elders. A homestead head reported that "boys [had been] behaving in a most contemptuous manner to men much their senior [in] years. They even struck those with head-rings [male elders] who happened to interfere when fights arose. . . . This had never happened before." A "headringed man," elder Ndukwana said several years earlier, "was shown respect (hlonishwa'd) and never touched by a youth." In pointing to this model of hierarchy, Ndukwana was overlooking the bloody generational strife that roiled Zulu king Cetshwayo's military on the eve of the Anglo-Zulu War of 1879 to 1880.[50]

From 1900 to 1905, recorded faction fight incidents in the Eshowe, Mapumulo, and Kranskop divisions were multiplying from year to year. In Kranskop alone the number of faction fight cases tripled between 1904 and 1905. The resident magistrate of Mapumulo calculated that more people in his division were convicted of faction fighting than of any other criminal offense. In the Thukela basin, which had become the epicenter of such conflicts in Natal and Zululand, the six districts abutting the Thukela River south of Zululand had nearly 30 percent of all cases in Natal's roughly two dozen divisions. On the north side of the river, more than half the faction fights cases were heard in just two Thukela basin divisions, Eshowe and Nkandla.[51]

Elders Become "Veritable Wom[e]n at the Feet of the White People"

One chief of the Sithole in the Nkandla division, Matshana kaMondisa, understood all too well that young men were openly confronting their fathers. A 1905 court case pitted him against his son, Gudhla. The Nkandla magistrate tried in vain to mediate between the two. After wrangling with his "contemptuous" son over property and authority, Matshana said that he wanted to be "done with him for ever." Gudhla faced official charges of defiance of his "kraal-head," while Matshana considered his son to be on trial for ridiculing neighboring elders and for presuming a rank on par with him. At stake for the aged Matshana was vindication. "I am an old man," he told the magistrate, "and I do not wish to die and leave my words from my mouth to be left unsaid." But he was too "infirm," he said, to travel to a distant colonial court. Matshana achieved a coup in persuading the Nkandla magistrate to convene the latest proceedings "under instructions of the full Native High Court" in the chief's own "Sigedhleni kraal."

On 10 June 1905, two colonial officials sat down in Matshana's homestead, surrounded by the chief's supporters. The magistrate permitted Matshana full opportunity to state his case. The aggrieved father asked his son a series of rhetorical questions: "You actually claim your father's property when he is alive[?] Am I to be dictated to by you[?] Are you so greedy that you cannot wait until I see fit to give you what cattle I like, or that you cannot wait until I die?" His words hinted at Gudhla's insult to patriarchal respect, to Matshana as the living representative of the *isibuko sikababa,* the "looking glass" into the paternal ancestry. Gudhla had defied the spiritual tradition by which a "child of a man, the child which he has fathered, will declaim [only] the father's praises" and not his faults.[52]

Gudhla did admit to calling the elders "dogs" but asserted the right to do so because he was acting as a homestead head himself, although not recognized as such by his father. He went further to deliver an indictment of his own, charging that Matshana was an elder in name only, a father who did not fulfill his obligations. Gudhla asked: "Have I not paid for my mother's taxes, and found food etc. for her? . . . Yes I repeat to you father . . . Haven't I lobolaed [given bridewealth for] my own wife with my own cattle, earned by me?" He raised questions about whether a son's earnings should be controlled by that son or by his homestead head.

At the end of the open-air proceeding, Matshana refused to dignify his son's claims with an answer. To reply to questions put to him about taxes and bridewealth, he said, would be to admit publicly that his authority as a homestead patriarch and chief could be questioned. He urged a quick judgment: "nothing can ever soften my heart towards Gudhla, and nothing can force me to give anything to a son who has shown the contempt he has shown me his own father, and flesh and blood (amatumbu), I have done with him for ever, and I now ask the Magistrate to expel him from my tribe, as he is only brewing trouble, and causing discontent amongst my people." The chief decreed: "To you [Gudhla], I leave nothing, I disown you," a statement of disinheritance intended to serve as a warning to others in the homestead that if "at any time one treats me in the manner Ugudhla has done, I shall . . . disown you." The Nkandla magistrate granted Matshana's request for the banishment of his own son.[53]

This drama at Chief Matshana's homestead revealed how the colonial world attempted to buttress African elder authority, while not seeing how the colonial patriarchy had provided youths with the means of acquiring their own power. With wages from their migrant labor, young men like Gudhla could buy goods ordinarily associated with seniority, which led to earlier emancipation of sons from direct patriarchal control. Young men accustomed to turning over their wages to their father now often spent their earnings in the towns, returning home empty-handed.

By the early 1900s, they were withholding contributions "to the common purse," some opting to pay their homestead's taxes personally instead of surrendering money, as was the custom, to their homestead head. Collecting payment receipts in their own name, they became, in the government's eyes, registered homestead heads, though they were "heads" without homesteads. The "ease with which a refractory son could become a kraal head" impressed one Weenen magistrate, who wrote that "emancipation was hedged around with restrictions, but in practice all that was necessary was to ask to have a separate Hut Tax receipt."[54]

African patriarchs were understandably ambivalent about money, some considering it as a godsend, others as a curse—a blessing because after crop failures migrant earnings could purchase relief grain and alleviate homestead hunger, an affliction because cash in the hands of young men was upsetting strategic exchanges like marriages, which had been the elders' monopoly. Mapumulo homestead head Mbovu asked rhetorically: "Was it not right to keep money from natives?" His answer cut to the heart of the matter. "Money was brought by Europeans. We had none. Natives should not have been given money because they do not know its use. They should be paid in clothing and cattle." Mbovu was convinced that whites introduced currency only to collect it. "What is wanted from us is money. After we have worked, the money we earn is taken from us in every way. Our needs are increased and we are pressed in every way. We then go out to work and wages are reduced. . . . We know nothing of paper. How do we, how can we, know anything of these innovations?"[55]

In the days of Shepstone's stewardship, homestead head Ndhlovu recalled, the chiefs who had domestic problems could petition "Our fathers, . . . who were magistrates at Stanger, were men who governed the natives well. They knew them." By the early 1900s, however, Ndhlovu lamented that white officials no longer appeared as surrogate patriarchs: "Nowadays the younger generation have come up who do not know the people. It is to the present generations, the sons of such men as those referred to, that we look and expect them to take our cause in hand and to help us. We are a falling people and we need help." For many homestead heads this dependent relationship between them and the colonizers was insecure, never formalized for long. The homestead head Mbovu characterized it as an "in-between" state of defeat, *"sitela ngoba sahlulwa."*[56]

African patriarchs, "unable to maintain [their] authority and claim people's respect," had become "veritable wom[e]n at the feet of the white people," in the words of Mbovu. Senior rank had lost its luster, he said, adding that now homestead heads were "made of copper . . . whereas [they] should be of gold." The governor could now name commoner men as chiefs, who then would be "obliged to pick a [headman] sometimes who is of no rank, and yet owing simply to his . . . being known at the court house he is made not only equal to but above those of rank, who are regarded by the Government as ordinary people." The stripping away of fathers' powers fostered disrespect within homesteads. Mbovu heard the "younger generation say old people gave in to the white people," blaming "old people . . . for not having made stronger representation at the time of Sir T. Shepstone." He foresaw a widening schism because "the country belong[ed] to the new generation—*abatsha*" who "jeer at me saying we are all equal now."[57]

CHAPTER THREE

Disobedient Daughters and Discontented Wives: Competition and Alliance between White and African Patriarchs

"A Zulu Woman Had a Lazy Daughter"

"ONCE A ZULU WOMAN had a lazy daughter," began the nineteenth-century legend "The Rock of Two-holes," a story of two cliff caves in northern Natal that had "the power of drawing in any passersby." The lazy daughter "strongly objected to being sent upon any errands," such as lugging water from the Thukela River to her homestead. She preferred to while away her days gazing into the "two big eyes" of the precipice.

"I now warn you," said the mother, "that if you go on this way, wasting your time in playing near that rock . . . one of these days you will be drawn into it." The daughter "thought this was merely said to frighten her into good behavior," and when her mother sent her to fetch water she left "as slowly and unwillingly as ever." On her "way back she stopped [and] looked into the [cave, mocking] 'Open to me O! Rock and let me enter.'" A "magic sucked her . . . into the terrible rock," and she was "shut up evermore." When gusty winds brushed the caves, "sad moaning sounds," said "to be the wailing of the lost maiden of yore," washed over the river valley below.[1] The legend of the lazy daughter showed the consequences of female insubordination to elder family members. Yet other primary sources, such as the testimony of African elders, give more nuanced descriptions of the shared interests of young and old, and the parallel challenging of patriarchal power.

The recorded accounts of homestead heads at the turn of the twentieth century depict married women as responsible for delegating domestic chores, a right usually gained from their husbands. A wife's privileged position in part came from raising sons. Yet women were also autonomous agents. Among mothers, often the homestead head's widowed mother—as the most senior woman—earned higher esteem than her son's wives, her status entitling her to a lighter work load. A homestead head's widowed mother could be the most dominant female in polygynous family politics. Her training ground might have started with her ability to influence her husband, to outmaneuver his other wives, and to position her son as his heir. When the homestead head's mother died, his chief wife, usually his first one if he practiced polygyny, became the homestead's new ranking woman who oversaw female tasks. Rivalries between wives, between sisters, and between mothers and daughters created the friction that could sabotage collective work. Thus, good domestic management on the part of the chief wife required knowing not only the talents of the women in her homestead but also their idiosyncrasies.

If a homestead head who had only one spouse re-wed, his second wife assumed an inferior position to the first, unless he had arranged for the second to take over the dominant role. A new second wife of a homestead head who was living with his brothers and their wives tended to assume a status lower than that of any of his brothers' wives. And, until she bore a child, the union itself was not considered fully consummated. A male elder, Ndukwana, said in 1900 that if "a wife does not bear children, the husband will fetch back the [bridewealth] cattle from her father, saying, 'What is there to stand in the place of these cattle?'" As a mother gave birth to more and more children, her standing among women in her homestead rose, particularly above younger unmarried women and those without children.[2]

Mothers enjoyed greater prestige than childless females because they nurtured the next generation, teaching their children the "praise" stories of accomplishment once declaimed by their own parents. Homestead head Mtshapi explained in 1918 that in his experience, "the mother will give praises to her daughters as well as to her sons. . . . And when you marry, your wives will praise you with the praises given to you by your mother, for you will tell your wives what your praises are. You will say, 'My mother gave me such and such praises.'" A widow able to bear children had the option of inviting her deceased husband's oldest brother to "enter into" her homestead—*ukungena*—to marry her and "raise seed." She also had the option of rejecting *ukungena* and remaining in her own homestead or moving elsewhere to the homestead of her father or a paternal uncle. Sometimes a young widow had no alternative but to accept the advances of her husband's oldest brother. For poor men without enough cattle to offer bridewealth, *ukungena* was a principal way to gain multiple wives.[3]

With high status came the right to assign work. A homestead head conferred on his chief wife the authority to delegate labor to the unmarried women and girls of her homestead. If the homestead head was a polygynist, his chief wife could direct work to his other wives as well. Just as older wives had rights to the labor of junior wives and unmarried women, so young women had rights to the labor of older girls, who, in turn, held rights to the labor of younger girls. Adolescent girls and wives with small children tended to perform the harder tasks: hauling water, cleaning huts, washing clothing, and tilling the soil. Mothers helped daughters perform their duties or guided their work. Girls cared for their younger siblings. Women and female children of a homestead worked together, the younger learning from the older. Girls and young women were obliged to labor for their elders, and in exchange they anticipated rewards to come from the older generation, primarily garden plots. Yet mounting colonial land appropriations and environmental degradation curtailed homestead heads' ability to deliver benefits for unremitting work. Although young women did not control bridewealth themselves—only men could strictly possess livestock—they knew that cattle pledged for their hand in marriage was itself a kind of inheritance. This gift of cattle from their husbands signified that wives themselves achieved a position above that of single women. With greater access to productive resources, married women could manage more independently their own domestic arrangements and, in the process, gain in standing. A few women sold their agricultural surplus to Africans and colonists, using the profits from these sales to build up the store of livestock for their hut households and for their sons' bridewealth. Young men who could buy their own cattle with wages earned through labor migrancy probably relied on their mother or the female head of their hut household to supervise the herd boys tending their livestock.[4]

Wives had rights to products like milk and meat from their hut cattle, but those rights were theirs by virtue of their relationship to men who controlled livestock. With only narrowly prescribed property rights, women could neither inherit nor bequeath property. Their rank was largely governed by certain elders, principally by the homestead head, at the top of the hierarchy. One Thukela basin patriarch, J. Khumalo, explained in 1900 that a father hoped not only to "get [his] children to marry where [he] has found

... the most desirable direction, ... where he may acquire cattle (*lobola*), but [also] where he feels his child's welfare will receive the greatest care and attention." A homestead head might delay the marriage of a daughter until he found her a husband whose pedigree would help fulfill his own ambitions.[5]

Rituals of Fertility, Deference, and Chastity

Rituals marked the momentous changes in a woman's social standing. Special observances heralding menstruation, marriage, and childbirth reinforced both the generational hierarchy among females and the subordinate position of women. In homesteads honoring the avoidance rituals of *ukuhlonipha*, females showed reverence for their homestead head by "withdrawing" from him and other men of rank, using polite metaphorical language to address them. One homestead head, named Ndukwana, described an *ukuhlonipha* practice in which a woman would bow to her husband and "instantly cover herself, bringing the blanket or skin [clothing] well up under her neck so as completely to hide her breasts," speaking to him in a deferential tone, and substituting either a figurative phrase or another word for his surname. If a homestead head's surname was *Moya*, "wind," his wife could use an alternative like *Mphefumulo*, "breath." Or she could call her husband "Father of So-and-So," So-and-So being the name of one of his children. *Ukuhlonipha* evoked a code of generational respect; as Ndukwana explained, "unmarried girls who have arrived at the years of discretion act similarly as their married sisters—they hlonipha those she hlonipha's," adding that girls "respected one another, the younger the older ones," and "a man's wives hlonipha'd one another according to seniority."[6]

In matters of intimacy, married women were expected to remain monogamous. Adultery was a grievous infraction for wives and could, in some instances, lead to punishment by death. In 1900 Ndukwana described an incident when a homestead head, Mtini, "found one of his wives having a connection with a white man in [the] bush close to his kraal and the store [around which a small community of settlers lived]. The white man, as all the evidence tended to show ... was actually on top of the woman, and in the act of carnally knowing her, when Mtini violently assaulted both him and his wife with [a] stick at the end of which was an iron nut or head. The white man's arm, one of them, was broken by Mtini, and he so severely assaulted his wife on the head and elsewhere that, although she did not there succumb to her injuries, she soon did so at Mtini's kraal." To some homestead heads, adultery represented the act of a wife who gave up everything for sex. For derelictions less than adultery, a husband could summon members of his homestead to exact retribution. Mapumulo chief Mahlube said of a wife perceived as obstreperous: "the people at the kraal beat her, and tell her to go back to her father, and there apply for a beast with which to pay the fine for having taken such an extraordinary course."[7] Still, unmarried women could exercise a measure of freedom because parents were aware that they could not outlaw sexual curiosity. The parable of the "lazy Zulu daughter" not only ridicules a girl's enchantment with the treacherous caves of Krantzkop; it also warns against her desire to wander about. When hauling water or fire wood, girls could elude scrutiny by their guardians. Outside homestead compounds girls shared a world with boys who might be bathing, driving cattle, or roaming in packs.

Some homestead guardians reluctantly permitted young women to have foreplay with their boyfriends as long as both adhered to *ukuhlobonga* or *ukusoma* custom, where a "man begins intercourse just within the vagina, the girl having her legs crossed, and when he feels he is going to pass semen, he draws away and passes on the girl's thighs." This intimate coupling implied that immediate male pleasure took precedence over female sexual release. Homestead head Ndukwana explained the broader background of coitus interruptus in 1902: "Hlobonga was a universal custom, but it was one which must go on in secret. Every girl's mother, father and brothers knew of the custom, and that she probably acted in accordance with it, but woe betide her if she was caught by her elder brothers. . . . If caught [girls] would be beaten." Yet the threat of discovery and even of reprisal from the Zulu king Cetshwayo in the 1870s, who "said (by proclamation) that girls were not to be hlobonga'd with," was destined to fail "because," Ndukwana explained, "girls and boys slept out in the open by stealth."[8]

To enforce celibacy, elders sent chaperons, usually their older children, to supervise encounters between boys and girls. Parents preferred to keep their children close at hand; if a girl committed a wrong near home, elders could quickly assess the severity of her violation and punish her accordingly. One patriarch, Dhlozi, said that some parents preferred any sexual activity to occur within their own homestead to discourage more serious transgressions: "a lover was allowed to hlobonga at the girl's home, a hut being even set apart for the couple's use." An unmarried woman who had intercourse risked immediate censure from her family and perhaps prolonged ostracism. A girl who lost her virginity before marriage, according to homestead head

Mkando, "knew she would of course lose value when the amount of lobola was being fixed." However, three Thukela basin homestead heads admitted in 1900 that "bona fide accident[s] ('Kwehl' itonsi', as they say)" would occur; in other words, an unmarried woman could become pregnant. Parents wanted their daughters to remain chaste until marriage, hoping to assure their future husband that his bridewealth would guarantee a wife who had not "been mekezisa'd or deflowered." If a woman was sexually assaulted, her assailant could be "soundly beaten by the girl's relatives, and be liable to pay a beast in the event of the girl becoming pregnant." When unmarried couples were caught having premarital sex, boyfriends generally paid a fine, a "beast of reparation," either in goats or cattle, to their girlfriend's father as a pledge of good faith and by way of hastening their marriage. Some unmarried couples who were expecting a child eloped, although to do so was a grave move since they left the protection of family. In the event that a child born out of wedlock could not claim her father's *isibongo,* his lineage or clan name, the child's life would be disadvantaged by the absence of paternal, watchful ancestral spirits. An "illegitimate" baby was a great disadvantage in a woman's life. Women who violated norms of chastity risked the wrath of *amadlozi,* or ancestral spirits, as well as of elders. Yet, ironically, *amadlozi* were said to imbue people with the emotions that roused youths' temptation.[9]

Homestead head Ndukwana gave a personal account of the sexual mores of a married couple: "When a husband desires to have sexual intercourse, he pleads with [his wife]; he speaks to her gently [and] when the woman has stepped over to the husband's side of the hut, she will first face the other way. The husband will say, 'Hau! What are you doing? Turn round.' There may be some reason for her refusing; she may be menstruating, or she may be ill. The husband does not show ardour exactly, but quite a lengthy conversation might take place between the two before the [wife] will consent. . . . A woman always pretends not to want to have sexual intercourse for fear of being thought she is sensually inclined." Ndukwana's account is a small piece of the historical record; one would not want, therefore, to generalize on the subject of sexual behavior without more evidence. Still, rules governing female deportment and regulating procreation helped to sustain homesteads. A natural analogy was made between a mother's ability to carry a healthy baby to term and a rich harvest. Rituals that boosted the crops of a homestead head also were said to have enhanced the fertility of his wife.[10]

"Heathen Girls" Escaping to Missions as a Substitute Patriarchy

When young women abandoned correct behavior, as in the dramatic case of daughters and wives who ran away, they withdrew from their homestead their commitment to labor and their respect for the elders. This was the ultimate threat to domestic security and the development of family itself. But for women with limited futures and for other restless youths, the Christian missions seemed to offer sanctuary and an opportunity to explore another spiritual dimension. Flight from the homestead was a journey into a world of profound cultural differences, into another patriarchy. The religious congregations, led by European and American male ministers, preached a paternalistic theology. God was the creator of life and the spiritual father of heaven and earth, and Jesus, his son, the source of salvation. One of the missionary orders that attracted young women from the lower and middle Thukela basin, the American Board Mission, whose base was in Massachusetts, saw itself as a haven for the children of God.

In the early and middle 1890s, as colonial taxes and other exactions sapped homestead production and increased domestic burdens, more and more girls on the Natal side of the Thukela basin chose the refuge of mission stations. When the oldest brother of a deceased homestead head would not observe *ukungena* practice and marry the widow, sometimes the widow withdrew to American Board stations. After rinderpest caused "the marriage market [to go] slack," American Board teachers noted that "heathen girls [were] coming in [great] numbers" to the Congregationalist mission schools. In 1898 the Nkandla magistrate wrote that in his district "much grumbling is heard" among prospective brides; the "seriousness of the lobola question" forced them to accept that "no cattle at all [were to be] paid." When they objected to injunctions "to marry persons of choice who have a few head of cattle," their fathers treated them "badly in consequence." With herds vanishing throughout the Thukela basin, homestead heads continued to arrange hurried marriages with men who could at least promise cattle. But when fathers found it increasingly difficult to persuade young women to agree to a wedding without immediate bridewealth, some disgruntled daughters joined the stream of "heathen girls" making their way to the missions.[11]

Unmarried sons, too, entered the field stations, enticed by a new religion and education as well as by curiosity about colonial society. Some African boys who became Christians enjoyed greater prestige within their own homestead—especially after learning to speak, read, and write some English—because the few "parents who [sent their sons to missions] want[ed] to know how to act under various circumstances when coming in contact with the European, and also what is going [on] in the world around them." Among males of different rank, religious conversion could be a source of strain in family relationships; one African patriarch complained in 1902 that "[b]oys who become kolwas," or adherents of the Gospel, "reproach their fathers for having left them in the dark." The overwhelming majority of those venturing to mission stations, however, were young African females.[12]

In 1899 an American Board missionary wrote what she claimed to be a true description of one young African wife's transition from obedience to her homestead head to obedience to God. She had been exploring Christianity at a local mission while living in a homestead with her polygynist husband. "[T]rying to serve two masters," she "found no rest until she came out boldly and told her husband . . . that she could not please him to the sacrifice of her master and that he must free her. She had been trying to make herself believe that he would be a protection to her; but . . . when she was working in her garden [God] said, 'unamanga'—'You are with lies.'" She was said to have embraced God after "He called her by her name and asked her about what she was doing and when she tried to avoid Him [H]e said 'Do not be afraid of me. I have not come to scold you . . . but to warn you [of your sin]." This depiction may tell more about the missionaries than their neophytes, but it perhaps shows the techniques used by the missions to win over African women. Homestead husbands, fathers, and mothers did not take the missionary challenge passively. A Natal-based American Board school teacher, Laura Smith, wrote her father in Massachusetts about "two determined and in the end successful attempts to get the girls away from us by the parents." These parents "finally prevailed on the plea of alarming illness in the home," she said, "and while we did not believe the statements, we could not say certainly that no one was sick . . . nor could the poor girls know whether they were being lied to or not. So back they went to their heathen homes and we have known nothing of them since."[13]

Such tugs-of-war between missionaries and homestead elders cast the government into the role of final arbiter between two competing "fathers," with colonial officials being a third impinging patriarchy. The Mapumulo magistrate, for example, admonished some girls in his division who were captured after fleeing to missions in 1903 and warned mission teachers who lured them away against disturbing homestead life. He attributed an upsurge in "cases where children [fled] from their kraals [to] missionaries . . . encourag[ing] native minors to . . . defy the divine rights of parenthood." An American Board mission teacher, Fidelia Phelps, complained that the resident magistrate near her Durban school, "a Christian man friendly to missionary work, seems to think that a girl is never justified in coming to us without her father's consent." This magistrate was following customary law that required him to side with a father who "complains that his daughter is [in mission] school against his wishes." A homestead head could secure a letter from the court, "saying that if a girl refuses to go home she must go to him [the magistrate] on a certain day." Phelps noted that the young woman in question must "obey, of course; if she goes to the Magistrate, as she usually chooses to do, though now we tell her it is of no use, he hears her story, but always tells her to go home, sometimes adding that if she runs away again, she may be put in prison and we [the missionaries] may be also for keeping her." Homestead elders could petition the colonial courts to seize their runaways, invoking Section 289 of the Code of Native Law, which forbade all African children to renounce their parents and which permitted arrest of the wayward.[14]

Despite the government's intervention on the side of African patriarchs, proselytizing missionaries could effectively weaken the influence of homestead relationships. Young women who took refuge in American Board stations in Natal had to become literate in "general Bible culture." Their mission education, a mixture of Gospel and training in the European domestic arts, supposedly provided a conduit to colonial society. For example, Fidelia Phelps in 1908 organized an assembly of female converts "in rapid succession according to standard [academic class]" for an official visit by the governor of Natal, and presented her accomplished pupils as examples of her religious school. The governor asked aloud if a "bright-faced little girl in one of the front seats . . . can . . . speak English?" He urged Phelps to "please make her talk," whereupon he "proceeded to catechize [the female pupil] as to what standard she was in, the countries in Asia, etc., ending with 'Can you tell me the number of inhabitants in China?' He was evidently pleased with her . . . answers to most of his questions, and with her clear and prompt reply to the last, to which she said, 'no sir, I cannot.'"[15]

The missionaries generally imposed their own customs on new converts to build the "foundation . . . girls needed to become Christian women." Mission teachers insisted that girls who had recently arrived scrub off their clay facial ointments and discard their beads, bangles, and cowskin aprons. In some of their schools the American Board teachers provided cotton skirts and long-sleeved blouses, even during hot spells, lest their charges be uncovered, ensuring the elimination of the "nakedness of heathenism."

Female students also were required to learn useful "industrial" tasks, such as sewing and washing clothes, skills expected of servants in South African settler society. Even traditional perceptions of time and order had to go. One American headmaster, who introduced the bell to his mission school in Natal, described its disciplining and liberating functions:

> If you were to spend a whole day here you would find a regular order adhered to in everything. Another step up for people who know nothing of order or time in their homes. At 5:30 in the morning a bell rings . . . 15 minutes are given for dressing and folding blankets. Another bell and they go out for . . . prayer. . . . A third bell calls all to receive orders for the morning work, . . . bringing water from the spring, chopping wood, digging in the garden [and] sweeping paths around the house. [Students] submit themselves day in and day out to the discipline and routine of school life [which] means a great deal to them to leave the drudgery of a Zulu woman's life.

By the beginning of the twentieth century, some missions were transformed into virtual placement agencies, becoming intermediaries for girls seeking domestic employment and, possibly, a monogamous union with an African convert husband.[16]

In the end, both missionaries and homestead elders would watch girls slip from their grasp, as many young women left mission stations for jobs in towns. Missionaries complained of wasted investment in time and effort. Parents lamented the loss of labor, bridewealth, authority, and continuity of their homestead. Perhaps most distressing to parents who knew only the world of homestead patriarchy was their daughters' abandonment of the universe of their forefathers, their rejection of a long-standing social hierarchy in favor of what the parents believed was a hostile colonial world.

A Man Who Struck His Wife Could Be Punished as "a Rascal"

Certain elders may have felt relief after some girls fled their homes; these runaways may have been the most defiant juniors in their homestead at a time when there were also growing concerns about young wives willfully challenging their seniors. A homestead head who argued with his wife could strike her for speaking up. When asked by a colonial official in 1882, "What does a husband beat his wife for usually—is it because she does not work enough?" an African patriarch from Umvoti replied: "It is usually on account of misunderstandings. Quarrels arise and the woman will not hold her tongue, so the husband gets a stick and hits her."[17]

By the 1890s, colonial laws protecting minors from mistreatment allowed

African women to pursue legal action against abusive African men. For example, contrary to indigenous customs that denied divorce to wives, the colonial government's 1869 marriage law granted African women in Natal the right to end their marriages if they could prove to a magistrate they had been seriously injured by their husband. When divorce was authorized more regularly in Zululand in the early 1890s, magistrates heard testimony from Africans about wives who "deserted" and then "claim[ed] a divorce . . . on the grounds of cruelty." Homestead wives might also leave their husband because of sexual problems, as in the case of a woman in southern Zululand who ran away from her husband in 1903, citing his attempts to compel her to take herbal drugs to enhance her fertility as a cure for his "impotence." Divorced women had a chance to salvage their social standing and avoid disgrace by finding another husband, but failed marriages broke valuable alliances between homesteads, causing tensions between estranged wives and their kin.[18]

The Natal government, supporting homestead patriarchy, limited the ability of married women to escape the domination of a husband or a father. The 1869 law required the return of a wife to her former homestead head and allowed a divorced man to reclaim his bridewealth; the failure to relinquish *ukulobola* cattle spawned disputes that were adjudicated by colonial magistrates. In some instances, where a wife created grounds for divorce by living with another man, white officials simply charged and punished her for "illicit intercourse" and refused to grant her a divorce. In Umsinga, the magistrate in 1894 charged an African wife with "fornicating here, there and everywhere." When questioned in court about why she violated her marriage vows, the accused blamed her husband for having "disregarded me" and said he had "neglected to provide for . . . necessities." Her testimony is a rare illustration of an African woman's voice being heard over the usual editing by colonial reporters. The verdict was to "return [her] to her husband." Although it took some time before magistrates began to enforce the divorce laws, by the 1890s, wives in ever greater numbers were able to end their marriages after proving in court that they had been abused.[19]

Chief Sibindi from Mapumulo, irked because the local magistrate was granting some married women legal redress, complained that "if an altercation arose between a wife and her husband, and the man happened to strike the woman, she would make a terrible fuss and charge him with assault before the Magistrate. The Magistrate then took her side and punished the man. The man might be punished or fined, and sometimes the Magistrate ordered the woman to go back to her own parents. Then she . . . procured a divorce." When women could achieve some legal justice, Mapumulo chief Mahlube's world was turned upside down. "If a man should reprove his wife, she would think nothing of striking him, and, when a case came before the Magistrate, the latter accepted the word of the woman, and called him a rascal." The "Magistrate would say it was clear from the evidence that the husband no longer wanted his wife, and would give his decision against the former. Even if a man had only one wife, they could find cases of women going to the Court as a result of some quarrel, and a divorce would actually be granted." A neighboring headman expressed similar bitterness over those women who "on the slightest pretext, ran off to the magistrate, and complained of the ill-treatment of their husbands, and, in most cases, the word of the woman was taken in preference to that of the man." Homestead heads felt emasculated by the intrusion of colonial patriarchy in their marital relations. Chief Sibindi blamed "Government . . . for caus[ing] men to lose status and dignity in the eyes of their women."[20]

Lost status and authority to discipline their wives threatened the continuity of the fundamental homestead rituals that were at the core of African patriarchy. The avoidance rituals of *ukuhlonipha,* for example, could not function without obedient wives. The complaints of senior men monopolize the written record about such matters, but ranking women, too, stood to lose from intrusion by the magistrates. The oldest wives who expected their married daughters to weather spousal abuse were undermined by the divorce statute that enabled a husband to claim back his *ukulobola.* The mother of a divorced woman may already have channeled the bridewealth cattle received from her son-in-law to her own unmarried sons. Moreover, when young women obtained divorces and left polygynous homesteads, senior wives may have had to perform the heavy tasks of the absent ones.

The 1869 marriage law also vexed both fathers and mothers by introducing paid "official witnesses" to protect the right of women not to marry against their will. Official witnesses were African men appointed by a magistrate to ensure that a chosen bride had selected her spouse without compulsion. Another requirement stipulated that the official witness enforce the immediate delivery of bridewealth, contrary to the custom that had permitted *ukulobola* cattle to be pledged in installments. For one homestead head from Umvoti, this new freedom of daughters to seek a husband could weaken their respect for their elders. "We object to the Marriage laws," he stated in 1882, "on account of the liberty it allows girls to choose their husbands; formerly a father found a husband for his daughter to his liking, and he directed his daughter to accept him for her husband—his authority was

then respected. The girls will select young men, . . . and an old man is left
with no one to attend him." Another Thukela basin chief mourned that "as
fathers, we can't dispose of the daughters where we would, nor can we [as
homestead heads] obtain the girls as wives."[21]

During the rinderpest epidemic of 1897, male elders urged the government to direct official witnesses to drop the requirement for prompt delivery of *ukulobola* cattle. The secretary for native affairs contemplated "a return
to the old . . . 'lobolo' [system] where a marriage could take place without
. . . any cattle on the understanding that the whole or balance of the 'lobolo'
agreed on should be delivered when the husband was able to do so." But talk
of reinstating the "old practice" did not satisfy homestead heads who continued to protest to magistrates. Some elder men attempted to circumvent
bridewealth restrictions by exacting "gifts," such as money and blankets, in
lieu of cattle, and by initiating secret marital negotiations, deliberately
neglecting to inform the official witnesses. Still, these diverse strategies to
perpetuate the authority of homestead heads did not reverse the trend
toward comparatively greater autonomy for women. Resident magistrates
heard from chiefs that the practice of polygyny was declining and that marriages between youths were rising in consequence.[22]

A "Girl's Other Father, the Government"

Homestead heads felt increasingly unable to prevent their daughters from
exercising independence in their personal lives. In 1900 homestead head
Mabaso noted the "disharmony between father and daughter [who] follow[ed her] own desires. [A]s soon as children reached the age of 21 they cry
out that, having reached their majority, they are independent of father and
mother and may do as they like." A competing paternalism was providing
protection. As Natal Midlands chief Mkentengu testified in 1907, a "girl
defied her parent, knowing she had another father on whom she could place
reliance, viz., the Government, and if her natural father made her marry
against her will, the other father would step in and prevent it." Another
Natal chief said wistfully that "parents formerly were allowed to marry their
daughters off to people who were property-holders, even though the girls
did not wish it, and, if they demurred, they used to beat and drive them to
their husbands." "To-day," he said, "owing to the Government's actions [the
1869 marriage law], a girl did as she liked." In southern Zululand, Eshowe
chief Nkomo explained that elders in his division had trouble placing
daughters in homesteads with "property" because a "man's child was no

longer his own." He asked "How was it . . . the Government supported the girls in their action?" He answered his own question: if "a father insisted on a girl marrying a person of property, a complaint was laid, and the Magistrate punished him. Not being in a position to oppose the Government, they gave in in the matter."[23]

Male elders tried to prevent their sons and daughters from exercising the new freedom to ignore practices of "the olden days, [when] natives themselves . . . fix[ed] lobolo [for] their children." Natal Midlands chief Mkentengu said that "authorities sided far too much with the girl and the young man as against the parent." Homestead head J. Africa reported in 1900 that "the loose morality of native girls seem[ed] to resolve itself into a conflict between the Government and parental authority." The "highest respect" had been replaced by "all the mischief [of] girls [and] disrespect shown by young men towards their fathers." Elders regretted the end of "the old days in Zululand [when] there was never any conflict between the state and the parent; all heads of kraals were treated with the very highest respect, were in fact the true kings of Zululand." Now in "Natal there is a struggle; the Government stands in direct opposition to the householder. And this opposition arises out of the will to protect whatever appears to be oppressed."[24] These patriarchs exaggerated the glories of the past, ignoring the tensions between homestead heads and the Zulu royal house over the labor of youths, to make their point about the present.

A Daughter "Marry[ing] Whomsoever Her Own Heart . . . Fancies"

At the height of the Anglo-Boer War, many youths upset the marital plans their elders had for them. Young women in the middle Thukela basin were pursued vigorously by young men who warned that if their sweethearts did not consent to intimacy, British troops would kidnap them as war booty. Colonial officials tried to dismiss such talk as an artful ploy, but in divisions where bridewealth cattle had succumbed to rinderpest, young men maintained that fathers would allow the abduction of their daughters without seeking customary recompense. Some daughters themselves used the talk of lustful colonial soldiers to gain leverage in the marriage market, suggesting a dire fate if their fathers did not allow them to marry suitors of their own choice. The alternative, they cautioned, was to be spirited away as plunder by foreigners who understood little, if anything, about *ukulobola*.

In November 1900 the Weenen magistrate elaborated on this "mischie-

vous report [that] has worked its way . . . from [southern] Zululand [into
northern Natal], to the effect that all marriageable Native girls who have
not been wedded to their lovers are to be given to the soldiers." Tracing
the source of this "invention" to the "young men without cattle [who
hoped] to secure their brides on credit," he employed the powers of "Chiefs,
Official Witnesses, and Police in denying the report," but to no avail. In
the adjacent Umsinga division the Weenen magistrate observed the "marriage of girls ha[d] been hastened to such an extent that no marriageable
girls . . . remain[ed]." The Kranskop magistrate said that the "silly rumour"
led to a "boom in marriages . . . whether the husband had cattle to pay
lobolo or not."[25]

Certain young women who claimed that they were being seduced by
magic said they had eloped after their boyfriends had administered "unheard
of drugs." Reports "of this drug having got such a hold" had a contrary
effect, as well, allowing youths to wriggle free of parental expectations that
love affairs would lead to marriage. One headman said girls took concoc-
tions that induced them "to cry . . . out like dogs and owls"; the sound of
"barking like a dog" then served as an excuse for "a young man who had
fallen in love with a girl . . . to break off his engagement."[26] A number of
young women employed a similar strategy of feigning possession to discourage unwanted advances. They now had more options to marry, including choosing from the growing pool of labor migrants who received wages.
A daughter's outright refusal to marry a man might no longer jeopardize her
future. A young wage earner who purchased his own bridewealth could
replace the rival someone else had chosen for her. When rinderpest made it
difficult for parents to marry off their daughters, single women became
more selective about who their husbands would be.

Many older girls revoked the commitments made by homestead heads to
polygynous suitors; marriage to such husbands would have moved women
into a lowly position in a homestead where other wives held higher status.
An elder from the Thukela basin reported in 1900 "an apparent . . . disinclination to be one of the women of a household with many wives." He said
that when "a young man has been chosen by say three girls and he proceeds
to the father of one of the three to ask his consent, the other two will immediately break off their engagements because they feel the chosen one will be
the main wife, and so above them in rank, whereas they hold they are in
every way her equal. And these two girls will be laughed at by others for
having been passed by." Homestead head Mabaso lamented that "in these
days . . . one's effort is often destroyed by the influence of others, [although]

many may naturally desire to bring about a marriage of his daughter with a particular young man; this girl if left alone, might have married the proposed person quite contentedly and lived happily afterwards, but she will associate with others of her own age and these girls will suggest to her that she may successfully withstand her father's wish and marry whomsoever her own heart most truly fancies."[27]

Fathers "Len[t] Their Girls to Their Lovers"

To cope with these unprecedented challenges elders tried to modify customs and reluctantly permitted violations of generational obligations to preserve what they could of their authority. Homestead heads earlier salvaged prestige when the rinderpest epidemic reduced their capacity to deliver marriage pledges by suppressing "the uncontrollable caprice of . . . children." They had devised new forms of bridewealth and determined a new schedule for converting pledges into *ukulobola*. Evaluating the wealth of their daughters' suitors, some homestead heads sought money, horses, sheep, and goats as collateral for the future promise of the usual cattle. Now fathers needed to accept certain limits on women's marriage rights. They had to wait more patiently before responding to "a young man who had fallen in love with a girl." Homestead head Majumba envisioned more deception in engagements where "prospective husbands [after making a commitment] threw everything to the winds and started courting some other girls." A "boy might lobolo, or begin to lobolo, a particular girl, and, when he had continued paying for her for some time, he would throw her over, take the cattle that had been set apart for her lobolo, and proceed to repeat this performance in regard to some other girl. This took place even where the father was quite willing that the marriage should take place."[28]

Elders also had to become more flexible in allowing the young greater leeway in matters of premarital sex. Patriarchs were afraid of upsetting their daughters' courtship with young men who were in a position to produce future *ukulobola*. Homestead heads preferred to "lend" unmarried daughters to their boyfriends, permitting intimacy, although not to the extent of intercourse, in exchange for a promise of *ukulobola*. One homestead head complained that at "the present time the law insisted on the whole of the lobolo cattle being paid on or before the day of marriage. . . . Girls were [already] in the habit of going to their lovers before marriage." He saw danger in "keeping [daughters] at their kraals," fathers "running a serious risk [when] other young men would come to court those girls, and would bring medicine with which to drug them. By reason of these risks they . . . len[t] their girls to their lovers, although the latter were not in a position to pay the lobola."[29]

Those African patriarchs who could command an audience with colonial officials often complained that the "vagabond life" stimulated greater sexual adventuring. A group of chiefs delivered this joint statement in 1905 to the Pinetown magistrate just outside Durban: "towns and women of bad fame in them . . . ruin[ed] our sons." Ziboni, a spokesman, pressed the "Government [to] do everything in their power to stop our young men [and] daughters from deserting their kraals and settling down for good in Durban. These women are really the treacle which draws our young men like flies." He suggested a solution: "if these women were hounded out of Durban it would go a long way towards putting a stop to this evil, for only those men who have adopted theft as a means to a livelihood would then remain for good in Durban." Punishment could follow: "The Government must remove all these bad women from Durban for our sake and as an example to those females who still are virtuous and leading moral lives." Ziboni ended his plea with a provocative question: "Can't these bad women be put into a kraal . . . all by themselves?"[30]

Homestead heads already had protested the havoc created by youths who came back to their homesteads after a dose of city life. When the mines suspended production during the Anglo-Boer War, and labor migrants began moving back into their districts, the return of sons en masse caused widespread mischief among unmarried men and women in the countryside; "idle" migrants, as resident magistrates called them, offered opportunity for amorous interludes. In 1900 Thukela basin elder Mabaso told of "young men coming [home] with concertinas, . . . the playing of these drawing audiences, and here again the sexes coming together brought trouble, for they went home, when they dispersed, two and two etc. in the dark."[31] Musical instruments like concertinas were alluring props in the sexual theater.

Magistrates in Kranskop, Nkandla, Mahlabathini, Melmoth, and Eshowe divisions especially attempted to clamp down on young women who were, they believed, straying about looking for trouble. Colonial officials sentenced increasing numbers for "wandering away from [their] kraal without [their] guardian's consent," subjecting some to a verbal warning, others to imprisonment, hard labor, solitary confinement, or lashes. In 1900 an African father protested that "[p]arents have practically lost control over their girls [who] leave home; no time is fixed for their return and, if fixed, the time will be overstayed, leaving the father . . . to get on at home with the young children and food as best as he can." He yearned for what he believed were rosy prewar times when "girls . . . rarely left home, except on special occasions—a wedding, etc.—and when they went they would return all together with their brothers." Homestead head Ndukwana linked "the cause of boys making girls pregnant" to the fact that "boys and especially girls have defied their parents"; he referred back to an ideal time "when admonished about their behavior, they were obedient." In Thukela basin courts, an increasing number of young men were being prosecuted for "seduction" and "abduction" of unmarried women and for gang fighting over their affections.[32]

In the opinion of one homestead head, Nkantolo, the behavior of young married and unmarried women was to blame for the surge in immorality. He "found [y]oung wives left their children quite unattended at home and took part in these drinks. The kraal-head had no authority to send them about their business, because, if he told them to go home, they would simply say they would not." Around the brew pot, older girls met young men who "were not content with courting girls, but made love to women." Chief Majozi, alert to the volatile mixture of youths and beer, called on the government to combat the "trouble." A statute was already on the books, but Majozi advocated "a very strong law . . . which would prohibit women and girls [from] attending beer drinks." Majozi's counterpart, Chief Mafahleni, "agreed [about] bringing in a law to prevent women [from] attending beerdrinks." The intention of these patriarchs was doubtless to encourage white officials to crack down on the volatile young men and women. Homestead head Khumalo and two other male elders believed that "the amount of seduction (making pregnant) of girls is altogether abnormal and a matter which calls out urgently for treatment." They insisted that pregnancy in the past had been the consequence of "sheer accident," but they admitted "[t]here were [always] seductions, but a girl who became pregnant was looked upon as having disgraced herself [and] was immediately married off." Although this account of rising "seduction" cases alarmed the three male elders, they may have overstated the unprecedented nature of the episode. Stories were still circulating among homestead heads about the young women of Zulu king Cetshwayo's *iNgcugce* female regiment of 1876 who defied his order to marry older soldiers and ran off to have sexual relations with their younger boyfriends in forest hideaways. But now the untoward pregnancies seemed to confirm the trend toward disobedience and to offer an occasion for hand-wringing.[33]

Parents like homestead head Khumalo sought to preempt the need for "inspections" by preventing young men and women from pairing off in the bush, where, in the words of Chief Swayimana from Umvoti, "the girl and the young man met . . . with the result that the young woman became pregnant." Khumalo hinted at the causes of these trysts, recounting in 1900 his recent counseling of a Thukela basin "man in great distress about his daughter [who] was engaged to a young man [with] no cattle to *lobola* and yet [he] wanted to marry the girl." Khumalo had advised the worried father "to demand *lobola* openly for his daughter and, if not paid, to break off all further dealings with her. The man took the advice, demanded the *lobola* [and] the young man gave his usual answer, but when the girl next met the lover, the father followed them up at once and found him *hlobangaing* [engaging in coitus interruptus] with her." The father "seized him and [brought] him before the magistrate, [who took] the father's side and fined the man."[34]

Patriarchs Securing Daughters' Obedience and Curbing Sons' "Unrest"

Despite the objections of homestead heads to colonial interference with courtship and marriage practices, the government continued to use the Code of Native Law to shield daughters and to punish their suitors. Resident magistrates shared some of the homestead patriarchs' concerns and subjected young men charged with "seduction" to additional damages for "indecent assault" and "immorality." Thukela basin criminal court records show that, from the late 1890s to the middle of the next decade, the number of "seduction" and "abduction" cases jumped dramatically, with magistrates sentencing the convicted to heavier punishments than mere fines, including "flogging and imprisoning." Khumalo and his two elder friends were skeptical that such punitive responses could achieve the desired ends. "Under the British Government," they said, "there are many laws devised to check the evil [premarital sex], but fine, (imprisonment), and even lashes, if for such offence they might be awarded, are all equally ineffective." Thus, Natal chief Mkentengu begged "the Government [to] devise some [other] remedy for the evil which now existed of young men running off with their girls into the veld and seducing them."[35]

Not all elders blamed passionate youths for the apparent trend toward premarital sex. Homestead head Nkantolo suspected that calculation rather than ardor was behind the illicit liaisons. Boyfriends were impregnating their lovers "before . . . getting the parent's permission to marry the girl" as a means of forcing the bridewealth exchange. According to one male elder, a scheme of this sort could have grave consequences for a vulnerable unmarried woman if word leaked out that she had shamed herself by having sex. Public censure was supposed to make youths circumspect about sexual intercourse since a loose girl, according to certain African patriarchs, faced "great contempt" as an *isirobo,* a "whore." Homestead head Mkando said in 1902 that "people spat at or towards [an *isirobo*] to show the disgust they felt for [her]." So scurrilous was the charge of *isirobo* that a woman so "maliciously" denounced could confront her accuser in an effort to save her good name; homestead head Ndukwana explained one possible course of action in which "[s]uch a girl will communicate the fact to other girls, . . . her relatives and friends, and they will, in a body—having divested themselves of every shred of covering—proceed to . . . where the person who insulted her lives." In their nakedness they would announce to the offender that "they have been insulted . . . If he . . . acknowledges himself to blame, having spoken hastily in anger, he will proceed to give them a goat, not necessarily a large one. This goat they will then take off and kill, cleansing themselves with its stomach contents, and then washing at the stream."[36]

The Kranskop magistrate linked the rising incidence of premarital pregnancies to the custom of "cohabitation" or coitus interruptus, commonly known as *ukuhlobonga* or *ukusoma,* the very act that incited Khumalo's friend to seize his daughter's excited boyfriend. In his 1905 annual report the magistrate wrote that "[w]eary of waiting, [a young man] throws off the moral restraint which has held him in check and cohabits with his fiancee or other women in spite of protests from father[s] and the threatened vengeance of the law." Most homestead heads themselves were probably unimpressed by this official explanation, with fathers turning a blind eye to *ukuhlobonga* or *ukusoma* because, though risky, these practices were supposed to thwart pregnancy. Although, as noted, a young unmarried man caught in the act of having sex with an unmarried woman was required by colonial authorities to pay fines in the form of cash and cattle to the woman's homestead head, no similar financial penalty was assessed against the woman. One homestead head named Mabele inquired of the Pinetown magistrate in 1905 why "are our girls not punished as well as our boys for seduction?" Mabele suggested that "if this was done, it would in many cases cause more carefulness on the girls' part when hlobongaing; there would be fewer seduction cases and thus many of our boys would save the . . . fines, usually imposed," implying that when young men forfeited wages to magistrates they likely diverted needed income from the homestead purse.[37]

Confining Irrepressible Homestead Daughters and Sons

The Natal government's alliance with African patriarchs was a matter of favoring known homestead practices over the provocations of youths. Officials in the local courts tried to keep abreast of community and domestic discord, canvassing local opinion and investigating "infractions of [customary] rule . . . and the offenders or offenders" involved. Their surveys helped to frame legislation intended to bolster homestead patriarchy. Colonial authorities saw that the escalating tensions between homestead elders and youths could easily become a source of "disloyal" action against settlers themselves.[38] It was a domino theory: if a youth was disdainful of his elders, the next disloyalty could be to white rule.

When the Natal government conducted an all-race census in 1904, the enumerators obtained permission from Thukela basin chiefs to enter homestead compounds to take the count. The unprecedented white presence stirred rumbles among young men that government officials "boded them ill." Some male youths suspected that the census was a prelude to higher taxes. Officials who toured the districts along the Zululand banks of the Thukela River encountered "[r]umours of Native unrest." On the Natal side as well, young men and some other followers of Chiefs Bhambatha and Njengabantu in the Umvoti division threatened an uprising if they were forced to comply with the head count. The secretary for native affairs, intolerant of threats, held Njengabantu responsible for the unrest and promptly removed him from his position as chief, a move that did little to stifle the angry young men. In light of the uninhibited behavior among male and female youths involving sex and alcohol, which distressed both homestead elders and resident magistrates, the discontent over the new census seemed a symptom of something graver. It triggered a new wave of resistance to colonial rule from a martial element in African homesteads: the young men who, in the eyes of many white settlers urging law and order, were the most dangerous people in the colony.[39] From late 1905 onward, the accounts of errant daughters faded in official documents as the stories of violent sons came to dominate the record.

In provoking social change on such a wide scale, the colonial patriarchy had widened existing cleavages between African elders and youths and between African men and women. The Code of Native Law liberated females in marriage and divorce laws but reshackled them when magistrates intervened at the insistence of African patriarchs. Labor migrancy, stimulated by the expanding colonial economy, depleted homesteads of workers and created emancipating benefits for both young men and young women. Male wage earners could now buy their own *ukulobola* cattle. They could become active suitors without their fathers' permission, and their girlfriends could have greater options in a marriage market traditionally controlled by homestead heads. The rinderpest epidemic and the chaotic climate created by the Anglo-Boer War contributed further to the fraying relationships between African daughters and their male elders and between young wives and polygynous husbands. In combination, these diverse factors encouraged a significant number of young African women to take advantage of the loosening patriarchal customs that had long prevented them from exploring independent choices.

African chiefs and homestead heads now operated to a significant degree within the rigid framework of the Code of Native Law. The Natal government acted to safeguard the position of African elders only insofar as their control of juniors helped to keep colonial patriarchy itself paramount. White authorities and African elders competed to protect, guide, and control African women, especially unmarried daughters. Yet in times of crisis between African elders and youths, it was the colonial government, a chief said later, that imposed itself as the "father on whom [Africans had to] place reliance."[40]

Gathering of settlers and officials, Pietermaritzburg, c. 1900. Photograph courtesy of the Natal Archives, Pietermaritzburg (C260).

Africans in native administration, including chiefs and headmen, Pietermaritzburg,
c. 1900. Photograph courtesy of the Natal Archives, Pietermaritzburg (C558).

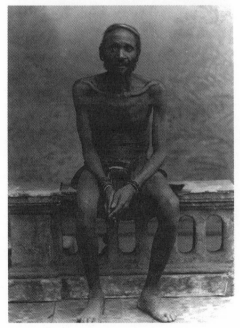

Children of African Christians, *amakholwa*, c. 1900 (top) (C747); famine victim, c. 1900 (bottom) (C690). Photographs courtesy of the Natal Archives, Pietermaritzburg.

The colonial military: Colonel George Leuchars, 1906 (top) (C231);
Colonel Duncan McKenzie's troops marching to Nkandla, May 1906
(middle) (C3534/25); Natal militia righting toppled wagon in moun-
tainous rebel country, May 1906 (bottom) (C3534/29). Photographs
courtesy of the Natal Archives, Pietermaritzburg.

CHAPTER FOUR

"Taxing Our Young Men . . . Separating Us from Our Sons"

The Poll Tax Weakens "Control of the Father over His Sons"

In the beginning of 1906 the colonial government collected a poll tax from unmarried white, "Asian" (Indian), and African men eighteen years and older. This revenue-raising device further upset the generational hierarchy within homesteads, giving young men both new power and new obligations. To meet heavy costs incurred during the Anglo-Boer War, the Natal legislature in 1905 considered instituting a house tax on white-owned properties but dropped the plan after homeowners reacted angrily. Some legislators opposed a hut tax increase as adding another burden to homestead heads.[1] There was no substantial opposition by settlers to the poll tax because they were convinced that African young men were avoiding fair tax responsibilities.

First promulgated in August 1905, the poll tax, like other taxes assessed on a per capita basis in the British colonies of Rhodesia, Transvaal, and Orange Free State, seemed the best available option for boosting revenue without inciting vocal colonial constituencies. Earlier taxes in the Natal colony had singled out African homestead heads, headmen, and chiefs. Male elders would still pay the hut and the marriage taxes imposed on homestead members and property, but the unmarried men were solely responsible for payment of the poll tax. Although single males, and some females in domestic service, had earned most of the homestead cash after the mid-nineteenth century, few African homestead heads had allowed them to pay taxes directly; the payment of taxes, like the giving of tribute, was considered the patriarch's responsibility. Formerly, the receipt for payment issued by the government bore only the name of the homestead head. The new poll tax arrangement circumvented this homestead ranking by age and social standing, demonstrating how the colonial patriarchy could, wittingly or unwittingly, undermine the authority of elders. It was apparent to some government authorities that the receipt young men would now receive in their own name from resident magistrates symbolized power for junior men.[2]

Chief Mafingo visited a resident magistrate outside Pietermaritzburg in late 1905 to point out that the rise in the "seduction" of young women as well as "faction fights" among male youths was a result of a government that "instead of helping us . . . oppress[es] us." Colonial taxes were draining both Mafingo's wealth and the respect he enjoyed as a male elder. He, like other homestead heads, warned that the annual tax collections caused a serious erosion of their patriarchal authority. Such somber caveats were intended to stir Natal government officials. "We have to pay, pay and always pay," Mafingo complained, "that is all the interest in us that our Government shews; our own sons now, when we seek access to the izinkobe (mealies) in the pot, elbow us away from them, saying the izinkobe are theirs, whilst our wives deliberately stare at us, look on, and thereby back up our own sons to defy us." At the time of Chief Mafingo's protest, the Umvoti magistrate reported that "headmen are unanimous in saying 'This [poll tax] Act will now emancipate all the young men from parental control.'" The Eshowe magistrate conferred with chiefs in his southern Zululand division and reported that "the Poll tax will . . . remov[e] the control of the father over his sons." Further north in the Mahlabathini division, a deputation of "alienated" fathers warned the magistrate that "imposing . . . a separate tax upon their sons will have the natural effect of causing them to assume an independent attitude." Chiefs in neighboring Entonjaneni division echoed this protest. To Chief Tulwana in Nkandla division, "taxing our young men" meant "separating us from our sons."[3]

A 1907 native affairs commission, a colonial investigative body, wrote that in "kraal-life," the poll tax had driven a wedge between "mutuality of interest and reciprocity of assistance" and had weakened the ties that bound young men and their sisters and mothers to their male elders. To African patriarchs living near Durban, the "fresh tax" was, in Chief Ndunge's words, "the last straw to break [their] back." In September and October 1905, the months immediately following the government's announcement of the new poll tax, African male elders warned of greater disobedience from restless sons. Umvoti fathers on the Natal side of the Thukela basin "contemplated a deal of trouble from their young men, who would decline to assist their parents . . . on the grounds that [they] were now independent and had to

provide their own . . . tax." In Umlazi division surrounding Durban, prominent homestead heads predicted that the poll tax would propel the last duti-
ful young men into the world of their wayward brothers: "the imposition
of this tax will most assuredly part us for good from the affections of the
very few well-meaning sons that still support us." Chief Faku in Zululand's
Nquthu division complained that fathers had only recently learned how
to cope with "bad sons [who] deserted their kraals [and led] useless,
vagabond lives in . . . towns." The poll tax would be as destructive as labor
migrancy: "the 'Zulu' people are crying at this as it threatens to 'scatter' our
kraal system." Umlalazi chiefs on the coast of southern Zululand dramatically predicted "the disappearance of all control by fathers over their sons."
Underlying their alarm was the habitual objection to the mounting defiance
against older African fathers.[4]

The sons themselves, while accepting their increased individual status,
rejected their additional financial burdens. In late September 1905 a group
of young men responded angrily to the poll tax proclamation at the Lower
Umfolozi courthouse on the southern Zululand coast. The "hot-headed,"
wrote the division magistrate, "remarked that the Government might as
well shoot them down as thus severely tax them." Amid "hoots and groans,"
a "dwarf, hump-backed, epileptic" played the joker, jumping up and asking what money could be received for his "faulty" head "which might at any
time cast him into fire or water or other dangers and destroy him."[5]

Colonial officials and male elders in other divisions reported "anything
but a reassuring manner" among "young bloods," who "would sooner fight
than submit to the measure." With a surge of faction fighting so well documented in magisterial records, the mere mention of "young bloods" con-
jured up images of widening disorder. The Nkandla magistrate in Zululand
wrote that murmurs had been "overheard at beer drinks between young
men," with "veiled threats . . . levelled at [chiefs]." On the Natal side in the
Mapumulo and Kranskop divisions, male youths, according to several resident chiefs, spread whispers of revenge against African patriarchs. In nearby
Umvoti division, elders who told their migrant sons "returning from Durban and Pietermaritzburg [about] the tax" were interrupted by "a song of
defiance." The young men, "reproved . . . for having . . . oppos[ed] the
Government's wishes said that they would not pay, and that if their fathers
wished to pay, they could do so; the Chiefs, thereupon, threatened to
arrest and take them to the authorities. . . . When the boys persisted in
their refusal, the Chiefs sold their [the young men's] cattle in order to pay
the tax."[6]

The furor between fathers and sons sparked demonstrations among labor migrants in Natal cities, and in southern Zululand resentment rose among young men who were earning wages far from their homesteads. In contrast, in the northern reaches of Zululand where colonial interference and labor migrancy were less pervasive, few disturbances occurred. Colonial officials in Ubombo and Igwavuma divisions near the border of what is today Mozambique noted only the "quiet" and "loyal" demeanor of young men and others in the chiefdoms.[7]

Dead Animals and a "Burning" Sky, Portents against Patriarchy

A rumor spread throughout the Thukela basin in late 1905 that the spiritual ancestors had issued an *umhlola,* a portent of a purer world. The landscape, so the *umhlola* predicted, would be filled with pots and pans and with freshly killed pigs and white cows, goats, and fowl. Such millennial rumors had gripped rural Africans seeking to cope with the colonial invasion elsewhere in southern Africa. In 1856 and 1857, when British imperial authorities were imposing indirect rule on portions of Xhosa territory in the eastern Cape, a prophecy swept through chiefdoms there calling for the destruction of cattle and grain and promising, in return, the eradication of white rule. The scale of the ensuing tragedy known as the Xhosa cattle killing was dreadful: four hundred thousand cattle destroyed and roughly forty thousand people dead of hunger in one year.[8] By contrast, the impact of the 1905 *umhlola* was much less than the earlier Xhosa prophecy.

The colonial record provides only hints as to why the *umhlola* called for Africans to slaughter farm animals whose "coats" were the color of European settlers' skin; although racial animosity was probably a factor underlying the *umhlola,* the youths involved in the poll tax protests, by most firsthand accounts, directed the thrust of their aggression against compliant African patriarchs. The pots, pans, and pigs were probably seen as representative of colonial contamination. Homestead heads had first acquired pigs from European traders in the middle nineteenth century. They raised them for lard and for sale in settler markets, but they rarely ate pork, which was taboo. The *umhlola* also foretold that a "burning" sky would send lightning into the huts of those who failed to heed the ancestors' warning, especially the "loyalists," a widely used term for male elders who complied with white rule. It appears that those who were the principal owners of the now-taboo articles were the main target in this effort to destroy the "foreign" wealth. To some patriarchs the *umhlola* would "make people abandon their homes" and the privileges linked to the colonial patriarchy. The portent did not prohibit cash, which was possessed by the young men, the predominant wage laborers. If they chose not to hand over a share of their earnings to their homestead heads, migrant workers could have hoarded money more easily than European goods or white farm animals.[9]

Government officials trying to locate the root of the disturbing prophecy suspected that Dinuzulu, son of Zulu king Cetshwayo and outspoken critic of colonial rule, was responsible for spreading the *umhlola*, but they could never prove it. Several African policemen had gathered intelligence and claimed to have traced the rumormongering to "two strangers" from Umvoti and Umsinga divisions, young men who were going "up-country," pausing at homesteads, telling awful tales of sharpened spears, of the slaughter of pigs, and of an impending revolt of Africans. This story illustrates the broader purpose of rumor: it allowed young African dissidents to criticize both homestead heads and colonial power without risking punishment for libel or sedition. In a patriarchal world, dissent could operate by metaphor, jokes, and storytelling. A wave of pig slaughtering in December 1905 hit Natal's Umlazi, Weenen, and Umvoti divisions. Late in the month, the ancestors' spirits seemed to intervene when lightning demolished Chief Silwane's Weenen homestead, killing his "child and four head of cattle." Animal slaying spread to the coastal areas of southern Natal, north to Lower Tugela, Lower Umzimkulu, and Umlalazi, the shoreline divisions in the Thukela basin. Some Africans began to hide their European-manufactured pots to avoid having them destroyed (map 7).[10]

In January 1906, magistrates summoned from the chiefdoms those liable for the poll tax, despite the governor's fear of "unrest [among] young men of the tribes [now] more out of control of kraalheads." Magistrates anticipated substantial poll tax revenue before the May 1906 deadline, and the colony's need for money had overcome official apprehension. Most chiefs well north of the Thukela River, where the Natal government had no less of a presence, obeyed the government, with the *Greytown Gazette* reporting that the "poll tax [was] paid all right in Zululand, and the deeper one gets into the country the less one hears any discrimination to do so." But in Natal, where magistrates had become keepers of law and order and where colonial officials deposed and appointed chiefs as they saw fit, "native[s] were] fomenting mischief." Fearing more unrest, the minister for native affairs and his undersecretary visited the mutinous northern Natal region to remind homestead heads of their loyalties and, through African patriarchs, to broadcast a warning to young men. The undersecretary for native affairs,

Events Leading to Rebellion
Colony of Natal
Natal (Proper) and Zululand

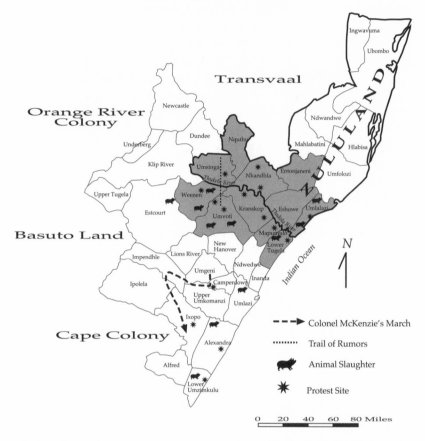

intending to draw the support of male elders in January 1906, convened an assembly of Weenen chiefs and headmen, the "hands and the eyes of the Government," and read to them a passage from the Code of Native Law that included these words: "every kraalhead was directly responsible for the upkeep of good order. . . . they were expected to arrest . . . any disorderly persons, and have them brought to justice before a Magistrate." The colonial government expected African patriarchs to support it, but the chiefs and homestead heads had less and less power to do so because of the very policies foisted on them by white rulers.[11]

Defiant Youths "Ungovernable by Either Myself or Their Chief"

In southern Zululand's Nkandla division young men offered "veiled threats" against elders who were "loyal" to colonial authority, especially those "who obeyed" the magistrate's order to have their sons pay the poll tax. In Empangeni, on Zululand's southern coast, a police sergeant named Matthews witnessed more than 1,500 young men displaying "exceedingly insolent" behavior; at a tax collection site the young men "stated that they would not pay until they saw one of their Chiefs step up and pay first." Twenty miles south of Empangeni, Chief Ngokwana accompanied "over three hundred" young men to within "50 yards of the veranda of the Umlalazi Court House." The resident magistrate saw "young men carrying . . . small shield[s] rush[ing] together, shouting defiantly and lifting their sticks." The chief had "told the boys to leave their sticks and shields some distance away, but they did not listen to him."[12]

On the Natal side of the lower Thukela basin, Mapumulo chief Gobizembe (alternatively spelled Ngobizembe in the colonial record) brought his own young men on 22 January 1906 to a poll tax collection site, and there he ordered them to squat and to hail the magistrate, Ernst Dunn. But instead of the chorus of *"inkosi,"* the respectful greeting of Africans before a magistrate, the male youths called out abuse, whereupon "the chief got up and asked his young men why they didn't salute the Magistrate but they made no reply." Dunn said to Gobizembe, "'these men are defying you and not me seeing they won't obey you.' The Magistrate then told Gobizembe to tell his men that he had come there to collect the Poll Tax. Gobizembe then repeatedly ordered his young men to pay. They replied 'we know nothing about the Poll Tax. We haven't the money.'" A week later on 29 January at Butler's Store, a trading post in Mapumulo, Dunn set up a table under a tree to record the names of those who handed over their one pound sterling. Chief Swayimana and "300 men all fully armed with sticks and shields" had gathered there. Swayimana's men "saluted" the magistrate but then thrust their weapons skyward rather than placing them aside. The chief commanded his followers to "put down their sticks but they refused to do so," and they told the magistrate "they had no money." Their headmen pleaded for peace. Swayimana, who "appeared anxious to preserve the peace," struck some of the young men with his *sjambok,* a tapered whip of cowhide, but as Dunn testified later, the lashing "had not the desired effect, it only drove [them] back from near my collecting table." As the chanting throng surrounded Dunn, he backed up against the tree that shaded his tax collection book and "wait[ed] for someone of them to throw a stone." Suddenly the young men dispersed, leaving Dunn greatly relieved; he wrote afterward that "the whole were regardless of restraint and completely ungovernable by either myself or their Chief." In his report to the Department of Native Affairs in Pietermaritzburg, an African police sergeant described the mustering youths at Mapumulo as a Zulu regiment encircling an enemy.[13]

Dunn's escape was brief. On 1 February, four hundred armed men, wearing white combat insignia (*ubushokobezi*), assembled with their chief at Dunn's collection table outside Galliard's Store, a trading post in Chief Meseni's territory. They stomped their feet and jeered that they would "not pay this tax," nor would they be "eaten up by Government." "If they were here to pay," Dunn recorded later in his minute book, "well and good, if not they had to go." In the principal isiZulu-language paper of Natal and Zululand, *Ilanga Lase Natal,* published and edited by an African Christian, John Dube, an editorial described how the "young men of three Chiefs" met the Mapumulo magistrate who came to exact the poll tax and "broke away and danced in a defiant way." Dunn's own letter to the undersecretary for native affairs revealed a more detailed version of his humiliation. He began: "For the sake of my family, I shall run no further risks"; he continued:

> If I was sent here to put right what others before me had made wrong I should have been told so and be given extra pay or something. . . . I do think I should have been told what I was coming to. You cannot realise how I have felt since 11 a.m. on the 28th. ulto. to 1st Feb., each day I had to sit and look on and listen to downright cheek. . . . the brutes here, I must call them this, when I say "Amabuku avuliwe telani" (The books are open, pay ye), shout at me "Iya asikutela gade satsho enza ngokutanda" (Get away. We are not going to pay. We have long said so. Do as you please), and gwiya [dance aggressively] at me fully armed. I never saw Natives anywhere else arm like this, in fact all Messeni's men wear the "Tshokobezi." To be brief there is open defiance.[14]

In this letter Dunn had employed two isiZulu terms, *tshokobezi* and *amabuku,* to suggest his knowledge of the African people in his area, an *ubushokobezi* being a bushy white ornament made from cow tails, part of a Zulu soldier's apparel, and *amabuku,* being slang for "book." If slurred, especially by a nonnative speaker, *amabuku* (which really means a "bull's neck") resembled *amambuka,* the term for traitor, an epithet used by youths to deride African patriarchs and their supporters who abided white rule. K. S. Makathini, who was born in 1907, recalled in 1981 what his father said about the *amambuka* African loyalists; they "hob-nobbed with the Europeans and had received their authority from the Europeans."[15]

As the first telegrams warning of "trouble" in Mapumulo circulated among officials in Pietermaritzburg, a group of armed young men from Chief Mveli's territory was organizing a protest eleven miles south of the capital. On 7 February, the young men boycotted the Umgeni magistrate's call to pay the tax, and then they retreated with spears and clubs to a ridge above an isolated railroad junction. When a white policeman and two of the chief's representatives approached on horseback, the young men brandished their weapons and chased them away. Early the next day a group of policemen and troops set out from Pietermarizburg to confront the men. When the force first arrived near the railroad junction at twilight, only three men, including the supposed ringleader, were spotted and captured. A trooper named Armstrong, reconnoitering on a hill, discovered "an armed party." His squad galloped up the incline to find a crowd of some fifty young men carrying spears and taunting Armstrong: "You have come for our money; you can shoot us; we refuse to pay . . . you're afraid." Sub-Inspector Hunt brought the "ringleader," Mjongo, with him up the hill to plead for peace, but members of the armed band "rushed at, caught, and dragged him [the ringleader] in amongst themselves." In the falling darkness a hand grabbed Hunt's bridle, and "fierce" shouts filled the air. Hunt and Armstrong were killed, each stabbed many times. The remaining troopers fled on horseback.[16]

The government proclaimed martial law on 10 February, mobilizing rifle, carbine, and artillery units. A thousand-man company of troops under the command of Colonel Duncan McKenzie marched to Mveli's chiefdom, while the young poll tax protestors hid themselves in Enon forest. The soldiers began to burn African homesteads and crops in an effort to force the young men out of seclusion to protect their families. In addition, Colonel McKenzie enlisted loyalist followers of chief Mveli to search for the killers of Hunt and Armstrong. Two persons called "rebels" were caught, tried, found guilty of murder, and sentenced to death. On 13 February, they stood before a firing squad and were executed near Enon forest. Chief Mveli now promised McKenzie five hundred men to assist in ferreting out the remaining rebels, but "succeeded [only] in getting together two hundred of the older men, the younger men refusing to turn out." Mveli's chiefdom had recently split in a dispute between Christian followers of the Presbyterian Church of Africa and believers of ancestral (*amadlozi*) worship. The latter supported Mveli, but his authority as a leader was clearly diminished. No longer could he assemble male youths to defend or assist him as chief in a time of crisis. A. W. Cooper, a white Pietermaritzburg lawyer who had defended Mjongo, the supposed ringleader, at his trial in 1906, said of the loyalists' motives: "I do not think it was due entirely to malice, but so as to put themselves in a good position . . . in the hope of favours to come." Since the gradual establishment in the 1850s of the "Shepstone system," which relied on African patriarchs to help maintain white rule, colonial govern- ment had been doling out benefits and rewards to cooperative chiefs, head- men, and homestead heads. Such African patriarchs most likely stood to gain the most from "favours to come," but only so long as they could main- tain their authority over their homesteads.[17]

Colonel McKenzie now directed his troops west and south to Ixopo divi- sion, where whites were clamoring for protection from real or imagined roaming armed bands of tax protestors. On 19 February, the *Natal Mercury* published his reassuring report: "There has been no attack on the Europeans in any part of the Colony, nor has any loss of property been reported to the Government." But no sooner had the story appeared than new anti–poll tax demonstrations broke out on the border of Natal and the Cape Colony, mainly in the divisions of Alfred, Lower Umzimkulu, Ixopo, and Alexandra (map 6). McKenzie and his army responded swiftly, "cowing" the dissenters, as official reports boasted, but the rebel movement had gained support among "the young men of the tribes who work in towns," and talk of revolt spread, feeding settler alarm far beyond Natal. *Ilanga Lase Natal* reported: "They are now imprisoning the Natives at the Gold Fields. They saw one man sharpening an axe and asked him why he was sharpening it. He said 'I shall cut the white men in Natal.' They imprisoned him for two months." Labor migrants in the Transvaal were beginning to break their contracts. The Natal pass commissioner, the authority responsible for keeping track of labor migrants, heard from a colonial official in Johannesburg that the colony should expect a stream of returning workers because there had been "many reports from employers that Zulu natives have given notice to leave." In these accounts, workers who intended to become rebels were said to be safeguarding their positions in the world of wages; to "give notice" rather than leave with no notice perhaps allowed them to avoid jeopardizing their chances of being rehired by their former employer.[18]

Poll tax defiance among young male Christian converts (*amakholwa*) also created discontent within mission stations. Some independent African Christian preachers in Natal seized on the discontent to gain adherents for their decade-old "Ethiopian" ideology, a protest movement that sought to end African dependence on white religious patriarchy. The Natal governor said he had "reason to believe doctrines and seditious teaching of those con-

nected with the Ethiopian movement" were linked to "native disturbances."
African constables who had secretly observed Ethiopian congregations had
accused their young male firebrands of being "propagandists and prosely-
tizers of [a] semi-political creed." *Ilanga Lase Natal,* hardly a vocal defender
of the Natal government, reported that Ethiopian "exponents advocate disloyalty" and "preach . . . sedition."[19]

Youths were, in fact, focusing their wrath on the homestead patriarchs,
though apparently many white officials were blind to this. Young men in the
Thukela basin were instigating turmoil to show contempt for their own
fathers. In Kranskop "the sons and . . . relations of . . . two chiefs" satisfied
their poll tax, but the majority of the young men, when asked to present
their cash, "moved off [to] shouts . . . that they had no money." The
Umsinga magistrate reported that "the young men of Kula's tribe . . . would
rather fight than pay the Poll Tax," although "the headman Kwenje advised
the young men to pay and not to talk nonsense." Days later a young man
"named Jingi was arrested for . . . trying to incite local natives to rise." To
unmarried African men the Natal administration was not itself the principal
adversary: what many poll tax protestors demonstrated was that their male
elders were disloyal to their own sons. By late February and early March
1906, the government was enforcing martial law in selected divisions on the
Natal side of the middle Thukela basin. To quell what he called "malcontents" in Mapumulo, the Natal governor dispatched a squadron of mounted
troops under a former secretary for native affairs, Colonel George Leuchars,
who vowed to inflict heavy fines on Chiefs Gobizembe, Swayimana, and
Meseni. One of the three chiefs, however, was begging for military protection from his own young men. Swayimana acknowledged, "the Govr. have
saved my life by bringing the troops here." Poll tax protestors targeted him
as an elder who had accepted his place in the colonial patriarchy: "I paid the
tax for my own kraal. I say no one should defy the Government, I speak of
other tribes, the young said the first that paid the tax shall be killed, this was
the general feeling among all the tribes."[20]

Colonel Leuchars, convinced that a display of force would defuse the
strife in Mapumulo, on 2 March commanded Chief Gobizembe to turn over
three hundred poll tax evaders. About two dozen were produced. Gobizembe was either passively resisting or simply unable to compel the evaders
to give themselves up. After waiting an hour beyond his deadline, Leuchars
aimed cannons at Gobizembe's homestead, two hundred yards off, ordered
him to move members of his family out of range, and unleashed an artillery
storm that tore apart the chief's enclosure. Gobizembe surrendered, was put

on trial, found guilty, deposed, and banished to Zululand. *Ilanga Lase Natal* criticized Leuchars's punitive action. The military officials in Mapumulo were misinformed, it said, for "if the blame had been removed from the old people, . . . these young men who are so wicked, and contemptuous [would be] severely punished." A "chief [who] demands obedience from the young men is simply laughed at," the paper said, since the elders could no longer control the behavior of their sons.[21]

Bhambatha, Unwitting Catalyst of the "War of the Heads"

Unlike most of his fellow chiefs, Bhambatha strongly opposed the poll tax. Bhambatha had succeeded to the Zondi chieftaincy at the death of his father in the early 1890s, when he was a youth himself, perhaps in his mid-twenties, and by the end of his first decade of rule, he had many grievances against the colonial government. Officials had curtailed his hereditary powers and broken up his chiefdom. He had swallowed many personal insults, and when the opportunity arose he chose revolt over further accommodation.

The Code of Native Law, which had become more constraining in 1893 when the Natal Colony became nominally independent, weakened the capacity of chiefs to rule over their followers. Consequently, it was impossible for Bhambatha to match the standing of his father, Chief Mancinza, who once had many followers and the respect of Swazi and Zulu monarchs. Mancinza could bequeath his son only a diminished status and a scattering of followers, most of them in the Umvoti division. Like other chiefs in northern Natal, Bhambatha had faced continual challenges from external forces, primarily from white settlers who evicted his followers from private farms. Bhambatha adopted a confrontational stance toward his African neighbors, battling rival chiefs for communal lands and for the meager tribute of African farm tenants. For years civil claims and criminal cases arising from disputes with colonists trailed him. From the late 1890s resident magistrates sentenced him for unpaid debts, theft, seduction, faction fighting, and criminal trespass, occasionally remanding him to a prison cell.[22]

While Bhambatha, with no land of his own, was living on a private holding near Greytown in 1905, a faction fight among Zondi youths threatened the operations of a white farm in Umvoti, according to the owner, P. R. Botha. He complained to the secretary for native affairs that Bhambatha's followers "unhesitatingly . . . agreed that [Bhambatha] is not a fit and proper person to be their guide and philosopher." Other settlers joined with Botha and urged the government to curb Bhambatha and expel him from northern Natal. According to Umvoti division court records, Bhambatha was seen as both inspiring faction fights and begging colonial authorities for his own "location." At the end of 1905, he made a final plea to colonial authorities for a resolution of his legal troubles and for more land. But the undersecretary for native affairs offered no sympathy and replied disdainfully: "I hope that your character will be cleared and that it will be established that you were not a participator in this fight amongst your own people. If it is proved that you took part in the fight then your conduct will be taken into consideration together with previous reports about you, and I would not hold out much hope to you of retaining the Chieftaincy. . . . There is no land available for you or your people." After this rebuke, Bhambatha appeared to have attended an *indaba* (a political meeting) in December 1905 in Greytown, where he learned of the new "head tax." As 1906 arrived, Zondi youths openly rejected the new tax. At secret "meetings called at Bambata's" insistence, according to Zondi police informants, "loyal headmen spoke out . . . against rebellion," while young men urged revolt. The youths' "seditious utterances" were said to have swayed Bhambatha himself.[23]

Late in February, the Umvoti magistrate tried to collect the poll tax from Zondi followers, whereupon many young men declined and massed themselves into armed regiments. Bhambatha hesitated over what to do, eventually deciding to "order the young men to put down their arms and go to Greytown." When "[t]hey refused point-blank," he supposedly came down with a disabling headache and excused himself from standing before the resident magistrate. Prominent Zondi patriarchs professed obedience to the government and stated as much on their visit to Greytown. The *Greytown Gazette* offered this interpretation: "It happened that a trifling headache of the chief and courtship by 'young bloods' brought the old men to indicate [their] fidelity to the Government."[24] The growing generational divide that the paper revealed was to become more severe and to spread throughout the middle and lower Thukela basin, much to the chagrin of those African elders who had sided with colonial patriarchy.

In 1981, eighty-seven-year-old Mvuyane Gasa, who had been a herd boy in Kranskop division in 1906, contradicted the archival records of these events. He said that Bhambatha was at Greytown during the "head tax" collection, and that while there he "sound[ed] the alarm . . . and as he [did] so (bawusho) they [took] up arms completely (iqeda)." A one-hundred-year-old man named Mazibuko in 1982 recalled no "headache" excuse; he remembered seeing Bhambatha at Greytown literally spitting mad over the poll tax. "After the chiefs had time to reply Bambada stood up and asked what the head had done, this hut tax has been enough, of what use is this head that

I should pay for it, I carry it, how does this affect the Government; a heated argument started and Bambada spat at the Commissioner, spat on his head in an attempt to spit on his face, the saliva landed on his hat, this was the signal of hostilities." Both the oral accounts and archival evidence agree on the rage of Zondi young men and of Bhambatha himself against the poll tax. On 23 February 1906, the government deposed Bhambatha, appointing his older uncle, Magwababa, as acting Zondi regent. The minister for native affairs, perhaps in keeping with the promise of "favours to come," transferred Bhambatha's followers in the New Hanover and Lions River divisions to the leadership of Chief Mveli, Colonel McKenzie's ally in the search for the killers of Commander Hunt and trooper Armstrong. In March the governor, who thought it was "the very worst policy to allow any chief to defy the Government," dispatched a force of one hundred soldiers and policemen to arrest Bhambatha. The men arrived at the chief's homestead only to discover that Bhambatha had fled to Zululand to seek haven with Dinuzulu.[25]

At Dinuzulu's uSuthu homestead, the trail of Bhambatha's activities becomes muddled, and the available evidence about them contradictory. On 25 March 1906, Bhambatha apparently sought an audience with Dinuzulu but was rebuffed. The uSuthu headman who informed Dinuzulu of Bhambatha's arrival said that the fugitive chief warranted no special treatment: He "is a Chief, but to look at him he does not look as if he were a Chief." Colonial authorities were alarmed lest Bhambatha's flight through magisterial divisions bordering the Thukela River intensify "the disturbed state of affairs." There were some ominous signs. In Umsinga division in northern Natal, a touring minister for native affairs observed young men "running about the country carrying assegais [spears] and shields." Kranskop headman Mbovu reported seeing a "body of young men . . . armed with their sticks and shields [who] said they would never pay their Poll Tax [and] chanted the word 'Blood.'" During March, pockets of youthful protest had developed in the middle and lower Thukela basin, where the establishment of colonial martial law quickly followed. Magistrates prosecuted "defiant" young men in Eshowe and Umlalazi divisions who "unlawfully . . . disturb[ed] the tranquillity [of] Natal with an object to excite [an] insurrection."[26]

In late March Bhambatha returned home, this time traveling with Chakijana, a "young fellow [who] acquired a reputation for his daring in looting cattle during the Boer War, and stealing them after the War from the Boers." A migrant laborer not quite thirty years old, Chakijana could "handle a gun and shoot." With his knowledge of weaponry and guerilla tactics, he became a valuable tactician for Bhambatha during the future rebellion. Chakijana's service to the uSuthu homestead lent some credence to his claim that he received from Dinuzulu authority to foment a revolt. In this instance the evidence is inconsistent. An uSuthu attendant disputed Chakijana's claim that he carried the royal Zulu order for Africans to rise up in Natal and Zululand. In 1908, when a magistrate in central Zululand asked a group of uSuthu headmen if Chakijana was Dinuzulu's emissary during the 1906 uprising, he received this reply: "It is not likely Dinuzulu would send a boy on such an errand." At the beginning of April 1906 Chakijana, Bhambatha, and a band of Zondi rebels made their way to the newly appointed Zondi chief, Bhambatha's uncle Magwababa. There Zondi rebels dragged Magwababa from a hut, tied him with rope, beat him, and kidnapped him. Magwababa's wife told Greytown officials that Bhambatha had abducted her husband, but by the time the Umvoti magistrate mustered policemen to go to the scene of the kidnapping, Bhambatha had fled with a large band of young Zondi men for Zululand. After a skirmish with the police, Bhambatha pushed through dense bush toward the Thukela River, and on the night of 4 April his men ambushed mounted colonial troops reconnoitering from Greytown. Zondi fighters, with few rifles but many spears, attacked the rear of the mounted column and killed eight men, with no casualties of their own.[27]

The corpse of one of the dead troopers, Sergeant Brown, became part of a battlefield ritual; the victors "skinned and cut [him] open," removing his forearm and portions of his intestines to give Bhambatha special powers. It was an echo of a practice, so a veteran of one of Cetshwayo's elite army regiments explained several years later, in which the Zulu king's soldiers took "the enemy's flesh" to make themselves impregnable. To seize an opponent's "forearm (throwing arm)" and his internal organs was said to strengthen a warrior's abilities and resolve. A severed arm was said to improve one's aim in shooting a gun or hurling a spear, while abdominal organs, such as the rectum, created "fear [in the enemy] by causing 'agitation' in the stomach, [and] diarrhoea."[28]

Invoking Ancestors, Historical Memory, and Selected Rebel Elders

This ambush victory gave Bhambatha's fighters great confidence. They believed that the guns of the white enemy had not killed or wounded them because supernatural intervention made them impervious to bullets. To pre-

serve this spiritual euphoria, Bhambatha had Sergeant Brown's flesh converted into a drug, *intelezi,* to sprinkle on his regiments. The rebels moved
into Kranskop district as news spread of the spectacular colonial defeat and
of the ancestors' divine intervention. Stories filtered into southern Natal of
Bhambatha's *umlingo,* a magic invincibility enjoyed by all who volunteered
for war. Young men from middle and lower Thukela basin chiefdoms were
enlisting in the "impi" (body of soldiers), which was reported to have been
almost three hundred men. On 7 April the rebels forded the Thukela River
to Nkandla, setting out for the forests that bore the division's name.[29]

While word of Bhambatha's daring inspired young men to join the
rebels, many poll tax protestors headed to Nkandla because they "were [sim-
ply] attracted by the fighting and enmity." One such rebel, Mazibuko,
recalled in 1982, more than seven decades later, that when the revolt was
erupting, he had just taken leave from work as a domestic servant in Johannesburg to visit his family homestead in northern Natal. Once home, Mazibuko was swept into the current of resistance, and defying his chief's order
to remain calm and obedient, he and other young men from the district
decided to embark on a journey to Nkandla, resting "under rocks and in
holes in the land" for fear of being discovered and walking several days
before reaching their destination. When they arrived in the Nkandla forests,
Mazibuko said he saw "Bambada sprinkl[ing] the army with protective
medicine [and telling] the warriors they were then going to engage the
white force."[30]

Crossing into southern Zululand carried great strategic, symbolic, and
even magical importance. Few whites had yet settled in the divisions north
of the Thukela, and the rebels may have believed that colonists would hesitate
before venturing into virtually impenetrable terrain. In the Chube chiefdom,
Bhambatha anticipated a friendly reception because its eminent aged chief,
Sigananda, had been offered sanctuary by Zondi chiefs Jangeni and Mancinza, Bhambatha's own father, in the middle nineteenth century. Sigananda,
now about one hundred years old and recognized by some colonial officials
as the "king" of his small territory, had grown up in Nkandla as the favorite
son of Chube chief Zokufa, one of Shaka's closest friends and allies in a frontier of *amalala,* or potentially fickle second-class Zulu subjects. Nkandla and
its natural surroundings held symbolic importance as an area steeped in
nineteenth-century Zulu history. Rebels would have seen the Qudeni
Mountains, home of the blue monkeys, whose skins were worn as cloaks by
nobles of the Zulu royal house, and they would have passed Mome gorge,
Cetshwayo's secret refuge during the 1883 Zulu civil war. The rebels' trek

would finally bring them to the Nkandla forest where, in eluding his Mand-lakazi enemies, Cetshwayo reached a set of caves by following a route cut out by "marks of axes in the trees," an "enclosed path made with branches and leaves, high enough for one to walk if slightly bending the neck." In 1884, hunted to death by his Mandlakazi rivals, Cetshwayo was buried in a glade in the Nkandla forest. This legendary jumble of strangling vines, rock shelters, and hidden trails became the rebel stronghold and the base for guerilla warfare.[31]

At the rebels' arrival in Sigananda's chiefdom, they heard that Dinuzulu was championing their cause, but the story was later denied by uSuthu leaders. An uSuthu servant recalled in 1907 that he had heard Dinuzulu reject the requests for support from the rebels. In refusing aid, Dinuzulu alluded to a betrayal three decades previously, in which many in his family and in the Zulu kingdom died in the 1879 British invasion when most Natal Africans remained neutral. The servant recalled that Dinuzulu told Bhambatha's band: "'When the English came to kill my father . . . where were you then?' He said to them 'As you were not here to assist my father at the time the English invaded [the Zulu kingdom], then I shall have nothing more to do with you.'" Nonetheless, Bhambatha's fighters felt encouraged by the rumor of aid, drilling to the chant of "*uSuthu*" and donning *ubushokobezi* badges, honoring these past traditions of the Zulu army. Some rebels adopted a collective identity, calling themselves *abashokobezi,* that is, the people of *ubushokobezi* who launch a military campaign.[32]

White fears of a widespread African uprising, eased but not dispelled by Colonels McKenzie and Leuchars, now rose sharply in the wake of Bhambatha's flight. Natal officials called up detachments of the Natal Mounted Rifles, the Natal Carbineers, artillery, and policemen. Additional Natal settler volunteers were enlisted into a unit called the Natal Rangers. On 13 February a British battalion of the Queen's Own Cameron Highlanders arrived in Pietermaritzburg from Pretoria, and the next day an imperial warship arrived in Durban port carrying more reinforcements. Nearly four thousand white soldiers were assembled under the command of Colonel McKenzie, divided into contingents under four subcommanders, Colonels Leuchars, Mansel, McKay, and Barker. The army waited until late April before moving to Nkandla. Settlers in northern Natal had barricaded themselves in their houses, girding for the rebels' next offensive, but nothing happened. Armed poll tax protestors who came within sight of the remote white settlements ignored the colonists, including white families from outlying farms who were bundling their belongings into wagons for points south.[33]

Sigananda, hearing of the colonial mobilization from informants, was concerned about his chiefdom's future. During his long reign he had deliberately avoided taking sides in conflicts among Zulu factions and between the Zulu and British. One Chube elder later remarked that Sigananda "did not want to fight in the war[s], for he regarded himself as an independent chief." Now a war was brewing in his own backyard, where Bhambatha had taken sanctuary. Sigananda had limited options: he could either join an insurrection that was not his and that might well be lost, or not join it and risk the government's reprisal for sheltering rebels. Probably neither alternative was appealing. Sigananda reported Bhambatha's presence to the Nkandla magistrate but proclaimed himself neutral when colonial officials demanded that he turn over the Zondi "madman." Sigananda had other problems to face. His great age made him vulnerable to the growing resolve of the Chube male youths. Hundreds of newcomers were in his territory, brandishing spears, clubs, and old rifles, mingling among his followers already agitated by the poll tax. Chube young men and a coterie of Sigananda's sons and headmen, led by his sixty-year-old heir-apparent Ndabaningi, had come together to combat the poll tax. The principal body of elders, including Sigananda, remained cool to Bhambatha's overtures.[34]

The most telling evidence of a rupture between Chube elders and youths emerges from the testimony of rebels harbored by Sigananda on the eve of the revolt. An April meeting of Chube patriarchs was interrupted by a courier, Bhambatha's strategist Chakijana, who claimed to be carrying a message from Dinuzulu. According to eyewitnesses, Chakijana, a mere "boy" in the eyes of venerable Chube fathers, intruded on Sigananda's *ibandla* (chief's council) to berate the aged audience for indifference to Bhambatha's plight. Chakijana seemed an incarnation of his namesake in Zulu folklore, a "weasel . . . famous for its smartness, [on] the alert, ready to bite first." He was said to have hushed the elders, proclaiming that he was only an uSuthu emissary disseminating Dinuzulu's call to arms. When Sigananda questioned his credentials, Chakijana purportedly spoke without respect for the elders: "[A]fter Sigananda had said 'Is there any black community that can go against the whites?' Chakijana said 'It is none of your business. This has been entrusted to my care.'"[35]

A subsequent visit to Sigananda by Mankulumana, an uSuthu headman described as "most astute" by H. C. Lugg, a longtime official in the Department of Native Affairs, failed to change the course set by Chakijana and Sigananda's heir-apparent, Ndabaningi, who now assumed leadership of the rebellious Chube youths. In Mankulumana's own version of events, he arrived at Sigananda's homestead only to encounter a wall of silence. He told Ndabaningi: "I have come here to see Sigananda. I see gathered before me a hostile lot of men, unknown to me. I have no message to give them. It is to Sigananda I have come." Whereupon Mankulumana heard from the heir-apparent: "Sigananda has nothing more to do with tribal affairs or matters on which you have come about by reason of his extreme old age. He can only concern himself with those of the times of Tshaka Dingana & so on. i.e. men of his own age. I am Sigananda . . . and if you have any message for Sigananda you can state it to me." Mankulumana then warned that Dinuzulu did not support the rebels. Ndabaningi was said to have replied: "Do not put your foot here again."[36]

Youths Rebelling, Elders Avoiding "the Displeasure of White People"

In addition to the Chube young men, other male youths from Nkandla chiefs Mbuzo, Mpumela, and Ndube threw in their lot with the rebels, although their chiefs had "been asked by the Government to arm and search for Bambata." The new rebel recruits, before melting into the nearby forest camps, vowed to punish "loyal" elders. The Nkandla magistrate reported the consequences: Chief Mbuzo, "a very old man, deaf and almost blind, . . . fled for protection to Sibindi's ward in Natal." Chief Mpumela, an equally "old and infirm" man installed by the government as an acting chief, escaped across the Thukela River "to the Magistrate [of] Krantzkop." Chief Ndube also avoided danger by going "with a small following [to] the Magistrate [of] Eshowe." In the resulting leadership vacuum, the young Nkandla rebels attached themselves to the older men of rank who advocated revolt. Dissidents from Mbuzo's chiefdom followed the chief's brother and son. Defectors from Mpumela turned to Mangati kaGodite, the former chief-in-waiting who had been passed over at the government's insistence in favor of the loyal "acting" chief, Mpumela. Young men from Ndube's chiefdom obeyed two "prime ringleaders," one of them a headman.[37]

The pattern of youths threatening loyalist chiefs, defecting from chiefdoms, and ultimately finding new leaders among the few sympathetic African patriarchs willing to dispute the loyalists repeated itself in neighboring divisions. In Mapumulo, for example, where Colonel Leuchars had recently reduced the home of Chief Gobizembe to rubble, young men promised reprisals against loyalist elders before heading to the Nkandla forests. Homestead head Mkhonto, convinced that "the young men will kill

us all," begged the resident magistrate "to be given assegais [spears] to protect [the] elder men," at least until the government sent in the constables.
Military intelligence reported that fathers were lamenting the departure of
their sons to foment insurrection instead of earning wages. Disconcerting
to both officials and loyalist elders was the fact that Gobizembe's headmen
arranged the departure of the young men.[38]

During April and May young men streamed into the Nkandla forests,
some arriving in *amaviyo* (regimental formation), some straggling in. Most
came from other Thukela basin districts "where many . . . broke away from
their Chiefs" because "young men thought so little of the control of the
Chiefs [that they] acted purely on their own account." These rebels had
ignored traditional controls at home and had renounced elders' demands for
obedience. In Kranskop, the objections that male youths of the Bomvu chiefdom had to the poll tax overrode the hostility they had toward their antag-
onists, the Zondi young men then in Nkandla. Neither the years of faction
fights between Bomvu and Zondi, arising from disputes over land and stick
battles at wedding ceremonies, nor the long-standing feud between Chiefs
Sibindi and Bhambatha could sabotage the united action against the poll
tax. Refusing to heed Sibindi's instruction to capture Bhambatha and turn
him in, many Bomvu youths joined their Zondi rivals in the forest camps.[39]

Young men from the chiefdoms of Gayede and Hlangabeza, "old enemies and neighbors" according to the Kranskop magistrate, halted a cycle of
"serious fighting" to embrace "a general undercurrent of rebellious feeling."
As elsewhere, a son and heir apparent turned against his loyalist father, Chief
Gayede, and guided a combined force of young men from Gayede's and
Hlangabeza's chiefdoms to the Nkandla stronghold. Some rebel leaders saw
that joining the uprising was a way to take the power from their real and
political fathers. In May, when magistrates asked area chiefs to provide logis-
tical support for the colonial militia, young men simply refused to turn out.
They responded instead to a call from the few African patriarchs who openly
opposed the poll tax. As Colonel McKenzie marched his thousand-man column southeast across Nquthu division to support the colonial troops sur-
rounding the forest stronghold, Mehlokazulu, one of the few Nquthu chiefs
against the poll tax, led a guerrilla band in the same direction. The forces
moved parallel to each other toward Nkandla forests with different destina-
tions. Chief Mehlokazulu, with five auxiliaries—all sons of Chief Matshana
kaMondisa who had ignored their father's orders to raise loyalist troops—
sought to reinforce the Nkandla rebel camps with fresh soldiers. Although

Chief Matshana's son Gudhla had been disinherited for filial disobedience in 1905, his brothers were undeterred from joining the rebellion. Matshana declared the rebels outlaws of the colony, but he was so little respected that the young male recruits en route to join the camps in Nkandla forests plundered the cattle of loyalists in Matshana's chiefdom.[40]

Since the onset of rebellion, the rebel youths understood that most of their political fathers were not going to risk their lives to confront the white government. Acquiescent chiefs far outnumbered defiant chiefs. Out of 321 chiefs in Natal proper, only 25 openly supported the rebellion, and out of that number fewer than a dozen took active military roles. Almost all rebel chiefs were from the Thukela basin. Many chiefs had promised to aid Bhambatha but backed down when they heard the stern government warning against revolt. In 1981 Mvuyane Gasa recalled that when he was in the Kranskop division in 1906, he had heard chiefs say, "'the word spoken by Bambatha is ours,'" yet in reality "they went in a roundabout way and paid the money to whites." Most chiefs "were not intending to fight," and Bhambatha was left "to fight alone." Other chiefs whose young men chose to take up arms, such as Chief Mtamo in Kranskop division, avoided taking a strong stand either way. Mtamo, so an elder follower of his said, "pretend[ed] that . . . [he] didn't see the enemy [the rebels]," hoping not to incur "the displeasure of the white people."[41]

In their mass defections from chiefs in Nkandla, Mapumulo, Kranskop, and Nquthu divisions, the young rebels made clear their willingness to break the customary ties with loyalist elders, particularly when led by African patriarchs who defied white rule. Yet despite the support of a few ranking men, the forest fighters often took the initiative in deciding what course of action to take in the rebellion. The revolt ultimately hinged upon the spontaneity of young men. The stronghold in Nkandla served as a haven for rebels eager to steer their own destinies.

The young rebel Mazibuko left his father's homestead near Weenen to release his "enmity" in battle. He was "not going to miss a war . . . to find out why we were made to pay for our heads." He covered nearly fifty miles of rugged terrain over several days, sleeping when it was light, walking during the night. On the final leg of his journey he risked fording the swollen Thukela. In 1982 an aged Mazibuko recalled his tale of adventure: "those of us who joined [the revolt] followed roundabout ways, having armed ourselves secretly . . . our chiefs did not see us, our fathers did not see us, we met without a plan, we just decided to join this fight which caused us to pay

the [poll] tax. . . . We were recruited by the word that Bambada was fighting [but] we liked, as strong young men, to go there. . . . The forest was full
of warriors . . . others had come on their own [from] areas like Maphumulo
[and] even the other side of Zululand, none had been called up by Dinuzulu
but they had come on their own."[42]

Another rebel, Mzili, from Mapumulo, had also "first heard about some
of our people going over to join the rebels at a beer drink [where] we spoke
in secret outside." He said that he and his friends were "drunk and . . .
decided in going with the other young men of our tribe," insisting that he
had "not [been] induced by any one to join." Mzili and other youths took
no weapons, with the result that when they arrived at the stronghold they
had to scrounge for loose spears and shields. The rebels tended to share a
generational perspective. Some were married and thus not subject to the
poll tax, but most were older than adolescence, under thirty years old, and
unmarried—thus liable for the poll tax. Numerous African and colonial eyewitness accounts confirm that the men who emigrated to the Nkandla
redoubt were overwhelmingly between the ages of twenty and thirty years
old; this generational range was confirmed after the rebellion, when the ages
of many captured fighters were recorded. Out of nearly 4,600 rebel prisoners held at the close of the struggle, fewer than 400, according to colonial
estimates, were more than fifty years old.[43]

Most rebels came from the middle and lower Thukela basin, a region
long on the periphery of nineteenth-century Zulu influence and British
administration but by 1905 being drawn into the core of colonial power. The
basin sat on the upper fringe of the most populated white settlements. Since
the 1850s, magistrates in the bottom third of Natal imposed an increasingly
strict brand of the Code of Native Law on homesteads, and many African
patriarchs owed their positions to good relations with the secretary for
native affairs, the "great white father," Theophilus Shepstone. Although
African young men sparked violent demonstrations against the poll tax in
magisterial divisions south of Pietermaritzburg, these outbursts could not
be sustained due to the overwhelming firepower of the colonial militia and,
in large measure, to the lack of a unifying goal among protestors to punish
amambuka patriarchs.

North in Zululand, chiefs and homestead heads endured far less magisterial interference in their affairs. In effect, they were able to contain domestic strife. During poll tax collection colonial officials in Zululand's middle
and northern divisions recorded few hostile encounters with African young

men. By contrast, the "war of the heads" erupted in the Thukela basin precisely because recent colonial encroachment not only inflamed homestead struggles over patriarchal control but also emboldened youths to overturn conventions of generational authority. While the rebels were reluctant to launch an offensive against white settlers, they raided and killed *amambuka* Africans, most of whom were homestead heads seeking to comply with white rule and preserve their own privileges, usually at the expense of an ascendant generation.

CHAPTER FIVE

"The War of the Heads":
Youths Rebel against Elders
and Colonial Power

The Oxtail Badge of Legendary Zulu Power

ON 5 May 1906, the poll tax rebels camping near Bhobe ridge awoke to the hiss of shells hurtling toward their Nkandla forest stronghold. Mvuyane Gasa, a herd boy in the Kranskop division roughly thirty miles south, was roused before dawn by blasts and muffled shouts of *"uSuthu"* resounding across the Thukela River; in 1981 he recalled the fight between the Natal militia and the rebels: "the battle was being fought in the early morning at 4:00 A.M. By 5:00 A.M., they were tearing [the rebels] apart (kwakuthi dlephu-dlephu). I have forgotten who was the man with whom we were left here in the hut. He stood up, put his hands to his back and said: 'Oh how the young men are being decimated.' There was a thundering of field guns and rifles."[1] This bombardment was the first salvo of a colonial invasion that by September 1906 had suppressed the "war of the heads."

A month before the assault, the young rebels in Nkandla forest had been buoyant, resurrecting symbols of a legendary era when a formidable Zulu patriarchy, founded by King Shaka, had slowed the pace of colonial encroachment; as Shula Marks was first to argue, the poll tax upheavals exhibited elements of a "restorationist" revolt. Donning bushy *ubushokobezi*, the badges of the soldiers of the Zulu army, the rebels chanted *uSuthu*, the name of King Cetshwayo's royal house, and sought revenge against *amambuka* African elders who obeyed colonial authority. As one veteran of the king's military recalled, "We of Cetshwayo's army used the cry, 'USutu!' We all had on the ox-tail (umtshokobezi) badge. . . . To tshokobeza means to evade the law, i.e. the white people's law, for we [joined] Cetshwayo. . . . The others were amambuka, i.e. those who had deserted (hlubuka'd) the king."[2]

In the view of the colonial government, the Zulu monarchy was an anachronism, but when the rumor of Dinuzulu's call to arms filtered into Nkandla, the rebels united behind the belief that the *umntwana*—the prince of the Zulu kingdom and counterweight to colonial power—was now sanctioning the poll tax revolt. To the young men irate at *amambuka* African patriarchs, Dinuzulu was a patriarch worthy of loyalty. Although the colonial government forbade Dinuzulu to act as "Paramount of the Zulus," his hereditary and political pedigree, in the eyes of the forest fighters, transcended white law and dominion. His imprisonment by the British on St. Helena Island in the Atlantic from 1888 to 1898 was viewed by many as clear evidence of his resistance to the settlers' government. In late April 1906 intelligence officers of the colonial government reported that the Nkandla forest burial site of Dinuzulu's father was now a training area, with young soldiers drilling around the grave. Rebels continued to invoke the spiritual armor of the *intelezi* "medicine" that had long been employed as protection against the hazards of war. Bhambatha was said to have assured them: "When bullets come to you do not be afraid and run away, all those who will give the enemy their back will die, but those who will go on until they engage the white impi [army] physically, will suffer no harm." For all their homage to the Zulu kingdom, the rebels did not use specially designated male elder healers who assured battlefield invincibility, although this practice had been used by Kings Shaka and Dingana during the preceding century.[3]

Youthful rebels so distrusted those African patriarchs who refused to join in the rebellion that they taunted them "from the hilltops . . . to 'plait a long rope with which to climb to the heavens,'" and they looted the livestock of those suspected of aiding the Natal government in collecting the poll tax. One Nkandla homestead head, Lumbe, reported that "old loyalist[s]" were being warned that they would be "killed by the Rebels." The forest fighters summoned self-declared African doctors, young men such as Bhambatha's guerilla strategist Chakijana, to sprinkle *intelezi,* protective medicine, on the regiments, contravening the customs of the Chube chiefdom in Nkandla that forbade seeking out "doctors from foreign parts." Age was one means of determining who was an ally and who was not. So was expressing allegiance to the youths who made the "extraordinary" sacrifice to repudiate the head tax and confront the patriarchs responsible for its imposition. The rebels' passwords were heavy with such generational connotations. Mazibuko, a guard at one Nkandla military camp, demanded "the password" from unknown African men passing through—"to which group do you belong?" He acknowledged only: "Something extraordinary, the money of the head."[4]

Beginning 3 May, four separate columns of Natal colonial troops, each ranging from four hundred to a thousand men—one from the east, two from the south, and one from the west—snaked across the spurs of the Thukela basin on their way to the rebel positions. Supply wagons toppled from precipitous ridges as soldiers made the arduous journey over the hills of "Thorn Country," passing through Umsinga division, where Chief Kula's young men had followed one of the chief's uncles, Mtele, to join the rebels. Kula, a prominent colonial-appointed chief who had warned the Umsinga magistrate of the uprising, was himself arrested on suspicion of treason. On 4 May one of Bhambatha's bands confronted a Natal troop detachment on the border between Umsinga division and Zululand and suffered some casualties before escaping. The next day, in the first major clash between an army of poll tax protestors and the colonial militia, the rebel movement received a devastating blow. The battle at Bhobe ridge in Nkandla division on 5 May pitted four hundred rebels against eight hundred Natal soldiers equipped with cannons. Half of the colonial troops were African troop levies or "loyalists," armed with spears and similar weapons and assigned to intelligence gathering. The artillery units moved to higher ground and bombarded the forest fighters, who appeared surprised by the fierce attack. The rebels, with few firearms, were trapped by the big guns of the field force; they crouched behind rocks and mounds of earth and made periodic charges with spears at the colonial positions, only to encounter withering rifle fire. About one hundred of Bhambatha's men were killed, some escaped into the Nkandla forests, and a substantial number surrendered. The Natal detachment had no casualties. British newspapers reported that the white troops had surrounded and destroyed the Bhobe rebels. An *Ilanga Lase Natal* article likened the flattening of rebel positions to the devastation of the San Francisco earthquake of the same month and year.[5]

Bhambatha's medicine had failed to bestow invincibility. The young men's earlier tactics had avoided direct confrontation by securing refuge in forests and caves. As a veteran of the 1879 Zulu victory over the British at Isandlwana, Mpatshana kaSodondo described the debacle at Bhobe ridge: "Bambatha's warfare . . . differed from that of Zulus for taking refuge in forests and fastnesses until hunted up by the Europeans. Zulus would have taken up a position in the open and come face to face with the foe. They waylaid Europeans wherever they could. We laughed at them for this." White troops now converged on the military camps in Nkandla near Cetshwayo's grave and in the nearby Macala Hills. By mid-May several skirmishes had ended in rebel defeat. The colonial soldiers, supplemented by hundreds of "native [troop] levies," "burnt many kraals," and drove the forest fighters deeper into the bush. During one encounter grass and bush around the king's burial stones caught fire, and messengers from both rebels and the government rushed to inform Dinuzulu. Some officials called the fire a regrettable consequence of war. Others voiced suspicions that although Bhambatha blamed whites for the blaze, his men were responsible for setting the fire themselves. Dinuzulu was said to have expressed concern that the fire and the "blood being shed in the vicinity" would disturb the spirit of his father, King Cetshwayo.[6]

Colonial Patriarchy Provoking Triangulation of Generations

While the colonial army was exploiting the tactical errors of rebel forces, the colonial administrators were effectively co-opting homestead patriarchs who feared retribution from the poll tax protestors. The Natal government played the elder African generation and their supporters against the rebel youths to the advantage of the Natal military. When colonial troops learned of rebel movements from African troops mustered by loyalist chiefs Sibindi, Mbuzo, Mpumela, and Sitshitshili, the chiefs were given permission to confiscate livestock from the homesteads of young rebels in their chiefdoms.[7]

The ages of African troop levies are unclear, but patchy archival evidence suggests that they tended to be considerably older than the young fighters in Nkandla forests. Photos of troop levies on the march to Nkandla forest, for example, show headringed older men in frock coats. The policy of mustering such Africans to fight the rebels had exacerbated existing generational tensions and forcibly aligned African patriarchs in times of crisis with white power. After defeating the Zulu kingdom in 1879, imperial authorities in Natal had employed a similar strategy by installing procolonial chiefs to stifle dissident, uSuthu-supporting homestead patriarchs in southern Zululand.[8]

The rebels, their morale eroded by routs on 5 May and later in which African allies of colonial power played a critical role, were hardly in a position to take the offensive. When they left their stronghold, they limited themselves to hit-and-run attacks. In one assault on 14 May, sixty rebels armed with only spears and sticks descended on a community of Nquthu loyalists and were repulsed by the rifle fire of two African men who had become levies for the colonial troops. At the edge of Nkandla forest, white soldiers "were sniped [at] by enemy," seemingly by rebels with rifles, but military reports said the snipers "evidently cannot shoot." After the clash at Bhobe ridge, colonial soldiers were scouring hill slopes near the Nkandla forests, seeking to flush out rebels and funnel them into Mome gorge, an area with few avenues of escape. Colonel McKay's column placed its big guns above the gorge, and after several days of shelling, patrols came upon scores of rebel dead under rocks and in the mouths of caves. On 31 May McKay wired Natal militia headquarters in Pietermaritzburg: "The rebels were hiding in caves and rocks and they built up palisades and had blocked up and loopholed their caves. Consequently it was a most difficult task to dislodge them. This entailed exceedingly hard work but it was cheerfully carried out by all ranks. Many dead bodies from the previous day's fight were found having been carried away and hidden in caves, one cave alone containing 12 bodies. There were also signs of others having been buried in the vicinity so that I am confident that I have not over estimated the enemy's losses."[9]

The rebels and their leaders, among them Bhambatha, Chakijana, and Mehlokazulu, now consolidated their forces in an effort to revive the sagging rebellion. Hearing of this alliance, Colonel McKenzie invaded Mome gorge on 10 June, ten weeks after the first rebel outbreak. In the next two days Bhambatha and Mehlokazulu and about five to six hundred rebels died in a rain of rifle fire. According to a 1912 account, reported by homestead head Mpatshana, the forest fighters made a fatal error. "Bambata and company," he said, "failed to put out scouts or even listen to the boy who said the Europeans were coming [to attack], except . . . the elderly men of Sigananda's tribe, who went up the gorge past the little burnt kraal on the right to the main [Nkandla] forest, Eziwojeni, where they simply stayed and kept quiet. A messenger was sent . . . to tell them to return as the Europeans were coming, but [the] company [of old men] refused to go back." In the ensuing fight, the young men, of course, suffered heavy casualties; the old men who "kept quiet" survived.[10]

When defeated rebels began emerging from the forests on 13 June, a great many women were among them. Militia spies, some of them African men from Nkandla, had earlier reported seeing young women around the Nkandla rebel camps. They were probably camp followers attending to domestic duties for the fighters or visiting their rebel boyfriends. There is no evidence in the archival record that women were organizing their own regiments, that they fought alongside the young men, or that they were even armed. The considerable number of women who emerged from the forest to surrender suggests that they probably survived the battle at Mome gorge, like the "elderly men of Sigananda's tribe," by seeking refuge from the range of colonial guns.[11]

Sigananda and other leaders surrendered on a blustery cool mid-June day, winter in the southern hemisphere. Military photographers who recorded the exodus from the Mome stronghold captured images of weary forest fighters holding aloft sticks bearing white rags of surrender, and of beaten rebels corralled into tight circles by colonial troops. The foreground of one photograph depicts young men, and a scattering of young women, crouched with knees drawn up to their faces. Victorious white soldiers are visible in other military photographs displaying booty salvaged from the battlefield—spears, shields, leopard skins, and *ubushokobezi,* the oxtail war badges.

In a lull in the fighting, one squadron combed Nkandla forests for Bhambatha's corpse, found it, and decapitated it, supposedly to preserve the head for identification. On 24 July 1906, the *London Telegraph* published a story about the search for Bhambatha's body in late June; colonial eyewitnesses claimed that "the medical officer to whom the head was delivered after its decapitation was in receipt of a telegram from Colonel McKenzie an hour afterwards, saying that the latter was on Bambata's hills in pursuit of the fugitive chief. He [the medical officer] despatched an amusing message in reply, saying: 'You can keep the hills; I've got the beggar's head.'"[12]

Hundreds of rebels, including commanders Chakijana and Mangati, managed to get away. Most headed either toward Dinuzulu's residential enclosures in Nongoma and Babanango or toward migrant hideaways in cities such as Durban and Johannesburg. One rebel, Mazibuko, made the dangerous journey to his father's homestead, a several-day walk to the north and west of Nkandla. Recalling his escape in 1982, he described how he eluded swarming colonial soldiers and traversed the "mountains of the baboons" to apparent safety. At home he discovered that the chiefs in his magisterial division were angry, "hot like chillies," and "all of us who had joined [the revolt] secretly had been listed. We were not many, just 13 young men." Mazibuko slept "only once, [then his] father . . . reported [his] return to the chief." Before "the police arrived," he decided that he was "helpless and [fled, wearing] no coat and no shoes, just a shirt and a pair of trousers," making his way to Johannesburg, where he found work as a domestic servant. Seven months later, early in 1907, he was arrested outside his employer's home for joining the poll tax insurrection and transported in a locked train compartment to Natal. He may "not have been found," so he claimed, "if I had not sent money home . . . and addressed [the envelope] to my father." Although it is unclear whether his father alerted the police in Johannesburg, Mazibuko believed "[t]hat is how I sold myself away."[13]

Distrusting their homestead heads and chiefs, many poll tax fighters refused to go home after June 1906. As the captured young men filed into court in northern Natal and Durban to face charges before magistrates in hastily arranged treason trials, some African fathers stepped forward to testify for the prosecution of their sons, seeing that their own continuing survival as patriarchs was dependent on cooperation with the colonial regime. Some homestead heads who appeared for the Crown exhibited a vindictiveness that reflected their sense that they had been betrayed by their sons. Nkandla chief Matshana, embittered over earlier disputes with his heir, Gudhla, described the defection of his five other sons as the final insult and urged the colonial authorities to execute two of his sons for taking up arms against the poll tax. In cases where African patriarchs did not testify for the prosecution, the accused rebels tended to receive greater leniency. The rebel Mazibuko recalled that when he entered the dock in a Durban courtroom, "on the floor" he saw a "brown rifle" he obtained during his service as a scout for the British during the Anglo-Boer War. Ballistic tests confirmed that Mazibuko's firearm was responsible for the death of at least one white soldier, but the prosecutor could produce no witness to prove that Mazibuko was the killer. In his summation the judge told Mazibuko that he "would not be hanged [but] would serve a long sentence" and would "build roads and bridges" in northern Natal.[14]

Since the Bhobe ridge fight in Nkandla, magistrates in Thukela basin courts had been trying captured rebels for treason, on charges that a secret African plan existed to overthrow the Natal government. In their arguments to the court, prosecutors could offer little direct evidence to support such a claim; the treason trial proceedings centered, instead, on the testimony of African elders that youths had vanished from home to join rebels in the forests. Nearly 1,800 young men and several hundred older men were found guilty of sedition between 1906 and 1908, with an average sentence of six months to two years in prison. Some youths were flogged before their incarceration; not quite 40 were sentenced to death and executed by hanging or firing squad. The government established a system of farming out convicted rebels to Natal coal mines and for public works; as word spread of the new reservoir of laborers, Transvaal and Kimberley employers competed for convicts as indentured workers. In December 1906 one Nkandla homestead head, Socwatsha, said, "these young men who were . . . being arrested were in the habit of exclaiming 'happy are those who have already fought and are now dead.'"[15]

Teaching Africans a "Severe Lesson"

While despair seemed to grip the surviving combatants from Nkandla, colonial officials stationed on the Thukela basin coast reported "turbulent" young men, and widespread rumors of a possible uprising in late May 1906 spread through northern Natal's Mapumulo and Lower Tugela divisions. Although there was no apparent connection with Colonel McKenzie's operation in Mome on 10 June 1906, the next day followers of Chief Ndhlovu kaTimuni stormed a store at Thring's Post in Mapumulo, killing the Norwegian owner and a white trooper. Over the subsequent week the Mapumulo rebels revived the poll tax rebellion, producing a second uprising.[16]

In mid- to late June Chief Ndhlovu kaTimuni, a "prince" of Zulu lineage, converted his young followers and those of deposed chief Gobizembe into a rebel brigade. Neighboring chief Matshwili, a grandson of Zulu king Shaka's one-time overlord, Dingiswayo, did the same with the young men from his own chiefdom. Followers of Chief Meseni formed regiments in alliance with Chief Ndhlovu. The coastal protestors, like the fighters of the forests, ignored old rivalries to embrace the anti–poll tax cause. Many migrant workers in Durban had left their jobs en masse to answer a call from their Mapumulo and Lower Tugela chiefs. Chief Meseni convinced "loyal" chief Swayimana's young men to arm themselves and join him, despite Swayimana's rivalry with Chief Bhambatha.[17]

The coastal rebels sounded the *"uSuthu"* cry and wore the oxtail *ubushokobezi*. Their commanders furnished them with medicine said to protect them from battlefield injuries, once again using the flesh of a slain settler, postal employee Mr. O. E. Veal, to concoct a potion able to confer ritual protection. Veal had strayed into a mutinous section of Mapumulo division when Chief Meseni's young men marked for punishment anyone connected with the colonial government. Suspecting that he was a government spy, rebels killed him on 1 July 1906 and removed some body parts for *intelezi*, the so-called drug of invincibility. These coastal fighters also marked for retaliation homestead heads who did not openly support the revolt, especially patriarchs who "were first to pay Poll tax" for their sons. Chiefs labeled as traitorous, *amambuka,* started to flee across the Thukela River to Eshowe during the week after the Veal murder.[18]

The colonial army had reacted slowly to the unfolding events around Nkandla during the first outbreak from April to June. In the second uprising the field force sped to the coast. During the final week of June, Colonels Leuchars and McKenzie had moved their troops along opposite banks of the Thukela River to keep the armed poll tax protestors from reaching Eshowe to the north or the Midlands of Natal to the south.

Without the natural advantages of the inland Thukela basin—the forest canopy and caves in which to hide—the rebels found themselves in a death trap. The colonial soldiers arriving in Mapumulo fanned out toward Lower Tugela division to search for the enemy across the rolling grasslands. The forces, nearly three thousand men, saturated the coastal belt, burning homes, killing livestock, and shooting armed and unarmed African men indiscriminately. A colonial medical officer noted "isolated instances of savagery" by Colonel McKenzie's column, but among "some hundred dead rebels," he saw "no instance of a disemboweled or otherwise mutilated one." Uncoordinated counterattacks by the rebels served only to expose them to the superior firepower of mounted troops.[19]

In 1979 an aged woman from Mapumulo, Mrs. Sibisi, recalled that the hunted young men along the coast traveled in dread of being discovered, with some concealing their identities: "[D]uring the fighting . . . some of the young men decided to resort [to] what we call 'isidwaba'—it's something that is worn by women, Zulu women. They were now disguising that they should not be seen that they are actually men, because at that time once a white soldier sees a male, he was going to be shot. So they resorted to this dressing as women."[20]

The government's field force depended on support from loyal African chiefs. Chief Swayimana in Mapumulo and Chief Mfungelwa in Eshowe, for example, supplied scouts, porters, and fighters to the colonial militia; they and their "loyal" men later received cattle confiscated from rebel homesteads. But Swayimana now had few recruits to offer. Since the young men's protest of magistrate Ernst Dunn's tax collection in late January and early February 1906, they had targeted Swayimana for revenge. By the third week of July 1906, the Natal forces had crushed the second uprising, in less than a month killing more than one thousand rebels from the chiefdoms of Meseni, Ndhlovu, and Matshwili. Mounted units conducted mopping-up exercises throughout the lower Thukela basin into August. The government's treason trials were to continue into 1908; magistrates commanded fathers to turn in their rebel sons, threatening to confiscate cattle and other possessions if the fathers disobeyed. Not all elders complied with the order;

many found ways to turn a blind eye to the order. The government punished some homestead heads with "hard labour and 10 whipping lashes" for such acts as supplying clothes to a rebel. Young men in hiding heard stories of rebels being "turned out of [their] kraal[s by their homestead heads and] handed over . . . to the Court" to be "tried and sentenced [to] imprisonment." By late 1907, an estimated 4,600 prisoners had already stood trial for sedition, and 4,342 were convicted.[21]

The July 1906 military operations left behind gutted homesteads and charred fields. The Reverend Goodenough, an American Board missionary, was quoted in the *Natal Mercury* as saying of the destruction: "thousands of houses and huts have been burnt. With the huts have gone the amabele [sorghum]. Most of the mealies [corn] were still unshelled in the little grass granaries. These were burned, and the mealies with them. Cattle and goats are gone. Hoes, and ploughs and carts were destroyed. Since the burning of their mealies, many people have been living on their sweet potatoes. . . . These are almost gone." When the growing season began in September, the *Times of Natal* reported that "bodies [of rebels lay] in the Government roads . . . after the battles in which they fell . . . mutilated by dogs and hogs."[22]

Ilanga Lase Natal likened the government's incursion into Mapumulo and Lower Tugela divisions to lynchings in the American South, "where the Native is falsely accused of doing violence to a white woman and taken from gaol and shot without a trial." Among the letters *Ilanga* published in October from Africans in the rebellious areas was one from a man (doubtless a member of the *amakholwa* because he was highly literate) who criticized the government for putting so much faith in "this man Leuchars . . . a red visaged whiteman who appeared to be a heavy drinker of liquor." "Cruelty," he wrote, knew no bounds among Natal military commanders, particularly "this good for nothing whiteman. He is harsh, . . . remorseless. It would have been well had he been killed by Bambata's bullets in Nkandhla. The country would be better if whitemen such as Leuchars, a wizard of the worst type, were removed." In November 1906, *Ilanga* reacted once more to the government's scorched-earth tactics: "What would have been said had 3,000 whites been shot . . . and their bodies left out in the open without burial to be eaten by dogs and pigs? [H]ad they been whites, it would have been said they were slaughtered unprepared. But in our case of the 3,000 [Africans estimated by the militia to be] killed, [the] white flag was not respected, prisoners were shot, homes burnt, foodstuffs trampled under foot, and cattle seized of those fighting."[23]

Colonial forces had killed between three to four thousand, mostly young male rebels; approximately twice that number were wounded. Harriet E. Colenso, a critic of the government's excessive violence, compared the ratio of killed to wounded to that in a European war: "In the Franco-German war, the proportion was three wounded to one killed. In our recent trouble the proportion of prisoners (included wounded) was something very different. The total given by the middle of June [1906 before the coastal outbreak] was 2,000 as against 3,500 killed." In addition to the numerous dead and wounded, nearly 7,700 men said to be poll tax protestors were held in jails, where a "large majority," according to the assistant commissioner of police in 1907, would "serve sentences of two years imprisonment with Hard Labour." The loss of young men to death, maiming, prison, and flight meant the loss of breadwinners in African homesteads. On the coast of the Thukela basin, one out of three Africans was homeless in 1907. A soaring population of "destitute women" had no homes. The commandant of the Natal militia offered to "hand [them] over to a reliable chief, who will have power to allot them to trustworthy kraalheads." In the razed interior a famine loomed, with the Nkandla magistrate warning that "families are at present leading discontented lives scattered all over the District with relations [and] it is difficult to feed them."[24]

By comparison, the losses suffered by whites were insignificant. Six civilians were killed; two dozen soldiers died; three dozen suffered serious wounds. Six African levies were killed, and thirty were wounded. Only a few white-owned stores or settler houses were damaged. Nothing short of a "severe . . . lesson," the Nkandla magistrate maintained, could teach Africans that they would "have not much stomach for repetition." In May 1907 the Natal governor offered a rationale for the merciless slaughter: the white settlers wanted to prove their "spirit of self-reliance and pluck" and to take their place in "British history." He believed that "the suppression of this Rebellion mark[ed] a new era. . . . A small Colony such as Natal has, at its own expense and with its own resources, successfully carried out the operations without any aid from Imperial troops except their moral support."[25]

Rebel "Reign of Terror" against "Loyal Natives"

Underlying the "severe lesson" and the invocation of "British history" was an insecurity in Natal colonial society. Since white settlers had gained political power by responsible government in 1893, they had heard garbled rumors from various African reserves from 1903 onward to the effect that Britain would not come to the aid of Natal in a time of trial and would leave the colonists by themselves to face internal threats. Natal officials hoped to dispel a belief that had acquired credence among both colonists and African chiefs: that the departure of imperial troops in 1893 reflected Great Britain's displeasure with the Natal Colony, and that in a future conflict between whites and Africans the king of England would send no troops to protect the colonists. Since Dinuzulu's return from exile in 1898, this rumor and others like it had circulated widely in settler politics. Resident magistrates and police spies in the vicinity of the uSuthu homestead in Nongoma claimed that Dinuzulu would challenge the Natal forces, after 1893 made up of colonists, but would never challenge imperial troops. In May and June 1906, when poll tax fighters were performing poorly in battle, Dinuzulu was said to have considered backing the rebels since "the King in England ha[d] nothing to do with" the Natal militia. The rumor that the British government would not necessarily support Natal forces remained a serious matter for settlers and the government even after the rebellion had been quashed and its participants punished.[26]

At the close of 1906, Natal officials estimated that approximately one thousand rebels still remained at large in the middle and lower Thukela basin, scattered in small bands in unpopulated pockets of bush, mostly in "Thorn Country" and in the hills around Dinuzulu's Nongoma enclosure in central Zululand. In this uSuthu region scores of rebels found a refuge far from the arm of colonial law, ploughing and weeding Dinuzulu's gardens in exchange for shelter, food, and cattle, and engaging in communal activities, such as sports in the nearby Dalala flats. Some of these young men hoped to acquire bridewealth cattle after prolonged service, just as earlier regiments in the Zulu kingdom had been rewarded. For the men who hid out at Dinuzulu's residence, their faith may have been restored in elders who could deliver security in exchange for loyalty. Isolated and for the time being undisturbed by colonial forces, the uSuthu homestead represented an equilibrium between the generations; the elders ruled and the younger men obeyed those who protected them.[27]

The uSuthu homestead had been transformed into a rebel command center from which attacks could be carried out against the loyalist Africans, who were the enemies of this outpost of Zulu patriarchy. The fugitives in Dinuzulu's enclosure were encouraged to rid the countryside of traitorous *amambuka* by Chakijana, who had settled into the uSuthu residence. One rebel was quoted by the *Times of Natal* as saying that Chakijana "required men to go and shoot certain bucks, [and] that these bucks were certain chiefs who did not rebel." The rebels were said to be training for attacks against African supporters of the government. In early February 1907 the Nkandla magistrate wrote that he had heard from an African informant that the young men at Dinuzulu's had vowed that "when the crops had been reaped, the real Rebellion would take place when they, the Rebels, . . . take the first opportunity of wreaking their vengeance on the loyalists (Amambugas) who had assisted the Government." Chief Sitshitshili, a loyalist appointed to his position by the Natal government, had become a special focus of hatred for having marshaled African levies against the forest fighters. An African government informant reported that "it was often heard a young Native named Nomapekepekana who [would] giya [dance martially] and shout, 'Umdumo weMpukana ziyongena egolo lesipakanyiswa Usitshitshili', (swarms of flies will enter the anus of the appointed Chief Sitshitshili)."[28]

The rebels at uSuthu homestead disseminated stories that Bhambatha was alive and planning vengeance against his enemies, stewing potions to bewitch loyalists. Hopes for retaliation occupied the minds of the girlfriends of rebels, who expected that their boyfriends would swoop down on unsuspecting *amambuka*. So convinced were young women in the middle Thukela basin of the eventual success of the reprisals that they wore "as a distinguishing badge the . . . 'umfingo' charm as a necklet, to enable the impi [the attacking rebels] to distinguish them from other women."[29]

What the Nkandla magistrate called "an echo of the late rebellion" reverberated through his division when an African Natal militia scout narrowly evaded "a deliberate attempt by a body of men to murder him in revenge for his loyalty." The scout, Bebe kaGawu, had been the only one of seven adult sons in a Nkandla homestead to remain loyal to the government during the uprising. Six of his brothers "rebelled, five of whom were sentenced to two years' imprisonment and the sixth named Sopela was shot and killed by his brother Bebe in attempting to escape capture." The incident, the magistrate predicted, would be "the precursor of others attempted by the rebels still at large to terrorize and possibly murder natives who thoroughly demonstrated their loyalty."[30]

The attempt on Bebe's life inaugurated a campaign against Thukela basin loyalists, a campaign that, with each "diabolical outrage," as the commissioner for native affairs reported, escalated into a "reign of terror." The Umvoti magistrate had reported that "rebels belonging to the late Chief Bambata [were] wandering about the hills in the Impanza District." They intruded into the public eye "by stealing goats belonging to the loyal natives." The Umvoti magistrate called the livestock thieves a "nuisance," but "certain loyalists . . . who were witnesses at the treason trials last year against friends and relatives of the rebels" feared "being murdered." The magistrate in Mapumulo recorded similar sentiments; loyalists in that district had felt endangered by rebels who were "wandering about trying to evade arrest." The first of several retaliatory assassinations occurred on 5 April 1907, when Gence, a medicinal healer to Dinuzulu, was shot by at least "two ex-rebels" according to the Kranskop magistrate. Before Gence died of his wounds, he identified one of his assailants as a bodyguard of Dinuzulu's. Colonial officials debated the motive for the murder; some believed that Gence was sleeping with one of Dinuzulu's wives and was the victim of a jealous husband, but loyalists in the Thukela basin suspected that Gence died because of his pro-government stance during the poll tax uprising. Unbeknownst to the victim, Chakijana had accompanied the group of assassins and probably had a hand in the shooting. The murder confirmed the widely held belief, according to an African policeman in Nkandla, that "all those of position who assisted the white people in the late rebellion will suffer later on, [and] will be wiped out."[31]

On the night of 25 August 1907, a young man murdered Chief Sitshitshili, who had unwittingly invited the killer into his homestead in keeping with his custom of "entertain[ing] strangers." According to his brother, the chief had ignored the warnings of his wives and headmen. He was blunt about his contempt for the rebels; he had used a now familiar scatology, "suggesting to the Authorities that the . . . Rebels be 'joja'd' (spiked through the rectum)." The young stranger had stopped on 23 August at the southern edge of Zululand's Nquthu division, where one of Sitshitshili's brothers lived, sipping beer with him late into the night. Excusing himself from a daylong "beer drink" the next morning, the assassin set out for Nkandla and arrived at Sitshitshili's on Saturday afternoon of 24 August. Sitshitshili "placed confidence in this youth who did not even give his name" and offered him a place to rest for the night. The women who took bedding to the stranger's hut remarked how he "refused a pillow saying he preferred to use the mackintosh [a raincoat] which he carefully folded." Afterward, the speculation was that he hid his gun in the coat. The next morning, Sitshitshili took "the stranger . . . to the kraal of Hlwakele [to drink] beer" for hours; the two walked back to the chief's home and sat "in the sun near the Cattle kraal." By early evening Sitshitshili "complained of feeling downhearted and old" and retired to his bed, the stranger following him into the sleeping hut, where one of Sitshitshili's wives found the two around "a small fire." As the women prepared a meal, a short distance from the chief's sleeping hut, one of his wives heard shots and rushed to her husband "just in time to see the stranger run past her hut, and out at the opening in the reed fence at the back." Family members found the chief "shot dead" with two bullet holes near the navel. The police found one "of the bullets . . . under the bed," along with a "small piece of the bone." Ballistics suggested that the killer's weapon was a Natal police issue said to have been stolen from a white trooper. After killing the chief, the assassin had made off with two of his victim's guns, but in his haste he left behind his walking stick, which proved to be a decisive piece of evidence that helped to convict him. The rebel, Mjombalwana, was arrrested, convicted of the murder, and executed in December 1908.[32]

In September 1907, a month after the assassination, members of Sitshitshili's family and his headmen visited the Nkandla magistrate for a public mourning. "My heart speaks but my mouth is silent," said Sivela, the first speaker and brother of the slain chief. He pointed out that Sitshitshili's death was caused by his

> loyalty to the Government [as the] first to pay the Poll Tax [in early 1906], in spite of it's being said that the Chief who first paid "would cause the assegais [spears] of others to be sharpened." After paying the Tax he [Sitshitshili] went out from the Court Room, the people assembled outside called him an "Ambuka" saying "you are the first to pay." Shortly after this the Rebellion broke out, my brother . . . was the first to come in when the Levies were called out, and he was again called an "Ambuka." They said the "AMBUKA" Chief is the first to arm for the Whites. He was accused of burning Cetewayo's grave.

Sivela himself asked the magistrate for protection in a roundabout way: "I say if my brother did all this, it was for the Government, the rulers of the land to punish him [Sitshitshili]. . . . I say let them kill us all, let them take all we possess, do not let our Chief suffer alone."[33]

Sitshitshili's assassination was a shock to Thukela basin loyalists. In September 1907 the Natal governor sent a telegram to the colonial secretary in London informing him that "the recent murder . . . frighten[ed] those chiefs who have hitherto been loyal." Shortly after, the Mahlabathini magistrate observed that "several chiefs, uniformly expressive of horror at the prevailing lawlessness [regard] their own lives as in danger, so that they 'eat their meals with closed doors.'" According to the Natal governor, during late September and early October "hardly a day pass[ed] without [loyal chiefs] coming [to Pietermaritzburg] to represent the unsatisfactory state of affairs and the danger they are in of being murdered." On 7 October armed rebels emerged from hiding and shot at Mapoyisa, heir of loyalist chief Mbuzo and a leader of African troop levies, but missed and fled in pursuit of a new target in a homestead four miles away. There, on the same day, they attacked Mapoyisa's right-hand man, Ndlezana, another commander of African levies, but this attempted assassination failed as well. To quell the disturbances, the government proclaimed "an amnesty in favour of the rank and file of those who had participated in the 1906 Rebellion . . . in the hope that this would induce them to return to their homes," but the proclamation had little effect. No sooner had the colonial authorities offered amnesty than the reprisals began again. On 20 November two armed men killed Mpumela, another Nkandla loyalist chief, who in peacetime organized his noncombatant followers to testify against jailed rebels. Chakijana was later alleged to have directed the murder. A week after Mpumela's death, a Nkandla loyalist marked as an *amambuka* had to fend off two assassins to save his life; during the rebellion forest fighters had looted his homestead in a raid, and he was known as an enemy of the poll tax protestors.[34]

The assaults and the killings induced the government to initiate another crackdown, and in December 1907 the Natal militia mounted new operations, led by Colonel McKenzie, who had experience fighting against the rebels. His assignment was to quash those "ruffians who are continually killing people in Zululand." McKenzie announced that "those who are loyal have no reason to fear the troops," but warned that the "troops were not brought . . . to play [and] if fighting starts it will be my business to teach you a lesson you will not readily forget." The mission had an obvious political motive as well: to seize Dinuzulu and "to impress upon the natives the seriousness of the position in which they stand, and the readiness of the Colony . . . to uphold its authority and punish sedition by a resort to war." Reuters described the arrest of Dinuzulu on 11 December: "This morning Dinuzulu was called up before Col. McKenzie, and to get to the Colonel . . . it was necessary for him to pass before the gaze of several hundred of his people and the people of other tribes. The Chief was escorted by a file of Natal Police with fixed bayonets. He was a somewhat impressive figure, despite his inordinate girth, and marched . . . at the head of the file quite composedly. He certainly was not humbled."[35]

With the military occupation of Dinuzulu's Mahlabathini division, the fugitives had lost their sanctuary. Even before Dinuzulu's capture, the rebels had been turning themselves in to the police, and now a welcome peace settled over the Thukela basin. At the end of 1908, martial law was lifted. The magistrate of Ndwandwe division in central Zululand heard from homestead heads that "[o]ne can eat one's evening meal now by the light of a fire and door open, and without having the feeling of being shot at."[36]

Images of rebellion: Chief Bhambatha and retinue before 1906 rebellion, Umvoti, c. 1900 (top) (C1393); seated, captured rebels guarded by standing African levies, Nkandla, mid-June 1906 (middle) (C569); Natal carbineers with rebel trophies from Nkandla battles, mid-June 1906 (bottom) (C566). Photographs courtesy of the Natal Archives, Pietermaritzburg.

Chiefs captured and tried by colonial authority: Sigananda seated and in custody, mid-June 1906 (top) (C569); Dinuzulu at Greytown treason trial, 1908 (bottom) (C744). Photographs courtesy of the Natal Archives, Pietermaritzburg.

In Natal the government arraigned Dinuzulu for treason before a special court headed by Sir William Smith, chief justice of the Transvaal. The trial opened in Greytown Hall in November 1908 and concluded in March 1909. Dinuzulu faced twenty-three charges, including sedition and rebellion, high treason, murder, accessory to murder, inciting murder, and violations of the Natal Firearms and Ammunition Act of 1905. But the Crown case proved weak, and Dinuzulu's defense team of noted barristers—E. G. Jellicoe, W. P. Schreiner, who was the former prime minister of the Cape Colony, E. Renaud, and R. C. A. Samuelson—rebutted virtually all of the charges. In preliminary examination, for example, Jellicoe exposed gaps in the Crown's proofs, arguing that favorable evidence in support of Dinuzulu's innocence had been illegally suppressed by the prosecution. He also argued that the government had coerced witnesses, citing the testimony of Africans, who had been required to preface their depositions with "It is true, according to the authorities." Although the special court found for the Crown on only two and one-half of its counts, the presiding judge sentenced Dinuzulu to four years in jail and fined him one hundred pounds sterling, primarily for his role in harboring Bhambatha and other rebels. If convicted of the serious charges, high treason and murder, Dinuzulu faced the death penalty or, with a commuted sentence, at least several decades in prison. The final chapter of the rebellion ended quietly.[37]

Labor Migrancy Luring Young Men to "Put Away Their Fear"

The central historical event in 1908 and 1909 was not Dinuzulu's trial; rather, it was the surge of fugitive rebels and other African young men from the Thukela basin into labor migrancy. The forces of the industrial centers had already pulled more and more workers from Natal, and during Dinuzulu's treason trial, Transvaal labor recruiters conducted an unprecedented number of "tours throughout Zululand" with an eye to "supplying labour to the Mines." Wage labor was the most practical option for rebels who wanted both to avoid jail and make a living.[38]

The colonial army had cut a destructive swath through the rebel areas, devastating the agricultural economy. The militia had so reduced herds, damaged fields, and burned huts that the countryside had become a wasteland. Consequently, life in Thukela basin homesteads meant wretched poverty. Poor prospects for a future on the land, combined with colonial military operations, led to a sudden rise in labor migrancy toward the Transvaal, a 26 percent jump from 1906 to 1907. Between 1907 and 1909, the number of Africans from Natal and Zululand working in the Transvaal shot up by 60 percent. The Transvaal Government Native Labour Bureau attributed the sharp rise in the number of domestic servants on the Rand to the "increase in the number of Natives employed . . . from Natal and Zululand." In September 1909 the Transvaal minister for native affairs stated the obvious to the president of the Chamber of Mines in Johannesburg: "Zulus are now taking far more readily to mine employment than they have in the past, an appreciable increase may be anticipated."[39]

The Transvaal Native Labour Bureau kept records of this significant surge of labor migrants. It calculated that in 1904 roughly two thousand labor migrants from Natal and Zululand had gone to the mines, but by 1909 the number had increased more than sixfold. In March 1909 nearly thirteen thousand migrants from Natal and Zululand were working in the mines. For mining companies, the labor inflow could not have come at a better time. Thousands of Chinese contract mine workers had begun to return home after China protested the harsh treatment of its workers in South Africa, and the Transvaal government decided to phase out the use of Chinese labor. The influx from Natal and Zululand began to fill the labor void.[40]

The increase in migrancy revealed the desperate plight of homesteads and the young male itinerant workers who were their primary breadwinners. The fact that the primary source of employment, the mines, was dangerous did not impede the flow. From the 1906 revolt onward, African workers' dissatisfaction with their laboring conditions on the Rand grew, and by the end of 1908 the squalor and brutality of the mining compounds and underground shafts were so severe that the director of the Government Native Labour Bureau in the Transvaal quit his post in protest, writing in his resignation letter that "the Mines are becoming . . . unpopular among Natives, owing to the arbitrary and frequently unjust treatment accorded to them." A flood of correspondence ensued between labor officials in Pietermaritzburg and officials in the Transvaal on pass regulations, tracking labor migrants, and contract grievances. The migrants fueled a rivalry over labor "touting," or recruiting, among employers in Natal—white farmers, railroads, and coal mines—and between Natal employers and mine employers outside the colony. With the promise of lucrative agricultural work, colonists on the Natal side of the Thukela basin lured African migrants from idling trains en route to the Transvaal. Natal farmers and coal mine operators claimed that they were victims of both the migrant exodus and employers outside of the colony who, through labor agents, were enticing contracted African workers to the Rand.[41]

The Natal government was pulled into the labor dispute. Its aim was not only to soothe the settlers but also to put Africans to work and to reap taxes from their wages; hence it eased "the conveyance of natives travelling to and from the Mines by batching [bunching] them" on trains, ensuring that labor migrants got "the cheap rate." As the *Natal Mercury* observed: "the government . . . want[ed] the native to be able to pay his share of the necessary taxation to carry on the administration of the Colony, and they also desire him to become more of a . . . consumer than ever." Whether "the native" should earn income to pay taxes outside or inside Natal was a point of endless contention. In an article entitled "On the Mines," *Ilanga Lase Natal* even suggested that "the natives . . . put away their fear and go in for the work which produces the best wages and would make them prosperous." The newspaper promoted the resumption of such a headlong trend. The chaos of the "war of the heads" only interrupted what was an accelerating flow of young men from homesteads into the world of cash and labor migrancy.[42]

The elders, slowly recovering from destitution after Natal soldiers razed the countryside and demolished the agricultural economy, also urged a shift from homestead to mine. In 1908 a growing number of chiefs and headmen from the Thukela basin visited the mines on the Rand to investigate how mine employers arranged contracts, wages, housing, and safety. A year later E. P. Robinson, a Transvaal mining representative, sought to resolve with the Natal secretary for native affairs the coordination of future inspections, hoping to get the Thukela basin chiefs "to provide employment for 16,000 men" on the Premier Mine. By 1910 a delegation of Umvoti chiefs and headmen had visited several mining sites outside Johannesburg to "observe the manner in which Natives are treated . . . underground." It was only one of many such traveling delegations that year.[43]

"My Destination Is Durban"

During the rise in labor migrancy, the conflicts between elders and youths in homesteads, which had grown numerous over the decade, dwindled to a few recorded incidents. The rare occurrences were not notable for either severity or frequency. Most of the conflicts seemed to be connected to distant migrant centers rather than within homesteads. For example, in 1909 Chief Sibindi, whose loyalty during the rebellion had been rewarded by his appointment to take over Chief Gobizembe's following, urged the Mapumulo magistrate to extradite a former rebel, Qolota, from Johannesburg.

Sibindi wanted Qolota prosecuted for "subscrib[ing] money which he stated would be used for the purpose of employing a Solicitor to get me ousted from my Chieftainship." Qolota, working on the Rand, had also "threaten[ed] his father" back home in Mapumulo and "defiantly" disobeyed the order of his newly appointed chief Sibindi to return and face punishment.[44]

Other rumors never seemed to die, especially the one that declared Bhambatha alive and ready to start a new life in an urban world. Zwezinye, a labor migrant who fled from Lower Tugela division when his rebel band was broken up by white soldiers, told a representative of the Transvaal Department of Native Affairs: "Bambata has said 'they (Europeans) have been seeking for me—my destination is Durban.'" Zwezinye confirmed a widespread belief of other isiZulu-speaking young men in the mining compounds of Johannesburg: "I say it is common amongst Natives to be talking about Bambatha—it is a great matter and it is a great secret with them." The hold that the dead rebel chief had over these young men in the big towns was one indication that the rebellion to some degree survived the military's conquest. Many African patriarchs, for their part, were dismayed over the military crackdown, and some found a convenient scapegoat in the younger generation. *Ilanga Lase Natal* published an anonymous letter in isiZulu headlined "The Death of the Country," in which the writer faulted homestead heads for failing in their "duty to prevent the disruption of the country [and to] guard the interests of . . . (the elders)." He went on to say they "could not have said to be men unless there was something to show for it. It would be correct to say that the country was destroyed by the youths."[45]

Homestead relationships had indeed endured severe shocks. Immediately after the "reign of terror," a dull calm descended on the lower and middle Thukela basin. Gone were the widespread police reports of drunken boys confronting their elders at faction fights and beer festivals; gone were the unending complaints of fathers to magistrates that sexual misconduct by young men and women was upsetting domestic relationships; gone were the reports by colonial officials of elders' worries about "seduction," "abduction," and female "runaways," all threats to patriarchal control. Family disputes involving the disobedience of both youths and young wives were less often documented by magistrates, chiefs, or police. Young men in increasing numbers departed for the mines and urban centers for months at a time, removing them as a focus of potential strife. Meanwhile, African patriarchs were facing overriding problems of hunger in their homesteads. The rifts between elders and youths over unruly behavior appeared no longer to weigh heavily on the officials of colonial patriarchy.

By 1910, most young migrant workers were returning home to find homestead members in a precarious existence, and patriarchs were still try-ing to maintain their control over rights to resources and the labor of youths and women. The young men and women who so recently had challenged their fathers' compliance with white rule were still using the Natal judici-ary to advance their claims in family conflicts. Youths began to adjust to the postrebellion reality, where homestead survival and elder authority were clearly linked to a begrudging acceptance of colonial patriarchal order and its legal arm, the Code of Native Law. Young men, particularly, understood that the means of securing their own standing in African patriarchy depended on wages paid by white employers outside homesteads. These cash earnings gave them greater license to negotiate with their elders the terms of customary relations at home, especially with respect to personal freedom in work, play, and courtship.

A major theme in the historiography of African labor migrancy has focused on the struggles of homesteads to maintain subsistence agriculture, while African patriarchs sought to control the labor of itinerant wage earn-ers. Chiefs were seen to have a pivotal role in protecting rural resources from capitalist incursions, even as they recruited labor for white employers in exchange for cash advances. Yet if the scholarly view of labor migrancy included a broader perspective of African youths' unwillingness (even before entering labor migrancy) to delay privileges of seniority, historical interpre-tations would likely change. Labor migrants in early-twentieth-century Durban have been depicted as newcomers to the world of insubordination, seduced by gang associations, "shebeen" (beer hall) debauchery, and extra-marital sexual activity with prostitutes. Historians have described how facets of traditional African culture, when exported to industrial areas on the Rand, survived only in hybrid form, frequently as aggressive expressions of gender and generational identity, as in dance and "poetic-musical" com-petitions or in stick fighting bouts between rival bands of young men. But this rich scholarship occasionally overstresses the fact that newly arrived labor migrants could only effect social change after they abandoned their conservative inhibitions and embraced the opportunities afforded to indi-viduals in faster-paced urban centers.[46]

Before entering into itinerant wage labor, African youths in the Thukela basin in the 1890s were already innovators who, for instance, sought redress from the colonial courts in domestic quarrels. They were risktakers who were engaging in premarital sex, which led to pregnancy. They defied patriarchal law and order in faction fights and rowdy drinking festivals. As youths streamed into colonial towns and cities after the "war of the heads" in 1906, they carried their past with them. The continuity between this phase of rural generational conflict and subsequent African protest movements in the twentieth century awaits further research. Scholars might want to consider how prior cycles of youthful defiance and dramatically weakening African patriarchy fomented insurgent African politics in the 1920s and again in the 1980s. During these two decades of escalating resistance to white rule, Zulu nationalists chose to defend traditional authority against threats posed by, among other forces, assertive and independent African youths.[47]

In the months after the surge in labor migrancy beginning in 1906, the authority of African patriarchs was limited by magistrates eager to expedite for colonial employers a regular flow of workers. The cooperation of homestead heads in the treason trials had only bought them a semblance of renewed power. Where agriculture failed to support families, older African fathers were beholden to their sons who were sent off to the mines to earn wages and deliver cash to the homestead. African patriarchs saw their authority ebb further after 1910, as white settlers appropriated even more land and as magistrates continued to punish Africans for violating customary prohibitions.

When the round of competition between white and African patriarchies concluded at the end of the "war of the heads," colonial authorities prevailed. Their power was magnified by greater military, commercial, and agricultural resources. They benefited from ties with a burgeoning South African industrial sector, where new modes of African patriarchy were tested and tried by young rural migrants. By the early twentieth century, the ideal of African homestead life based on self-sustaining agriculture, on reciprocal obligations within a generational hierarchy, and the gradual attainment of higher social rank—the three-tiered system that had supported patriarchal respect and the obedience of women and youths—had further receded into history. The Natal Colony, for the time being, had effectively resolved a generational crisis within African homesteads by denying victory to Africans both young and old.

Postscript

Some studies of anticolonial violence herald the 1906 revolt against white rule in Natal as a forerunner of protests seeking political independence for Africa, overlooking the "war of the heads" that was the apogee of African youths' defiance of patriarchal authority.[1] Generational conflicts may have kindled other uprisings in twentieth-century Africa as younger Africans saw their material birthright exploited to buttress the waning privileges of some of their patriarchs. Whether more recent upheavals, such as the Mau Mau outbreak in Kenya in the 1950s and the "People's War" against South African apartheid starting in the 1980s, can also be viewed as an internecine struggle between African elders and youths and therefore as part of a historical continuum awaits closer investigation.

In a 1986 article, Shula Marks argued that the 1906 Natal rebellion "displayed all the classic features of a peasant revolt." She gave little weight to generational conflicts within homesteads, instead focusing on the "social banditry" of Africans, who, preaching "alternative ideologies" and resisting white rule, incited peasants to reject proletarianization. Marxist-oriented historians, Marks among them, have suggested that encroaching capitalism was the catalyst that ignited African poll tax violence. Thus, Chakijana, the principal military adviser to the rebel leader Bhambatha, is seen by Marks as being capable of "mobiliz[ing] beyond the village level." Marks translates Chakijana's nickname, *hlanya*, as "firebrand" or "anarchist," a metaphorical definition that illustrates how one radical leader kindled a backward-looking revolt. Yet there is an everyday meaning of *hlanya*, derived from the verb *ukuhlanya*, to be "crazy," "insane," or "prone to acting out," with no connotation of revolutionary motivation.[2]

Chakijana, as Marks notes, was a man of youth and low rank, "about thirty years old and without 'that customary sign of manhood and responsibility—a headring.'" During the 1906 revolt, several African elders described Chakijana as an interloper in the Chube chiefdom, where the poll tax protestors established military bases. He was said to have rebuked Chube chief Sigananda for refusing the path of insurrection. An eyewitness heard Chakijana tell Chief Sigananda: "It is none of your business. This [revolt] has been entrusted to my care."[3]

Ruling Chube patriarchs could have seen Chakijana both as a member of the *abasha,* "the younger generation [who said] old people gave in to white people," and an outsider crazy enough to challenge the one-hundred-year-old chief Sigananda. To Chube followers enraged by the poll tax, Chakijana's inflammatory statements may well have been decisive in ousting Sigananda from power and in paving the way for the "war of the heads." After Chakijana's harangue, Sigananda's son and heir, Ndabaningi, seized control of his father's chiefdom and released Chube young men to take the "extraordinary" step to resist the white and African patriarchs who collected the head tax. Hence the pointed and menacing question and password that rebels asked of African passersby around the Chube chiefdom: "to which group do you belong? Something extraordinary, the money of the head."[4]

The rebels' question, "to which group do you belong?" elicited a response from Marks: the peasant followers of the "hegemonic ideology of the Zulu royal family," the uSuthu. And yet in the middle and lower Thukela basin the outer trappings of Zulu culture—dress, language, and ritual—were more evident than political ideology. The rumored support of the uSuthu heir, Dinuzulu, buoyed forest fighters for a brief period, but the same royal house may well have revived memories of Zulu cruelty. In 1878, for example, Zulu regiments had stalked and killed dozens of young women in Nkandla and neighboring divisions after they refused King Cetshwayo's order to marry older soldiers. Moreover, Zulu ideology received a near-death blow during the civil unrest in the early 1880s, when "many knowledgeable men [keepers of Zulu 'traditions'] had lost their lives" in a war between uSuthu and Mandlakazi factions that decimated the ranks of King Cetshwayo's praise singers and oral historians.[5]

To Marks, however, Zulu tradition, the "moral universe" that resisted progressive change, had stifled the 1906 rebellion. With no "revolutionary political party 'willing and able to mobilise the peasantry,'" the poll tax protests could not rouse the rural poor to abandon their own parochial instincts to fight for a larger cause. Marks does not elaborate on why those rebels who sought out wage labor would now be motivated to abandon this new freedom in earning cash. Or why these youths opted to incite an uprising that attacked the grasping authority of *amambuka* African patriarchs and embodied the aggressive, forward-looking spirit of those who fought for "Something extraordinary," for emancipation from homestead constraints.[6]

The poll tax fighters had been propelled by diverse forces, a legacy of colonial encroachment and generational outrage perhaps foremost, but also

by the retaliatory violence of armed whites. Similar complex motivations
fomented Kikuyu support of the Mau Mau uprising in Kenya in the early
1950s, yet historians are just beginning to probe how, in the decades leading
up to Mau Mau, Kikuyu elders and youths had clashing expectations of customary obligations and patriarchal authority. During World War I, some
Kikuyu chiefs and headmen were paid to enlist young men in the British
Carrier Corps. Reluctant Kikuyu conscripts sought refuge in the neighboring White Highlands, where arable territory was set aside exclusively for
colonial settlement but was sparsely populated by Europeans. By the 1920s,
many more Kikuyu people had migrated from their barren reserves to the
White Highlands to become "squatters" living on land they could not own.[7]

Beginning in the 1930s, the white Kenya government, fearing that the
continuous Kikuyu influx would wear out the fragile soil in the White Highlands, selected compliant Kikuyu male elders to curtail indigenous cultivation and stock herding. Barred from the most productive land, many young
and poor Kikuyu squatters saw their politically acquiescent patriarchs as
oppressive, and they channeled their discontent into the Mau Mau outbreak. At the start of the uprising in 1952, Mau Mau rebels, like the poll tax
protestors in Nkandla, withdrew to remote forests to establish military bases
led by Kikuyu commanders who regarded any thought of cooperating with
the British as cowardly. From these strongholds in south-central Kenya,
Mau Mau rebels eluded colonial soldiers mobilized to seek and destroy
guerilla camps, and the rebels periodically attacked white settlers and the
Kikuyu who benefited from British favor.[8] The competing claims to Kikuyu
patriarchal power require further analysis, as do analogous antagonisms in
the national upheavals that thrust African youths to the fore of revolutionary change in South Africa.

In the 1976 Soweto uprising, students in black townships broke with
their more quiescent elders to fight the imposition of Afrikaans language
schooling. This nascent generational schism dominated political turmoil in
the next decade. African youths in the 1980s became the foot soldiers of the
Mass Democratic Movement and United Democratic Front, the principal
forces that championed a democratic nonracial South Africa. As self-pro-
claimed "comrades," African young men and young women sought to make
separate black townships "ungovernable" by drawing reinforcements from
workers in the townships, union organizers, the unemployed, and criminal
gangs. Their tactics included consumer boycotts, strikes, mass rallies, running battles with army troops, and "people's courts" conducted primarily by
youths who tried, convicted, and executed local police informants and other
perceived traitors.[9]

African young men in the eastern Cape appeared to focus their wrath both on the security forces sent by the state to quell street demonstrations and on older civic leaders who attempted to enforce calm and discipline in township schools and religious congregations. In one small town, Cradock, the historian Michael Tetelman writes that in the mid-1980s African "churches were ripped apart. . . . Younger activists labeled and threatened some elder church women as informers." Such demonstrations of "bravado," Tetelman argues, "had repelled many older men. They had become frustrated by the increasing power . . . displayed by younger activists."[10]

In Natal and KwaZulu, where Inkatha (and its successor, the Inkatha Freedom Party), a proponent of Zulu cultural nationalism, battled the United Democratic Front (UDF) and, later, the African National Congress (ANC), youths' defiance of patriarchal authority provoked widespread political killings. Clashes between UDF youth activists and older Inkatha supporters turned regional townships into theaters of combat. In the early 1990s, after the legalization of the ANC (and the disbanding of the UDF), what was in effect a civil war spread from Natal and KwaZulu to the Transvaal.[11]

Inkatha, an elder-controlled organization that claimed the martial legacy of the Zulu kingdom, embraced whites who were intent on shoring up Zulu patriarchal control "as a bulwark against radical change." In the 1980s, Inkatha, as the ruling party of KwaZulu, a black homeland dependent financially on white minority government in Pretoria, enjoyed considerable advantages, controlling resources such as land on which to build shacks and pensions for retired African workers. Inkatha called for negotiated and incremental change and for a decentralized government to allow sovereignty for Natal and KwaZulu. The more youth-driven UDF and ANC sought to dismantle apartheid and establish a democratic government within a unitary South African state. Inkatha was cultivating ties with traditional older isiZulu-speaking Africans, mustering fighters from urban hostels that housed rural Zulu migrants, from loyal chiefs who enlisted armed regiments or *amabutho,* from rogue security forces, and from township "warlords" who drummed up vigilante bands. This support included "older men [seeking] to put down the cheeky upstart youth who dared to think they could challenge the power of older men."[12]

In stark contrast, UDF and ANC youths strained against patriarchal control; some moved away from home and encouraged friends to join them in makeshift camps from which to assault Inkatha strongholds. According to Catherine Campbell, a psychologist who studied African family relationships in Natal townships from the 1980s to the early 1990s, severe "inter-generational tensions" stoked the civil strife, with African parents "complain[ing] stridently of 'a breakdown of respect' for adults," older men, especially, voicing "outrage at [the] failure to accord them the status and authority they deserve." One African patriarch from war-torn Natal told Campbell: "I grew up understanding the word father as meaning he is the only head of the house with the final word and decision-making power. This is no longer the case. They [the youths] are all disobedience and contempt towards their elders. Sometimes I wish I could ask the government to send officials to come to my house and pick up all these children and beat them heavily, and having got that lesson, bring them back."[13]

Many Inkatha supporters tended to see the ANC-led insurrection as a deliberate bid by youths "to destroy traditional Zulu power" and to impose a reign of youthful masculine authority. Thus, in a 1991 interview, Senzo Mfayela, a Central Committee member of Inkatha, told me that "[w]hen the ANC introduces new rules, they expect [traditional] people to change overnight. I can see more destruction . . . coming from this since the comrades [i.e., youths] introduce a new power game only they can play." Mfayela's lament echoed the tone of African patriarchs a century before, grieving their decline in the Thukela basin: "Don't you wonder," Mfayela asked rhetorically, "why it is that youths are able to control schools, people's courts, stayaways, boycotts? Does a community run by adults simply hand over power to children?"[14]

Literature probing the origins of the internecine conflict between supporters of Inkatha and the ANC focuses primarily on external causal factors —the apartheid legacy of poverty, political division, and social dislocation— ignoring or underestimating the consequences of African generational struggles. When sifting through this debris of a bursting domestic world, scholars may well find another, older legacy apart from the racist system established by South African colonialism and its heirs. As during the earlier "war of the heads" in 1906, the rebels in the "People's War" broke from African patriarchs, who appeared to the young to be more consumed by their loss of control at home than by the fight for liberation.

Notes

Note: Abbreviations in the endnotes are keyed to principal sources and archival locations. Most of the cited primary documents are located in the Natal Archives, Pietermaritzburg, South Africa. Other South African archives cited are the Transvaal Archives, Pretoria; William Cullen Library, University of Witwatersrand, Johannesburg; Killie Campbell Library, Durban; KwaMuhle Local History Museum, Durban; Natal Museum, Pietermaritzburg; and Natal Society Library, Pietermaritzburg. Also cited is Yale Divinity School, New Haven, Connecticut. The location of principal sources outside the Natal Archives appear in parentheses.

Abbreviations

Archival Locations

KCL	Killie Campbell Library
NAP	Natal Archives, Pietermaritzburg
TAP	Transvaal Archives, Pretoria
WCL	William Cullen Library

Bibliographic Categories

GR	Government Records
PT	Papers and Transcripts

Principal Sources

AGO	Attorney General's Office
BB	Blue Books
BPP	British Parliamentary Papers
CSO	Colonial Secretary's Office
CNC	Chief Native Commissioner
COM	Commissions
GH	Government House
GNLB	Government Native Labour Bureau

LTG   Lieutenant Governor
MR   Magistrates' Records
OHP   "Oral History Project Relating to the Zulu People"
PM   Prime Minister
PR   Proceedings
SNA   Secretary for Native Affairs
YB   Year Books
ZA   Zululand Archives
ZGH   Zululand Government House

Numerical Notation

The numbers in parentheses (e.g., 1/1/2/2) at the end of bibliographic citations refer to call numbers of document collections in archives.

Journals

Annals   *Annals of the Natal Museum*
IJAHS   *International Journal of African Historical Studies*
JAH   *Journal of African History*
JNZH   *Journal of Natal and Zulu History*
JSAS   *Journal of Southern African Studies*
RHR   *Radical History Review*
SAHJ   *South African Historical Journal*

Other Abbreviations

Mag.   Magistrate
Min.   Minute
MinP   Minute Papers
Rep.   Report

Sample Entry

A sample entry, with the translation in brackets, follows: Min. [minute] Mag. [magistrate] Lower Tugela, 11 Aug. 1894, 4/1/5 [call number of Lower Tugela Minute Papers in Natal Archives] 719/94 [number of a document in a large set], MR [Magistrates' Records]/GR [Government Records].

Introduction

1. In the early nineteenth century, a Zulu chiefdom forced some weaker chiefdoms (also known by lineage names such as Bomvu and Cele) in southeast Africa to adopt a Zulu identity. To avoid confusion over the names of many chiefdoms, and to avoid debates over terminology, I use "African" instead of "Zulu."

2. Frontier zones: Lamar and Thompson, *Frontier in History*. Thukela River as a porous boundary: Min. Mag. Lower Tugela, 11 Aug. 1894, 4/1/5 719/94, Lower Tugela MinP/MR/GR; Testimony, Ndukwana, 16 Sept. 1900, in Webb and Wright, *Stuart Archive*, 4:275; BB Natal 1879, JJ12, GR; Rep. Mag. Umsinga, B50, BB Supplemental, Departmental Rep. 1884, GR.

3. For example, Beinart and Harries have examined the effects of colonialism and labor migrancy on African subsistence production and local community politics, yet a full investigation of domestic relationships is not within the scope of their work. Beinart, *Political Economy of Pondoland;* Patrick Harries, "Kinship, Ideology and the Nature of Pre-colonial Labour Migration," in *Industrialisation and Social Change,* ed. Marks and Rathbone.

4. Control of African women and youths: Hunt, "Introduction," in *Gender and History;* Iris Berger, "'Beasts of Burden' Revisited: Interpretations of Women and Gender in Southern African Societies," in *Paths toward the Past,* ed. Harms et al.; Jeater, *Marriage, Perversion and Power;* Walker, *Women and Gender;* Peters, "Gender, Development Cycles and Historical Process"; Bozzoli, "Marxism, Feminism and South African Studies."

5. Father-son feud: *Ugudhla* v. *Matshana kaMondisa,* Min. Mag. Nkandla, 26 June 1905, 1/1/323 1741/1905, SNA MinP/GR. Matshana kaMondisa was the leader of the Sithole chiefdom in Nkandla (with followers in adjacent Nquthu). *Abafokazana* as epithet: Testimony, Mpatshana, 28 May 1913, in Webb and Wright, *Stuart Archive,* 3:316.

6. Criticism and fury of ancestral spirits: Testimony, Ndhlovu, 9 Nov. 1902, in Webb and Wright, *Stuart Archive,* 4:208.

7. Quotations from Matshana: *Ugudhla* v. *Matshana kaMondisa,* 1/1/323 1741/1905, SNA MinP/GR.

8. *Ukulobola* is a verb meaning to offer bridewealth. The noun, *ilobolo,* means bridewealth. Residents in the middle and lower Thukela basin now say that *ukulobola* was, and is, the preferred description of bridewealth cattle and the giving of it.

9. *Abasha* and "younger generation": Testimony, Mbovu, 16 Sept. 1904, file 41, notebooks, J. Stuart, Papers of Individuals/PT.

10. "It is useless to talk": *Ugudhla* v. *Matshana.* For more on the proceedings, see chapter 3.

11. Intelligence Rep., Nqutu District, 12 Oct. 1906, Claim 267, Gwintsha and Umgweni, 8 Oct. 1906, 1/1/358 4208/06, SNA MinP/GR. It is unclear whether Gudhla joined the rebels.

12. Local turbulence as opposition to Europeans: Guy, *Destruction of the Zulu Kingdom;* Marks and Atmore, eds., *Economy and Society in Pre-industrial South Africa.*

Demythologizing African resistance: Beinart and Bundy, *Hidden Struggles;* Peires, *Dead Will Arise;* Ranger, "People in African Resistance"; Isaacman, "Peasants and Rural Social Protest." East Africa: Glassman, *Feasts and Riots.* Criticism of resistance paradigm: Cooper, "Conflict and Connection"; Mamdani, *Citizen and Subject.*

13. Marks, *Reluctant Rebellion,* 308–10, 355; Shula Marks, "Class, Ideology and the Bambatha Rebellion," in *Banditry, Rebellion and Social Protest in Africa,* ed. Crummey, 351, 353–55. Welsh's *Roots of Segregation,* published a year after *Reluctant Rebellion,* also examined the colonial policies that impinged on Natal Africans.

14. Lambert, *Betrayed Trust,* 3; Lambert, "Africans in Natal, 1880–1899," Ph.D.

15. Bryant, *Olden Times;* Bryant, *History of the Zulu and Neighboring Tribes.* Bryant's "faulty" methodology: John Wright and Carolyn Hamilton, "Traditions and Transformations: The Phongolo-Mzimkhulu Region in the Late Eighteenth and Early Nineteenth Centuries," in *Natal and Zululand,* ed. Duminy and Guest, 49–57. Anthropological studies of generational tensions: Krige, *Social System;* Gluckman, *Order and Rebellion;* Wilson, *For Men and Elders;* Phillip Mayer and Iona Mayer, "A Dangerous Age: From Boy to Young Man in Red Xhosa Youth Organizations," in *Anthropology and the Riddle of the Sphinx,* ed. Spencer; Murray, *Families Divided;* Werbner, *Tears of the Dead.* Elsewhere in Africa: Aguilar, ed., *Politics of Age and Gerontocracy;* Berry, *Fathers Work for Their Sons.*

16. Precapitalist household: Claude Meillassoux, "'The Economy' in Agricultural Self-Sustaining Societies: A Preliminary Analysis," in *Relations of Production: Marxist Approaches to Economic Anthropology,* ed. Seddons; Meillassoux, *Maidens, Meal and Money.* See also Rey, "Lineage Mode of Production." Anthropological studies of family reciprocal obligations: Goody, *Production and Reproduction;* Maurice Bloch, "The Long Term and Short Term: The Economic and Political Significance of the Morality of Kinship," in *Character of Kinship,* ed. Goody. Different African household structures: Kuper, "'House' and Zulu Political Structure"; Stichter and Parpart, *Patriarchy and Class;* Vaughan, "Which Family?"; Guyer, "Household and Community." Meillassoux's methodology and studies of the Zulu kingdom: John Wright, "Control of Women's Labour in the Zulu Kingdom," in *Before and after Shaka,* ed. Peires; Jeff Guy, "The Destruction and Reconstruction of Zulu Society," in *Industrialisation and Social Change,* ed. Marks and Rathbone. Juniors choosing to labor for assorted patriarchs: Hammond-Tooke, "Descent Groups."

17. Eldredge, *South African Kingdom.* See also Schmidt, *Peasants, Traders and Wives.* Eldredge and Schmidt reassessed pioneering analyses of African patriarchy and gender oppression: Bozzoli, "Marxism, Feminism and South African Studies"; Guy, "Analysing Precapitalist Societies." Scholars delineating a generational dimension: Beinart, "Origins of the *Indlavini*"; Beinart, "Joyini Inkomo"; Delius, *Lion amongst the Cattle.* See also Iliffe, *Africans: The History of a Continent;* Freund, *Making of Contemporary Africa;* John Lambert and Robert Morrell, "Domination and Subordination in Natal, 1890–1920," in *Political Economy and Identities,* ed. Morrell; Mandala, *Work and Control in a Peasant Economy;* Berman and Lonsdale, *Unhappy Valley.* Scholars examining

generational struggles: McClendon, "Tradition and Domestic Struggle"; McKittrick, "Burden of Young Men"; Michael Tetelman, "In Search of Discipline: Generational Control, Political Protest, and Everyday Violence in Cradock, South Africa, 1984–85," in *Politics of Age and Gerontocracy*, ed. Aguilar; Thomas, "Ngaitana (I will circumcise myself)"; Akyeampong, *Drink, Power and Cultural Change*.

18. Bosman, *Natal Rebellion of 1906*; Stuart, *History of the Zulu Rebellion*.

19. Most Natal newspapers addressed a white settler audience, but *Ilanga Lase Natal*, first published in 1903, expressed the opinions of Africans in isiZulu and English. The editor, a mission-educated, African isiZulu-speaker, John Dube, urged extension to male Christian property-owning Africans of the franchise and liberal rights to buy and sell land.

20. Julian Cobbing dismisses Stuart as a white supremacist, manipulating evidence to exaggerate the brutality of Zulu rulers: Cobbing, "Tainted Well." The oral history in the *Stuart Archive* is nonethless valuable and demonstrates Stuart's rigorous methods of verification: Hamilton, *Terrific Majesty*, 130–67; "James Stuart and 'the Establishment of a Living Source,'" Unpublished Paper.

1. Competing African and Colonial Political Patriarchies

1. "Alarming suddenness": "Zulu Customs Etc. List of the More Important Mountains, Rivers," c. 1900, file 1, H. C. Lugg, Papers of Individuals/PT. Climate: Rep. Resident Commissioner, Eshowe, 21 March 1895, 763 ZGH/GR; Returns, Lower Tugela and Mapumulo, BB Natal 1892–93, GR; Returns, YB Natal 1894, GR.

2. Topography and elevation: Rep. Mag. Mapumulo, BB Departmental Rep. 1904, GR; Evidence and Draft Rep. 1917–18, SNA Correspondence re: Protests and Written Evidence (1913 Land Act), GR. *Imikhovu:* Testimony, Mkando, 13 Aug. 1902, Webb and Wright, *Stuart Archive*, 3:170; Testimony, Mageza, 21 Feb. 1909, ibid., 2:78.

3. Soil fertility and sowing cycle: BB Natal 1880 (JJ108, JJ111), BB Natal 1886 (X6–X7), BB Zululand 1890 (X3–X4), GR; Rep. Mag. Krantzkop, 1 Oct. 1896, 3/1/1, Kranskop MinP/MR/GR; Testimony, Sibisi, 13 March 1979, tape 207, OHP, Papers of Individuals/PT. "Thorn Country": Testimony, Induna Class, 30 Jan. 1882, *Evidence, Natal Native Commission, 1881(–2)*, 333, COM/GR; Rep. Natal Conservator Forests 1893, F49, BB Departmental Rep., GR.

4. Since at least 300 CE, there were homesteads in the Thukela basin: Maggs, "Ndondwane"; Mazel, "Mbabane Shelter." Sketchy census figures were a consequence of labor migrancy and mobile seasonal work. At the turn of the twentieth century, the population density among Africans in Lower Tugela and Mapumulo divisions was about ninety persons per square mile, about twice that in the divisions of Eshowe and Umlalazi across the Thukela River in Zululand. Arable acres available per African farmer on the coast were the fewest in the Thukela basin. The number of acres available to Africans doubled in divisions away from the coast, falling slightly as population density rose in the Thukela basin western divisions. See BB Natal 1880, JJ109, JJ113, GR; Return Popula-

tion, YB Natal 1899, GR; BB Zululand 1889–1895, 1897, 848–54, 856, GR; BB Zululand 1896, microfilmed/GR. An average of thirty-five people per square mile lived in northern Natal's Kranskop and Umvoti divisions, roughly forty-five persons per square mile in Umsinga and Weenen divisions. Basin population: Rep. Mag. Umsinga, B31, BB Supplemental Departmental Rep., 1888, GR; Population Return, Natal 1892, 1/1/161 1031/1892, SNA MinP/GR; Acres per Head of the Population, Persons to Square Mile Native Population, *Census, Natal April 1904.*

5. Small white population: Bill Guest, "The War, Natal and Confederation," in *Anglo-Zulu War,* ed. Duminy and Ballard; Guest, "The New Economy," in *Natal and Zululand,* ed. Duminy and Guest. Settler acreage and land appropriation: Rep. Mag. Umsinga, BB Natal 1883, GG10, GR; Revenual Auditor's Public Accounts, D52, BB Supplemental Departmental Rep., 1885, GR; Agricultural Department Annual Rep., BB Departmental Rep., 1902, GR. Absentee colonial landlords and homestead rents: Statistics, Schedules of Farms, etc. 1917–18, SNA/GR; Lambert, *Betrayed Trust,* 14–15.

6. White sugar planters: Min. Resident Commissioner, Eshowe, 11 Sept. 1895, 766, ZGH/GR; Memo Prime Minister, Pietermaritzburg, 20 Feb. 1895, 785, ZGH/GR; Peter Richardson, "The Natal Sugar Industry in the Nineteenth Century," in *Putting a Plough to the Ground,* ed. Beinart, Delius, and Trapido, 150–51. Christian missionaries and *amakholwa:* BB Departmental Rep., GR; Etherington, *Preachers, Peasants, and Politics.*

7. Late-nineteenth-century homesteads: Testimony, Mabonsa, 2 Feb. 1909, Webb and Wright, *Stuart Archive,* 4:30; Testimony, Ndukwana, 21 Oct. 1900, ibid., 4:313; *Greytown Gazette,* 13 Jan. 1906, Newspapers; Nkandla Homestead, c. 1890s, 57, Album of Zulu Customs, 3, KCL, Photographs; Nkandla Homestead, c. 1900, 27, Album of Zulu Customs, 2, KCL, Photographs; "A Picturesquely Situated Kafir Kraal in the 'Uplands of Natal,'" c. 1900, C4731, NAP, Photographs; Homestead, c. 1900, C599, NAP, Photographs; Zululand Homestead, c. 1900, 621.12, Buildings: Historic and Common Zululand, KwaMuhle Local History, Photographs.

8. Oldest son and choice portions of meat: Annexure A, Statement, Lugubu, 8 Feb. 1905, and Lukulwini, 7 Feb. 1905, 1/1/315 2525/1904 SNA MinP/GR. Pecking order among siblings: Testimony, Ndukwana, 9 Nov. 1903, file 61, notebooks, J. Stuart, Papers of Individuals/PT.

9. Political centralization and youth mobilization: Wright, "Pre-Shakan Age-Group"; Testimony, Mandlakazi, 23 May 1916, Webb and Wright, *Stuart Archive,* 2:18. See also Maggs, "Iron Age Sequence." Elephant hunting and youth: Alan Smith, "The Indian Ocean Zone," in *History of Central Africa,* vol. 1, ed. Martin and Birmingham, 234–37.

10. *Amabutho* activities and competition over trade: Hedges, "Trade and Politics in Southern Mozambique," Ph.D.; Phillip Bonner, "The Dynamics of Late 18th Century Northern Nguni Society: Some Hypotheses," in *Before and after Shaka,* ed. Peires. Bridewealth customs: Ndukwana explained in 1897 that "throughout Zululand before cattle multiplied" (prior to the late eighteenth century) *ukulobola* could be given in various forms: "Brass neckbands (izimbedu) or neckrings (imdaka) or armrings (amasongo) . . . , or goats were used for this purpose, or hoes." Testimony, Ndukwana, 19 Oct. 1897, *Stuart Archive,* 4:266.

11. Wright, "Political Transformations in the Thukela-Mzimkhulu Region of Natal," in *Mfecane Aftermath*, ed. Hamilton; Wright, "Dynamics of Power and Conflict," Ph.D., 39, 42, 55, 209, 259–60. Wright's research draws extensively from oral testimony recorded in Webb and Wright, *Stuart Archive*.

12. Certain authors who have studied despotic dictators such as Hitler have cited Shaka as the African prototype: Walter, *Terror and Resistance*. Fiction writers who highlight Shaka's cruelty: Becker, *Rule of Fear*; Ritter, *Shaka Zulu*. Critique of the mythic representations of Shaka: Hamilton, "Character and Objects of Chaka"; Julian Cobbing, "Grasping the Nettle: The Slave Trade and the Early Zulu," in *The Debate on Zulu Origins*, ed. Edgecombe et al.; Wright, "A. T. Bryant and 'The Wars of Shaka.'" Different interpretations of *mfecane*: Wright, "Political Mythology and the Making of Natal's Mfecane"; John Omer-Cooper, "Aspects of Political Change in the Nineteenth Century Mfecane," in *African Societies in Southern Africa*, ed. Thompson.

13. In early-twentieth-century Natal a white priest, A. T. Bryant, compiled European travelers' accounts of precolonial "Nguni tribes and clans" in *Olden Times* and presented a view of Zulu people as martial and fearsome, which, until the 1980s, most historians regarded as authoritative. See Omer-Cooper, *Zulu Aftermath*, 24–27, 156; Brookes and Webb, *History of Natal*, 13.

14. Historians reassessing the concept of Zulu belligerence have been influenced by anthropologists who attacked the accuracy of oral traditions and "origin myths." See MacGaffey, "Oral Tradition in Central Africa"; Vansina, "Is Elegance Proof?" Studies asserting that Shaka and his Zulu followers were not the principal transforming force: Alan Smith, "The Trade of Delagoa Bay as a Factor in Nguni Politics, 1750–1835," in *African Societies in Southern Africa*, ed. Thompson, 171–89; Hedges, "Trade and Politics in Southern Mozambique and Zululand," Ph.D.; Phillip Bonner, "The Dynamics of Late 18th Century Northern Nguni Society: Some Hypotheses," in *Before and after Shaka*, ed. Peires, 74–81. Violence and slaving in the Drakensberg and Cape region: Alan Webster, "Unmasking the Fingo: The War of 1835 Revisited," in *Mfecane Aftermath*, ed. Hamilton. Cobbing has claimed that the violence associated with Zulu aggression was caused by rapacious Portuguese slavers: Cobbing, "Mfecane as Alibi." Certain scholars who challenge Cobbing see little, if any, evidence for his hypothesis: Eldredge, "Sources of Conflict in Southern Africa."

15. Demographic interpretations of the *mfecane*: Omer-Cooper, *Zulu Aftermath*, 25–26; Gluckman, "Rise of the Zulu Empire." Environmental interpretations: Jeff Guy, "Ecological Factors in the Rise of Shaka and the Zulu Kingdom," in *Anglo-Zulu War*, ed. Duminy and Ballard; Gump, "Ecological Change and Pre-Shakan State Formation"; Hall, "Dendroclimatology, Rainfall and Human Adaptation."

16. Peires, "Paradigm Deleted."

17. Early 1800s trade from Delagoa Bay and Port Natal: Cobbing, "Mfecane as Alibi"; Wright, "Beyond the Concept of the 'Zulu Explosion,'" in *Mfecane Aftermath*, ed. Hamilton. British traders in Natal: Ballard, "Natal, 1824–44." Farewell and Fynn: Hamilton, *Terrific Majesty*, 36–48; Leonard Thompson, "Co-operation and Conflict: The Zulu Kingdom and Natal," in *Oxford History of South Africa*, vol. 1, ed. Wilson and Thomp-

son, 348–49; Hattersley, *British Settlement of Natal,* 13; Brookes and Webb, *History of Natal,* 18–21. "No ordinary man": Testimony, Jantshi, 19 Feb. 1903, Webb and Wright, *Stuart Archive,* 1:198.

18. Zulu power and clientage: Hamilton, "Ideology, Oral Tradition and the Struggle for Power," M.A., 184–86, 355, 361–62, 498; Wright, "Thukela-Mzimkhulu Region of Natal," 177. The Ngwane were different from the AbakwaNgwane, the ruling group of the Swazi. *Amabutho*: Testimony, Madikane, 27 May 1905, Webb and Wright, *Stuart Archive,* 2: 54; Wright and Hamilton, "Traditions and Transformations," in *Natal and Zululand,* ed. Duminy and Guest, 69–70.

19. Gender relations in the kingdom: Wright, "Control of Women's Labour"; Golan, "Life Story of King Shaka."

20. Rigid codes of conduct and privileges of hierarchy: Testimony, Lunguza, 13 March 1909, Webb and Wright, *Stuart Archive,* 1: 310–11; Hamilton, "Ideology, Oral Tradition and the Struggle for Power," M.A., 260, 317. *Amalala* who spoke "with their tongues": Testimony, Dinya, 9 April 1905, Webb and Wright, *Stuart Archive,* 1:118. Low status of *amalala:* Testimony, Madikane, 27 May 1905, Webb and Wright, ibid., 2:55; Wright and Hamilton, "Making of the *Amalala."*

21. Wright and Hamilton, "Traditions and Transformations," 70–71; Eldredge, "Sources of Conflict in Southern Africa," 156.

22. Patriarchal and generational structures of the Zulu kingdom: Kuper, "'House' and Zulu Political Structure," 469–87. Long-existing conventions: Mack et al., "Homesteads in Two Rural Zulu Communities."

23. Shaka eliminating possible male heirs: Testimony, Jantshi, 19 Feb. 1903, Webb and Wright, *Stuart Archive,* 1:198. Assassination plots: Slater, "Transitions in the Political Economy," Ph.D., 201–2.

24. "A new king cannot rule": Testimony, Ndukwana, 13 Sept. 1900, Webb and Wright, *Stuart Archive,* 4:271–72. Greater independence for African patriarchs: Okoye, "Dingane: A Reappraisal," 221. Dingana reinstituted regiments and launched campaigns: Wright and Manson, *Hlubi Chiefdom,* 24–28; Bonner, *Kings, Commoners, and Concessionaires,* 40–42.

25. Missionaries in southeast Africa: Etherington, *Preachers, Peasants, and Politics;* Taylor, *American Board Mission in South Africa.*

26. Fragmentation of the Hlubi and consolidation of the Ngwane: Wright, "Political Transformations in the Thukela-Mzimkhulu Region," 169–70.

27. *Voortrekker* relations with Dingana and "Battle of Blood River:" Thompson, "Cooperation and Conflict," 357–61.

28. Dingana's fight with the Swazi and Mpande's flight: Bonner, *Kings, Commoners and Concessionaires,* 41–45; Mael, "Problems of Political Integration," Ph.D., 86–90. Mpande was considered a "simpleton," but he emerged as the longest reigning Zulu king: John Wright and D. Edgecombe, "Mpande kaSenzangakhona, 1798–1872," in *Black Leaders in Southern African History,* ed. Saunders, 46–48. "Breaking of the rope": Testimony, Mbovu, 7 Feb 1904, Webb and Wright, *Stuart Archive,* 3:49.

29. *Voortrekkers,* Mpande, and confiscation of Zulu cattle and land: Kennedy, "Fatal

Diplomacy," Ph.D., 51–53. Refugees return to Natal: Kennedy, "Mpande and the Zulu Kingship," 33–34. Natalia, British fears, and imperial annexation: Brookes and Webb, *History of Natal*, 54–55; Galbraith, *Reluctant Empire*, 193–97.

30. Establishment of African reserves in Natal: Lambert, "Chiefship in Early Colonial Natal," 270–72; Charles Ballard, "Traders, Trekkers and Colonists," in *Natal and Zululand*, ed. Duminy and Guest, 124.

31. The son of a Methodist missionary, Shepstone spent his early childhood in the eastern Cape, learned to speak isiXhosa, which is similar to isiZulu, and won success with African patriarchs, in part because of this linguistic talent. See Testimony, Mtshayankomo, 15 Jan. 1922, Webb and Wright, *Stuart Archive*, 4:126, 153. Shepstone's rule through African patriarchs: Guy, "An Accommodation of Patriarchs," Unpublished Paper; Norman Etherington, "The 'Shepstone System' in the Colony of Natal and beyond the Borders," in *Natal and Zululand*, ed. Duminy and Guest, 170–71.

32. "Mere hereditary deputies . . . to the Crown": Welsh, *Roots of Segregation*, 15; Guy, *Heretic*, 40–42. Early colonial customary laws reflected the changing official interpretations of African "tradition." Customary law in Natal: McClendon, "Dangerous Doctrine." Customary law in British colonial southern Africa: Jeater, *Marriage, Perversion and Power;* Terrence Ranger, "The Invention of Tradition in Colonial Africa," in *Invention of Tradition*, ed. Hobsbawm and Ranger. British colonial west, central, and east Africa: Berry, *No Condition Is Permanent;* Chanock, *Law, Custom and Social Order;* Hay and Wright, *African Women and the Law.*

33. Shepstone's "wont to hold frequent intercourse with the Chiefs": Testimony, Joko, 1 Feb. 1882, *Evidence Natal Native Commission 1881(–2)*, 355, COM/GR.

34. Lambert, *Betrayed Trust*, 74–76; Welsh, *Roots of Segregation*, 20–21, 32–50.

35. Testimony, Mtshayankomo, 11 Jan. 1922, Webb and Wright, *Stuart Archive*, 4:115.

36. Remarks of homestead head: Testimony, Ndukwana, 16 Sept. 1900, Webb and Wright, *Stuart Archive*, 4:275.

37. The clash between Cetshwayo and Mbuyazi over Mpande's succession: Kennedy, "Mpande and the Zulu Kingship," 32; Norman Etherington, "Anglo-Zulu Relations, 1856–78," in *Anglo-Zulu War*, ed. Duminy and Ballard, 15. Battle between rival brothers: Peter Colenbrander, "The Zulu Kingdom, 1828–79," in *Natal and Zululand*, ed. Duminy and Guest, 104.

38. Dube, Thukela Mouth, Eshowe, 17 Sept. 1992, Interviews. The story of the slaughter and the place name, *emathanjeni*, was confirmed in an interview with the area chief, Dan Dunn, descendant of the white Zulu chief, John Dunn, ruler of Eshowe district in the late nineteenth century: Dunn, Gingindlovu, Eshowe, 18 Sept. 1992, Interviews.

39. Cetshwayo ceding a parcel of territory: Etherington, "Anglo-Zulu Relations," 29. Shepstone's acknowledgment of Cetshwayo as heir to Mpande: Testimony, Cetshwayo, Feb. 1880, "Cetywayo's Story of the Zulu Nation and the War," in *Zulu King Speaks*, ed. Webb and Wright, 18–21.

40. Small settler population and government agricultural policies: Hattersley, *Portrait of a Colony*, 124–26; Henry Slater, "Changing Pattern of Economic Relationships in Rural

Natal, 1838–1914," in *Economy and Society in Pre-Industrial South Africa,* ed. Marks and Atmore. 154.

41. The increasing indigenous population alarmed colonists; some urged that Zulu-land serve as a repository for Africans in crowded Natal reserves. Population in 1860s: Statistical Summary, Population, B2, BB Natal 1901, GR. Commercial hamlets outside Pietermaritzburg: Ballard, "Traders, Trekkers, and Colonists," 127–29.

42. White land speculators: Lambert, *Betrayed Trust,* 8. Settler agriculture in the 1870s: Charles Ballard and G. Lenta, "The Complex Nature of Agriculture in Colonial Natal, 1860–1909," in *Enterprise and Exploitation in a Victorian Colony,* ed. Guest and Sellers, 122–46. Natal Land and Colonisation Company: Hurwitz, *Agriculture in Natal,* 53–70. The Natal Native Trust also parceled out 144,000 acres (divided into nineteen reserves) to missionary churches from the United States, Germany, Norway, and Great Britain: Area 6, 7, and 12, Statistics, Schedules of Farms, etc. 1917–18, SNA/GR.

43. The Natal Colony taxed homestead rituals such as the marriage ceremony, in 1869 requiring African grooms to pay five pounds sterling to a magistrate before taking a wife; this highly unpopular tax was repealed a few years later: *Rep. Natal Native Commission 1881–2,* 36, Rep./GR. African revenues supporting Natal Colony: Public Debt 1847–1906, 7, YB Natal 1906, GR.

44. Migrant labor flow from Natal and Zululand: Rep. Mag. Lower Tugela, JJ109, Rep. Mag. Umsinga, JJ113, BB Natal 1880, GR. African taxes, fees, and customs charges going to upgrade colonial infrastructure: Total Revenue, 1847–1906, 7, YB 1906, GR; Ether-ington, "Shepstone System," 175.

45. Regulations protecting African patriarchy under scrutiny: Welsh, *Roots of Segre-gation,* 159–61.

46. "Guns . . . from the Portuguese": Testimony, Mpatshana, 2 June, 1912, Webb and Wright, *Stuart Archive,* 3:328. Firepower of the Zulu kingdom: Guy, "Note on Firearms in the Zulu Kingdom."

47. Testimony, Mtshayankomo, 15 Jan. 1922, Webb and Wright, *Stuart Archive,* 4:126. Mtshayankomo's recollection is an important indication of what leading Zulu men thought about Shepstone's patriarchal bearing. Zulu coronation and Natal government recognition of Cetshwayo's political mandate: R. Cope, "Political Power within the Zulu Kingdom," 11–17.

48. Testimony, Ndukwana, 13, 14, 15 Sept. 1900, Webb and Wright, *Stuart Archive,* 4:271–73.

49. Testimony, Mtshayankomo, 20 Jan. 1922, Webb and Wright, *Stuart Archive,* 4:133.

50. British subjugation of Xhosa chiefs: Peires, *Dead Will Arise.* Moshoeshoe and BaSotho: Thompson, *Survival in Two Worlds;* Eldredge, *South African Kingdom.* Per-ceived threat posed by Chief Langalibalele: Etherington, "Why Langalibalele Ran Away." "Stab [the inGobamakhosi]": Testimony, Baleni, 14 May 1914, Webb and Wright, *Stuart Archive,* 1:32. Another Zulu eyewitness: Testimony, Ndabazezwe, 23 June 1921, ibid., 4:184.

51. "English" and "Cetshwayo [was] taking his advice": Testimony, Ndhlovu, 10 Nov. 1902, Webb and Wright, *Stuart Archive,* 4:209. White confederation: Peter Colenbran-

der, "The Zulu Political Economy on the Eve of the War," in *Anglo-Zulu War,* ed. Duminy and Ballard, 84–91. Historian who emphasizes white settlers' reluctance to go to war: John Laband, "The Reduction of Zululand, 1878–1904," in *Natal and Zululand,* ed. Duminy and Guest, 193. Historians who argue for white settlers' support of invasion: Guy, *Destruction of the Zulu Kingdom,* 43–50; Guest, "War, Natal and Confederation," 61.

52. Wolseley design: Guy, *Destruction of the Zulu Kingdom,* 54–61; Laband and Thompson, *Kingdom and Colony at War,* 204–7.

53. John Dunn and Hlubi Molife: Laband "Reduction of Zululand," 195–97. Imperial rule and cooperative chiefs in Zululand: Resident Commissioner, Eshowe, to Governor, Pietermaritzburg, 17 April 1894, 44, Letters Despatched, Commissioner/GR; 8 Interim Rep., 27 Aug. 1904, 33, Zululand-Lands Delimitation COM, Rep./GR; "Brief Sketch of Zulu History," SNA/GR; Elaine Unterhalter, "Confronting Imperialism: The People of Nquthu and the Invasion of Zululand," in *Anglo-Zulu War,* ed. Duminy and Ballard, 106–9; Jeff Guy, "The Role of Colonial Officials in the Destruction of the Zulu Kingdom," in *Anglo-Zulu War,* ed. Duminy and Ballard, 157–59. Laband argues that Wolseley's settlement was part of a British plan to stamp out any Zulu resistance after 1880 and to avoid the costs of imperial annexation of Zululand. Laband, "Reduction of Zululand," 205–13. Wolseley design as a deliberate attempt to stoke a civil war: Guy, *Destruction of the Zulu Kingdom,* 75–78; Brookes and Webb, *History of Natal,* 146.

54. "Youths had come to defy the nation": Testimony, Ndhlovu, 10 Nov. 1902, Webb and Wright, *Stuart Archive,* 4:209.

2. African Patriarchs

1. "Cut for him by his elder brother": Testimony, Ndukwana, 11 Sept. 1903, Webb and Wright, *Stuart Archive,* 4:378. Meat as a luxury: Testimony, Gama, 18 Dec. 1898, and Bikwayo, 15 Oct. 1903; ibid., 1:142, 69; Testimony, Mahaya, 26, 27 Aug. 1905, ibid., 2:113, 122. Gender divisions, emphasizing male labor: Testimony, Madama, 21 Feb. 1882, *Evidence, Natal Native Commission, 1881(–2),* 248–49, COM/GR; Rep. Mag. Umsinga, B187, BB Supp. Departmental Rep. 1886, GR; Testimony, Mqayikana, 12 Nov. 1897, Webb and Wright, *Stuart Archive,* 4:34; Testimony, Ndukwana, 11 Sept. 1903, file 61, notebooks, J. Stuart, Papers of Individuals/PT.

2. Homestead resilience and steady production: Annual Statistics for the following years: 1879 (AA8–AA15, Mag. Rep., JJ6–JJ16), 1880 (AA7, Mag. Rep., JJ105, JJ111), 1881 (X7–X13, Mag. Rep., GG45), 1883 (X6–X11, Mag. Rep., GG11), 1884 (X6–X11), 1885 (X6–X11), 1886 (X6–X7, X14–X15), 1887 (X6–X7), 1888 (X6–X7), 1889 (6–7), BB Natal, 1879–89, GR. See also Veterinary Surgeon and Revenual Auditor, BB Supp. Departmental Rep., 1884–1889, GR.

3. Operations on white farms: Testimony, Umhini, 11 (labor recruitment), Botha, 39, Nel, 31, *Natal Native Commission, 1881–2, Evidence, Sub-Commission Umvoti,* COM/GR.

4. Attracting dependents and securing labor: Notice, Beer Drinking Act 1898, 1/1/296 2557/1902, SNA Minutes Paper/GR; Testimony, Ndukwana, 12 Sept. 1900, Webb and

Wright, *Stuart Archive,* 4:269–70; Testimony, Khumalo, 31 Dec. 1900, ibid., 1:250; Testimony, Mxaba, 2 Jan. 1901, ibid., 1:250–52. See also Rep. Mag. Lower Tugela 1902, 4/1/7 132/1903, Lower Tugela MinP/MR/GR; Statement, Bukwana, Min. Mag. Nkandla, 7 Oct. 1905, 1/1/328 2672/05, SNA MinP/GR. "Rights" to command labor: Stuart, "The Zulu Tribal System," c. 1907, file 26, notebooks, J. Stuart, Papers of Individuals/PT; Guyer, "Wealth in People," 84. Polygyny of male elders: Monica Wilson, "Changes in Social Structure in Southern Africa: The Relevance of Kinship to the Studies of the Historian," in *African Societies in Southern Africa,* ed. Thompson. 79.

5. Chieftaincy and activities of *izinduna:* Rep. Mag. Krantzkop, 31 Dec. 1898, 3/1/2, Kranskop MinP/MR/GR; Testimony, Khumalo, 20 Oct. 1900, file 59, notebooks, J. Stuart, Papers of Individuals/PT; Testimony, Ndukwana, 21 Oct. 1900, Webb and Wright, *Stuart Archive,* 4:316; Testimony, Mayinga and Dinya, 11 July 1905, ibid., 2:257–58; Holleman, "Structure of the Zulu Ward." *Ibandla:* Claim, Mhlakaza kaMpenzi, Eshowe, 30 Jan. 1901, 1/1/293 2047/1901, SNA MinP/GR.

6. Fluctuations in size of chiefdoms: Testimony, Mageza, 20 Feb. 1905, and Maziyana, 30 April 1905, Webb and Wright, *Stuart Archive,* 2:73, 300; Testimony, Lugubu, 4 March 1909, ibid., 1:281–83; Testimony, Mbokobo, 5 Nov. 1913, ibid., 3:6–15. Reciprocal obligations between chiefs and followers: Mag. Eshowe to Chief Dunn, Eshowe, 6 Sept. 1894, Letter Book, 1892–97, Eshowe MR/GR; Min. Civil Commissioner, Eshowe, to SNA, Pietermaritzburg, 21 Jan. 1898, 1/1/279 25/1898, SNA MinP/GR; Statement, Chief Kula, Umsinga, 26 Nov. 1902, 1/1/298 3531/1902, SNA MinP/GR; Statement, Headmen Sandanezwe and Mankamfana, Nkandla, 7 Oct. 1905, Min. Mag. Nkandla, 7 Oct. 1905, 1/1/328 2672/05, SNA MinP/GR. "Applicants wishing": Testimony, Ndukwana, 21 Oct. 1900, Webb and Wright, *Stuart Archive,* 4:312–13.

7. *Isibuko sikababa:* Annexure A, *Deyi* v. *Mbuzikazi,* 1 July 1897, 1/1/278 1962/97, SNA MinP/GR; Testimony, Mgidhlana, 5 June 1921, file 56, notebooks, J. Stuart, Papers of Individuals/PT. Contemporary modifications of *isithombe sikababa:* Mchunu (Makhabeleni, 13 Dec. 1992, 23 Jan. 1993), Nxumalo (Makhabeleni, 1 May 1993), Cube (Nkandla, 21 Nov. 1992), and Ntuli (Nkandla, 20 Feb. 1993), Interviews. Son's praises: Testimony, Mtshapi, 6 April 1918, 9 May 1918, Webb and Wright, *Stuart Archive,* 4:73–74, 89.

8. Testimony, Ndukwana, 3 Sept. 1903, Webb and Wright, *Stuart Archive,* 4:376.

9. Divine realm and choosing an heir: Testimony, Mkando, 12 Aug. 1902, Webb and Wright, *Stuart Archive,* 3:168–69; Testimony, Ndukwana, Mkando, and Dlozi, 13 Aug. 1902, ibid., 3:171–72, 174; Testimony, Msimanga, 28 Feb. 1922, ibid., 4:41.

10. Guidance and property of African patriarch: Testimony, Khumalo, 16 Dec. 1900, Webb and Wright, *Stuart Archive,* 1:237; Testimony, Mbovu, 7 Feb. 1904, ibid., 1:28; Testimony, Induna Class (30 Jan. 1882, 333) and Umnini (15 Feb. 1882, 193), *Evidence, Natal Native Commission, 1881(–2),* COM/GR.

11. Receiving bridewealth for daughters and taking a second wife: Min. Mag. Umvoti, 29 June 1904, 1/1/312 1341/04, SNA MinP/GR; Testimony, Ndukwana, 15 July 1900, Webb and Wright, *Stuart Archive,* 4:267–68. "Commercial advantage": Lambert, *Betrayed Trust,* 50.

12. Polygyny distressing colonists and 1869 marriage law: *Rep., Natal Native Commission, 1881–2*, Rep./GR. See also Welsh, *Roots of Segregation*, 90–91.

13. "Young men [who] can pay": Testimony, Umnini, 15 Feb. 1882, 193, *Evidence, Natal Native Commission, 1881–2*, COM/GR. "Girls and boys": Testimony, Joko (1 Feb. 1882, 354–55) and Madama (21 Feb. 1882, 249), ibid., COM/GR.

14. Rep. SNA, Aug. 1900, 1/1/290 1430/1900, SNA MinP/GR.

15. "To the internal conflicts . . . the parent body": Stuart, "Lectures and Notes of the Zulu," c. 1900, file 26, notebooks, J. Stuart, Papers of Individuals/PT. Natal government tightening control over chieftaincy: *Rep., Natal Native Commission, 1881–2*, 33–34, Rep./GR; Statement, Chief Kula, Umsinga, 26 Nov. 1902, 1/1/298 3531/1902, SNA MinP/GR; Chief Mtamo, Krantzkop, 28 Nov. 1902, 1/1/298 3668/1902, SNA MinP/GR; SNA to PM, Pietermaritzburg, 15 Aug. 1904, 1/1/311 1149/1904, SNA MinP/GR. See also PM Papers 1904, 49, 1120/1904, PM/GR.

16. Chiefs who enlisted young male laborers and enforced pass laws: Testimony, Matiwane (10 Feb. 1881, 148), Umnini (15 Feb. 1882, 199), and Teleku (13 Feb. 1882, 176), *Evidence, Natal Native Commission, 1881(–2)*, COM/GR; *Rep., Natal Native Commission, 1881–2*, 4–5, Rep./GR; Rep. Mag. Umsinga, B39, B46, BB Supp. Departmental Rep. 1885, GR. Magistrates' qualifications: Lambert, *Betrayed Trust*, 60. Young men in labor and fighting bands: Min. Mag. Weenen to Under-SNA, Pietermaritzburg, 29 Dec. 1896, 3/2/2 117/1897, Weenen MinP/MR/GR; BB Natal 1904, 120–36, GR.

17. Collapse of Zulu kingdom and rise of civil conflict: Guy, *Destruction of the Zulu Kingdom*, 201–9, 217–27, 243; Laband, "Usuthu-Mandlakazi Conflict." Deposing hereditary chiefs and destroying political autonomy: *Rep., Natal Native Commission, 1881–2*, 40–45, Rep./GR; Testimony, Mbovu, 25 Sept. 1904, Webb and Wright, *Stuart Archive*, 3:42; Min. Resident Commissioner, Eshowe, 8 Dec. 1893, 753, ZGH/GR.

18. New Republic: Dominy, "New Republicans." Partition of Zululand: Resident Commissioner, Eshowe, to Governor, Pietermaritzburg, 17 April 1894, 44, Letters Despatched, Commissioner/GR; Petition, Makongolo, Nkandla, to Governor, Pietermaritzburg, 4 July 1896, 1/1/279 298/1898, SNA MinP/GR.

19. Chiefs' tribute, fines, and loss of jurisdiction: Resident Commissioner, Eshowe, to Governor, Pietermaritzburg, 16 Feb. 1894, 44, Letters Despatched, Commissioner/GR; Min. Under-SNA, 22 April 1903, 1/1/300 1141/1903, SNA MinP/GR. Sec. PM to SNA, Pietermaritzburg, 7 May 1903, 1/1/300 1145/1903, SNA MinP/GR. Dinuzulu's 1889 conviction: Laband, "Dick Addison," M.A. thesis, 159–63, 175–80, 222–23, 238–41.

20. Population: Annual Rep., 851–53, BB Zululand, 1892–94, GR. Settler encroachment, delicate "question": Resident Commissioner, Eshowe, to Secretary, Governor, 21 Sept. 1895, 766, ZGH/GR. No "difficulty": Annual Rep. Civil Commissioner, 6, 851, BB Zululand 1892, GR. Chiefs' "obedience to the Government": Annual Rep. Civil Commissioner, 6, 852, BB Zululand 1893, GR. See also Correspondence, 1892–96, 748–52, ZGH/GR.

21. White farmers in Natal: Rep. Mag. Weenen, 98, BB Supp. Departmental Rep. 1893, GR. African farmers dominating Natal markets: Lambert, *Betrayed Trust*, 114.

22. Expanding Code of Native Law and prosecutions of young men in faction fights:

Minutes of Interviews with Native Chiefs, 1914–25, SNA/GR. This source discusses early 1890s legal practices of chiefs and resident magistrates. "Absolute power to appoint and dismiss chiefs": Welsh, *Roots of Segregation,* 288. Magistrates' intervention in chiefs' succession: Min. Mag. Stanger, 11 Aug. 1893, 1/SGR 4/1/4, SNA MinP/GR. See also 1/1/281 1109/1898; 1/1/290 1430/1900, SNA MinP/GR. Usurpation of chiefs' powers: John Lambert, "From Independence to Rebellion: African Society in Crisis, c. 1880–1910," in *Natal and Zululand,* ed. Duminy and Guest, 384. In the mid-1890s, amended sections of the Code of Native Law gave headmen the right to try civil cases and claim *ukulobola* privileges of a hereditary chief: Lambert, *Betrayed Trust,* 62, 124–25.

23. Rep. Under-SNA 1905, ii, BB Departmental Rep. 1905, GR. The 1905 Rep. describes the colonial administration following the 1897 annexation of Zululand.

24. To "recognize . . . on lands falling . . . special permission": Statement, Chief Bambatha, 4 Nov. 1895, 1/1/210 1353/1895, SNA MinP/GR. See also Min. Mag. Krantzkop, 1/1/210 1333/95, SNA MinP/GR; Chief Bambatha, 22 Aug. 1902, Min. Under-SNA, 25 Aug. 1902, 1/1/296 2277/1902, SNA MinP/GR. "Residence from one Magisterial . . . different tribes": BB Departmental Rep. 1905, vii, GR. See also Statement, Magqanqu, Lower Tugela, Min. SNA, 21 April 1900, 1/1/293 566/1900, SNA MinP/GR. Restricting the autonomy of chiefs: Min. SNA, 24 Nov. 1900, 1/1/290 2093/1900, SNA MinP/GR.

25. "That all chiefs . . . power to make chiefs": Resident Commissioner, Eshowe, to Governor, Pietermaritzburg, 3 April 1894, 44, Letters Despatched, Commissioner/GR. "Section 33 of the Laws and Regulations": Circular 471 1894, Min. Resident Commissioner, 28 Feb. 1894, Nkandla MinP, Confidential/MR/GR. Scaling back jurisdiction of appointed chiefs: Mag. Eshowe, to Chief Dunn, Eshowe, 11 June 1894, 313/94, Eshowe MinP/MR/GR. Magistrates reversing decisions of chiefs: Min. Resident Commissioner, Eshowe, 8 Dec. 1893, 753, ZGH/GR; Civil Record Book, Native Cases, 1895–1901, Eshowe MR/GR; Min., Meeting between Nkandla Chiefs, SNA, Civil Commissioner Zululand, and Mag. Nkandla, 29 Aug. 1898, 1/1/282 2419/1898, SNA MinP/GR. "Circumstances have changed": Statement, Resident Commissioner, 9 July 1896, Nkandla MinP, Confidential/MR/GR. "Without permission": Min. SNA, Pietermaritzburg, to Civil Commissioner, Eshowe, 29 Jan. 1899, 1/1/284 176/1899, SNA MinP/GR. The governor's title, the "Supreme Chief," like Shepstone's name, "Somsewu," or "great white Father," was doubtless well known among Africans decades before the Natal Colony annexed Zululand in 1897.

26. "To be employed": Min. Government House, Jan. 1898, 89, 1034, GH/GR; Memo Civil Commissioner, Eshowe, 6 April 1908, Native Rebellion Court Martial Proceedings, SNA/GR. Graves of Zulu kings: Lugg, *Historic Natal and Zululand,* 113. "The existing system": Min. Civil Commissioner, Eshowe, to Minister Native Affairs, Pietermaritzburg, 10 April 1905, 1/1/319 873/1905, SNA MinP/GR. In his correspondence the civil commissioner referred to the Zululand Annexation Act of 1897.

27. Homesteads consuming their harvests: YB 1904, 3, GR. Loss of environmental balance: BB Natal 1880 (JJ108, JJ111), 1886 (X6–X7), 1892–93, GR; YB 1894–1895, GR. African agricultural production, 1879–93: BB Natal 1879 (AA8–AA9, AA11), 1880 (AA7), 1881 (X7, X11), 1883 (X6–X7, X10–X11), 1884 (X6–X7), 1885 (X6–X7, X11), 1886 (X6–X7,

XII), 1890–91 (X6–X7, XII), 1891–92 (X6–X7, X12–X13), 1892–93 (X6–X7, XII), GR. Increasing African agricultural production: YB 1906, 6, GR. Livestock damaging environment: Lambert, *Betrayed Trust,* 110–11.

28. Young men departing from homesteads: BB Natal 1892, 1/1/161 1013/1892, SNA MinP/GR; Min. SNA, 6 April 1894, 1/1/184 431/1894, SNA MinP/GR; *Star,* 25 Oct. 1895, 1/1/210 1320/95, SNA MinP/GR; *Standard and Digger News,* 28 Oct. 1895, 1/1/210 1336/95, SNA MinP/GR. Young men working outside homesteads: Min. Mag. Lower Tugela, 8 Jan. 1895, 910/94, Lower Tugela MinP/MR/GR; Lambert, "Africans in Natal," Ph.D., 401. "Stream of the able-bodied": Annual Rep. Mag. Weenen, B5, BB Departmental Rep., 1893–94, GR. African young men leaving and breaking filial obligations: see homestead patriarchs' testimony in *Evidence, Native Affairs Commission, 1906–7,* 316, 767–8, 855, COM/GR. African migrants seduced by city culture: Van Onselen, *Studies in the Social and Economic,* 1:xvi; Rob Turrell, "Kimberley: Labour and Compounds, 1871–1885," in *Industrialisation and Social Change,* ed. Marks and Rathbone, 58–68.

29. Locust destruction: YB 1895–96, GR. Migrant sons' wages buying grain: Rep. Resident Commissioner, Eshowe, 21 March 1895, 763, ZGH Correspondence/GR. "Swarms of locusts": *Times of Natal,* 11 Sept. 1896, in 1/1/229 1540/96, SNA MinP/GR. "Great scarcity of food": Mag. Entonjaneni, 31 Aug. 1895, 281, Letter Book, Entonjaneni MR/GR. "Cost price" and "young men": SNA Circular 4, to Natal Magistrates, 12 Feb. 1896, 1/1/216 203/96, SNA MinP/GR.

30. Homestead heads "on the eve of being robbed": *Natal Mercury,* 7 Oct. 1896, in SNA Min., 18 Sept. 1896, 1/1/230 1676/96, SNA MinP/GR. Destructive path of rinderpest in southern Africa: Kevin Shillington, "Irrigation, Agriculture and the State: The Harts Valley in Historical Perspective," in *Putting a Plough to the Ground,* ed. Beinart, Delius, and Trapido, 326; Van Onselen, "Reactions to Rinderpest in Southern Africa." First cattle victims: SNA Min., 18 Sept. 1896, 1/1/229 1557/1896, SNA MinP/GR. Corrals and precautionary measures: SNA Min. 9 Oct. 1896, 1/1/230 1676/1896, SNA MinP/GR. Bile serum: SNA Min., 31 Aug. 1897, 1/1/252 1636/97, SNA MinP/GR.

31. General vaccination program: 1897 SNA MinP, 1/1/250–1 1401–1600, GR. "The natives . . . disease nearer to them": SNA Min., 11 Sept. 1897, 1/1/255 1972/97, SNA MinP/GR. Dead Eshowe cattle: Annual Rep. Mag. Eshowe, 192, 3/1/4, Letter Books, Eshowe MR/GR. Dead cattle in Kranskop: Rep. Mag. Kranskop, 16 Oct. 1897, 3/1/2 2021/1897, Kranskop MinP/GR.

32. "Nearly everything . . . blocks of cow dung": Rev. C. Johnson, Nquthu, to Secretary, Society for the Propagation of the Gospel, 12 Nov. 1897, 779, ZGH/GR. "Natives are in actual *want*": Min. Mag. Weenen to Under-SNA, 28 Dec. 1898, 965/1898, Weenen MinP/MR/GR. Colonial statistics, though sketchy at best, showed that African crop acreage and yield increased steadily (with the population increase) from 1855 to 1906. Homestead output plummeted from 1894 to 1896, but production recovered just three years later to match previous levels and then, in 1900, started to climb again. See BB Zululand, 1889–90, 2U, 848–49, 1891–95, 2Y, 850–54, GR. Cattle taking longer than crops to rebound: YB 1906, 6, GR.

33. A "man who has no cattle": Testimony, Dhlozi, 18 May 1902, Webb and Wright,

Stuart Archive, 1:94. "Because of the losses": Mag. Melmoth to Resident Commissioner, Eshowe, 14 Oct. 1897, Letter Book, Entonjaneni MR/GR. Anglo-Boer War: Warwick, *Black People and the South African War,* 1–3.

34. Food deficits and strategies to bolster production: BB Departmental Rep., 1902, C2, GR; Rep. Mag. Eshowe, 70, and Rep. Mag. Krantzkop, 34, BB Departmental Rep. 1903, GR. British military employing former migrants to fight Boer guerillas: Min. Resident Commissioner, Eshowe, 9 Sept. 1899, 32, Confidential Correspondence, Commissioner/GR; Magistrates' Reply to Circular 123/02, 1 Nov. 1902, 33, Confidential Correspondence, Commissioner/GR.

35. Settler farmers' advantages and increasing African tenancy: Rep. Mag. Krantzkop, 23 Jan. 1902, B32, BB Departmental Rep. 1899–1901, GR; Testimony, Chief Bubula (14 Feb. 1907, 68) and Chief Belebana (14 Feb. 1907, 770), *Evidence Native Affairs Commission 1906–7,* COM/GR. Pass restrictions: *South African Native Affairs Commission 1903–5,* 3:531–38, COM/GR.

36. In 1901 the Natal government estimated that 22,000 Africans lived in Durban and Pietermaritzburg; by 1904 the total had risen to almost 33,000: YB 1901, 13, GR. In 1905 the movement of labor migrants to Durban and Pietermaritzburg had gained even more momentum. "Outward Passes" and "Inward Passes": Rep. Mag. Nkandla, C5, BB Departmental Rep. 1902, GR; *South African Native Affairs Commission 1903–5,* 3:531–38, COM/GR.

37. Age range of labor migrants: Rep. Under-SNA, 20 July 1906, iii, BB Departmental Rep. 1905, GR. Fifty percent more women: Rep. Mag. Nkandla (1903, 73), Rep. Mag. Mapumulo (1904, 6), Rep. Mag. Kranskop (1904, 33), BB Departmental Rep./GR.

38. Migrant wages trickling into homesteads: Rep. Mag. Umlalazi, C12, and Rep. Mag. Mahlabathini, C15, BB Departmental Rep. 1902, GR. Doubling hut tax on Crown land: *Ilanga Lase Natal,* 28 July 1905. Homestead debt: Testimony, Dhlozi, 29 July 1902, Webb and Wright, *Stuart Archive,* 3:155–56; Min. Under-SNA, 25 Aug. 1902, 1/1/296 2277/1902, SNA MinP/GR. Usury: Rep. Mag. Krantzkop, 34, BB Departmental Rep. 1903, GR. Tenants burdened by higher rents: Testimony, Banana (16 May 1907, 871) and Nomdwana (15 April 1907, 863), *Evidence, Native Affairs Commission, 1906–7,* COM/GR. Evicting insolvent homesteads: Min. Assistant Mag. Umvoti to Under-SNA, 20 July 1905, and Min. Mag. Umvoti to Under-SNA, 1 Nov. 1905, 1/1/324 1912/1905, SNA MinP/GR. Elimination of African rights to purchase land: Bundy, *Rise and Fall,* 189–91.

39. White-owned acreage in Natal: BB Natal 1901, 13, GR; Rep. Secretary, Minister of Agriculture, June 1906, 8, BB Departmental Rep. 1906, GR. Population statistics: Director's Annual Rep. Natal Agricultural Department 1902, 15–17, BB Departmental Rep. 1902, GR. Homestead dwellers streaming from barren African reserves: Natal Agricultural Department Annual Rep. 1902, 2, BB Departmental Rep. 1902, GR; BB 1901, 13, GR; Under-SNA to SNA, 25 Aug. 1902, 1/1/296 2490/1902, SNA MinP/GR; Statement, Chief Nondubela, Umsinga, 1 May 1903, 1/1/301 1442/1903, SNA MinP/GR. "Islands" of "waste": Deputation, Chiefs and Headmen, 9 Oct. 1906, 1/1/328 2833/1905; SNA MinP/GR. "We are . . . unable": Testimony, Dhlozi, 29 July 1902, Webb and Wright, *Stuart Archive,* 3:156.

40. Agricultural output and land ownership: BB Natal 1901, 13, GR; Rep. Secretary, Minister of Agriculture, June 1906, 8, BB Departmental Rep. 1906, GR.

41. Before 1902, except for a section of Entonjaneni district (Proviso B) given over to Afrikaners in 1887 and 1888 and the small plots owned by European officials at eleven magisterial districts, Africans controlled virtually all the land in Zululand. At "least four-fifths": *Natal Witness,* 25 Jan. 1905. "Those who are under": Final Rep., 44, Zululand-Lands Delimitation COM, 1902–4, Rep./GR. No ambitious plan to remove Zulu homesteads: Third Ad. Interim Rep., 6, Zululand-Lands Delimitation COM, 1902–4, Rep./GR. "In many parts . . . the most densely populated: Eighth Ad. Interim Rep., 32–33, Zululand-Lands Delimitation COM, 1902–4, Rep./GR. Colonial fear of depleting resources in Zululand: Annual Rep. Natal Agricultural Department (1902, 96) and Rep. Conservator of Forests (1904, 32), BB Departmental Rep., GR.

42. "Two years ago, the Division": Rep. Mag. Mapumulo, 6, and Rep. of Natives in Zululand, 89–90, BB Departmental Rep. 1904, GR. "Cut the bush": Rep. Conservator of Forests, 3–4, BB Departmental Rep. 1904, GR. Ruined harvests, relief grain, and live-stock diseases: Min. Government Entomologist to Director, Agriculture, 31 Jan. 1903, and Min. Mag. Mahlabathini, 11 Feb. 1903, Mahlabathini MinP/MR/GR; Rep. Mag. Umlalazi, C12, and Rep. Mag. Krantzkop, 34, BB Departmental Rep. 1903, GR; Rep. Secretary, Min-ister Agriculture, 9, and Rep. Mag. Eshowe, 92, BB Departmental Rep. 1904, GR. "Buy, beg, and . . . steal": Rep. Mag. Eshowe, 70, BB Departmental Rep. 1903, GR. Livestock traders imported East Coast fever, a tick-borne virulent disease, into southern Africa after the Anglo-Boer War.

43. Timber planting: Min. SNA, March 1904, 1/1/310 638/1904, SNA MinP/GR. White sugar planters: Min. Commissioner Native Affairs, Eshowe, to Mag. Eshowe, 20 Sept. 1905, 1266/1905, Eshowe MinP/MR/GR; Commissioner Native Affairs to Minister Native Affairs, 13 Oct. 1905, 1/1/329 285/05, SNA MinP/GR; Rep. Mag. Umlalazi, 95, BB Depart-mental Rep. 1905, GR. Zulu elders "objected to paying rentals": Testimony, Chief Mkungo (3 June 1907, 893), Chief Nkomo (3 June 1907, 888), Nhlekele (3 June 1907, 890) and Mphuhlana (3 June 1907, 893), *Evidence, Native Affairs Commission, 1906–7,* COM/GR. "Past dry and rainless years": Statement, "Chiefs, District Headmen, Official Witnesses, and Kraal-heads," 7 Oct. 1905, 1/1/328 2833/1905, SNA MinP/GR.

44. Elders' remarks: Statement, "Chiefs, District Headmen, Official Witnesses, and Kraal-heads," 7 Oct. 1905, 1/1/328 2833/1905, SNA MinP/GR.

45. "Ploughing up": Testimony, Chief Bagibele, 3 June 1907, *Evidence, Native Affairs Commission, 1906–7,* 890, COM/GR. "Give praise": Testimony, Ndukwana, 29 July 1902, Webb and Wright, *Stuart Archive,* 3:156. "Principles that guided": Stuart, "The Zulu Tribal System," c. 1900, file 26, notebooks, J. Stuart, Papers of Individuals/PT. See also Min. Mag. Lower Tugela, 11 Aug. 1893, 99/93, Lower Tugela MinP/MR/GR; Testimony, Mcotoyi, 15 April 1905, Webb and Wright, *Stuart Archive,* 3:59–61, 69; Min. Mag. Nkandla, 5 Dec. 1904, 1/1/315 2525/1904, SNA MinP/GR.

46. Beer drinking etiquette: Statement, Chief Mabonjana, 25 June 1903, Min. Mag. Lower Umzimkulu, 25 June 1903, 1/1/302 2158/1903, SNA MinP/GR; Testimony, Mxaba,

2 Jan. 1901, Webb and Wright, *Stuart Archive*, 1:252–53; Testimony, Bikwayo, 18 Oct. 1903, file 61, notebooks, J. Stuart, Papers of Individuals/PT.

47. "Prospects of losing . . . occupation of herding": Rep., Esidumbini and Noordsberg Mission Stations, June 1897–1898, Annual Rep., 1898–1903, American Board Mission (NAP)/PT. "Assemblies . . . the host responsible": Government Notice, Act 5, 1898, Principal Under Secretary to Colonial Secretary, 5 Jan. 1903, 1/1/296 2557/1902, SNA MinP/GR.

48. Beer parties that exposed male elders to fines: *Regina* v. *Mamfona and others,* 27 Oct. 1897, 1177/97, Stanger Court Depositions, Lower Tugela MR/GR; Acting Chief Magqunqu, Lower Tugela, 21 April 1900, 1/1/293 566/1900, SNA MinP/GR; Min. Mag. Weenen, 1 Sept. 1900, 890/1900, Weenen MinP/MR/GR. "Formerly, boys": Testimony, Nkantolo, 15 Feb. 1907, *Evidence, Native Affairs Commission, 1906–7,* 774, COM/GR. *Isishimeyana:* Testimony, Mbovu, 8 Feb. 1904, Webb and Wright, *Stuart Archive,* 3:28.

49. Young men in fighting bands; Papers, "Faction Fight," Jan. 1898, 312/98, Stanger Court Depositions, 1898–1900, Lower Tugela MR/GR; Conditions of Natives, 1898, Annual Rep. Mag. Kranskop, 3/1/2, Kranskop MinP/MR/GR; *Rex* v. *Mvinjwa and 17 others,* 15 July 1903, Min. Mag. New Hanover, 17 July 1903, 1/1/302 1752/1903; SNA MinP/GR; Min. Under-SNA, 5 Nov. 1900, 3/2/8 577/1900, Umvoti MinP/MR/GR; Statement, Mutiwentaba (Mapumulo, 18 May 1905, 1/1/321 1234/05) and Nyandeni Mvalese (Umsinga, 28 Nov. 1905, 1/1/330 3213/1905), SNA MinP/GR. Analysis of faction fighting: J. Clegg, "'*Ukubuyisa Isidumbu*—Bringing Back the Body': An Examination into the Ideology of Vengeance in the Msinga and Mpofana Rural Locations, 1882–1944," in *Working Papers in Southern African Studies*, vol. 2, ed. Bonner. For *ukuphindisela* describing a revenge attack, see interviews: Mchunu (Makhabeleni, 19 Nov. 1992, 4 April 1993), Nxumalo (Makhabeleni, 19 Nov. 1992), and Cube (Nkandla, 21 Nov. 1992). Faction fights ignited by struggles for scarce resources: Min. SNA to Mag. Krantzkop (29 Jan. 1902), Statement, Zikizwayo, Umvoti (24 July 1902, 1/1/295 299/1902), Min. Mag. Umsinga to SNA (7 Feb. 1902, 1/1/295 R193/02), Min., Meetings between SNA and Krantzkop Chief Bambatha et al. (25 Aug. 1902, 1/1/296 2278/1902), and Rep. Mag. Krantzkop to SNA (16 July 1904, 1/1/305 3077/1903), SNA MinP/GR.

50. "Somewhat severe sentences" and soaring number of faction fights: Rep. Mag. Mapumulo, 33, BB Departmental Rep. 1897, GR. Harsh punishment of young men: Rep. Mag. Mapumulo, B33, BB Departmental Rep. 1899, GR. "Boys behaving": Testimony, Majumba, 14 Feb. 1907, *Evidence, Native Affairs Commission, 1906–7,* 773, COM/GR. "Headringed man was shown respect": Testimony, Ndukwana, 1 May 1903, Webb and Wright, *Stuart Archive,* 4:367. Young men raising their fists against elders: Min. Mag. Estcourt to SNA (28 Jan. 1902, 1/1/295 45/1902), Min. Mag. Umsinga (31 July 1902, 1/1/297 2567/1902), Statement, Chief Tulwana, Umsinga (16 Nov. 1903, 1/1/306 3601/03), SNA MinP/GR.

51. Statistics on faction fighting: Return, "Native Assault and Faction Fighting Cases," 31 March 1905, 1793, CSO/GR. Faction fighting by district: Rep. Mag. Eshowe, Rep. Mag. Mapumulo, and Rep. Mag. Krantzkop, BB Departmental Rep. 1904, GR; Rep. Mag. Krantzkop, BB Departmental Rep. 1905, GR.

52. "Contemptuous . . . until I die": Court testimony, 10 June 1905, SNA MinP/GR; Native High Court Civil Appeals in *Ugudhla* v. *Matshana*, Min. Mag. Nkandla, 26 June 1905, 1/1/323 1741/1905, SNA MinP/GR. "Child of a man": Testimony, Mtshapi, 6 April 1918, 73–74, and 9 May 1918, 89, Webb and Wright, *Stuart Archive*, 4.

53. Quotations from Gudhla and Matshana: 1/1/323 1741/1905, SNA MinP/GR.

54. "Common purse" and young men's privileges: Rep. SNA, Aug. 1900, 23, 1/1/290 1430/1900, SNA MinP/GR; Rep. Mag. Krantzkop 1901, B34, BB Departmental Rep. 1899–1901, GR; Testimony, Chief Mqolobeni (14 Feb. 1907, 767) and Tshwetshwe (13 April 1907, 855), *Evidence, Native Affairs Commission, 1906–7*. "Ease with which a refractory son": Testimony, Mag. Weenen, 4 Feb. 1907, 316, ibid., COM/GR.

55. Testimony, Mbovu, 8 Feb. 1904, Webb and Wright, *Stuart Archive*, 3:29.

56. "Our fathers . . . need help": Testimony, Ndhlovu, 2 Jan. 1903, Webb and Wright, *Stuart Archive*, 4:212. "In-between": Testimony, Mbovu, 16 Sept. 1904, file 41, notebooks, J. Stuart, Papers of Individuals/PT.

57. "Unable to maintain . . . be of gold": Testimony, Mbovu, 16 Sept. 1904, file 41, notebooks, James Stuart/PT. "Obliged to pick": Mbovu, 7 Feb. 1904, Webb and Wright, *Stuart Archive*, 3:28. "Younger generation say": Mbovu, 16 Sept. 1904, file 41, notebooks, J. Stuart, Papers of Individuals/PT.

3. Disobedient Daughters and Discontented Wives

1. Samuelson, "The Rock of Two-holes," c. 1900, 131, Faye, Papers of Individuals (NAP)/PT.

2. "A wife does not bear": Testimony, Ndukwana, 15 July 1900, Webb and Wright, *Stuart Archive*, 4:268. Social standing of mothers: Testimony, Chief Silwane and Joko, 1 Feb. 1882, *Evidence, Natal Native Commission, 1881(–2)*, 354 COM/GR; Njengabantu's and Pikana's Families, Min. Mag. Umvoti to Under-SNA, 29 June 1904, 1/1/312 1341/04, SNA MinP/GR; Testimony, Mbovu, 24 Sept. 1904, Webb and Wright, *Stuart Archive*, 3:40; Ngubane, *Body and Mind in Zulu Medicine*, 159; Vilakazi, *Zulu Transformations*, 21–23.

3. "Mother will give praises": Testimony, Msthapi, 9 May 1918, Webb and Wright, *Stuart Archive*, 4:89. Some magistrates saw their role as protecting women from unwilling sexual or marital unions and allowed widows to reject *ukungena* advances: Civil Record Book, Native Cases, 1892–95, Eshowe MR/GR. Other *ukungena* practices: Testimony, Induna Class, 30 Jan. 1882, *Evidence, Natal Native Commission, 1881(–2)*, 334, COM/GR; Min. Assistant Mag., Umvoti, 9 April 1892, 3/2/5 616/1892, Umvoti MinP/MR/GR; Statement, Headman Fokoti, 9 Nov. 1893, R2641/93, Correspondence, "Divorce and Lobola, 1890–96," Commissioner/GR; Ukungena Register 1894–97, Mapumulo MR/GR.

4. Women's work and rights to labor: Testimony, Mqayikana (12 Nov. 1897, 34) and Ndukwana (5, 18 April 1903, 363–64), Webb and Wright, *Stuart Archive*, 3; Mkotana, 1 June 1905, ibid., 2:228; Testimony, Ndukwana, 11 Sept. 1903, file 61, notebooks, J. Stuart, Papers of Individuals (KCL)/PT; Testimony, Sibisi, 13 March 1979, tape 207, OHP,

Tape Transcripts/PT. In the 1890s Sibisi spent her childhood in Mapumulo, observing how older girls "looked after the young girls." African women selling crops: Lambert, *Betrayed Trust*, 46.

5. Khumalo emphasized the discretion of fathers yet kept silent on young women rejecting arranged marriages. To "get [his] children": Testimony, Khumalo, 16 Dec. 1900, Webb and Wright, *Stuart Archive*, 1:237. Similar evidence from other African patriarchs: Testimony, Induna Class (30 Jan. 1882, 333) and Umnini (15 Feb. 1882, 193), *Evidence, Natal Native Commission 1881(–2)*, COM/GR; Testimony, Mbovu, 7 Feb. 1904, Webb and Wright, *Stuart Archive*, 4:267–68.

6. Woman would "instantly cover herself": Testimony, Ndukwana, 18 April 1903, Webb and Wright, *Stuart Archive*, 4:365. "Father of So-and-So": Testimony, Ndukwana, 18 April 1903, ibid., 375–76; Testimony, Mkando, 23 July 1902, ibid., 3:154. Rituals heralding a woman's change in social position: Testimony, Mkando, 20 Aug. 1902, ibid., 3:184–85. Early anthropological analyses of these rituals: Krige, *Social System of the Zulus*, 103. *Ukuhlonipha* is still practiced in Thukela basin homesteads: Cube (Makhabeleni, 31 July 1991), Sibisi (Mtunzini, 19, 20 Sept. 1992), and Mchunu (Makhabeleni, 19 Nov. 1992) Interviews. "Unmarried girls who have arrived": Testimony, Ndukwana, 1 May 1903, 3 Sept. 1903, Webb and Wright, *Stuart Archive*, 4:366, 376.

7. Mtini "found one of his wives": Testimony, Ndukwana, 29 Sept. 1900, Webb and Wright, *Stuart Archive*, 4:294. Examples of women being put to death for adultery: Rep. Mag. Nkandla, "Native Divorce and Lobola," 1893, R2641/93, Correspondence, "Divorce & Lobola, 1890–96," Commissioner/GR; Case 26, Adultery, *Hashi* v. *Similele (wife)*, 28 March 1904, Civil Record Book 1903–13, Eshowe/ MR/GR. "The people at the kraal": Testimony, Chief Mahlube, 11 April 1907, *Evidence, Natal Native Commission, 1906–7*, 848, COM/GR.

8. Comments on *ukuhlobonga:* Testimony, Ndukwana, 6 July 1902, 19 Oct. 1900, Webb and Wright, *Stuart Archive*, 4:353, 311. Colonial alarm over *ukuhlobonga:* SNA Rep. Confidential Circular 52 1894, 1/1/270 2951/97, SNA MinP/GR.

9. Parents keeping children close at hand: Testimony, Ndukwana, 7 Oct. 1902, Webb and Wright, *Stuart Archive*, 3:147. "Lover was allowed": Dhlozi, 6 July 1902, ibid., 4:353. "Knew she would of course lose value": Testimony, Mkando, 10 July 1902, ibid., 3:147. "Bona fide accident": Khumalo, J. Africa, and Ndukwana, 8 Dec. 1900, ibid., 1:225. "Been mekezisa'd" and "soundly beaten": Testimony, Ndukwana, 6 July, 1902, 21 Sept. 1900, ibid., 4:353–54, 287. Boyfriends paying fines: SNA Rep. Confidential Circular 52, 1894, 18 Sept. 1894, 1/1/270 2951/97, SNA MinP/GR. "Beast of reparation": Testimony, Ndukwana, 15 Oct. 1900, Webb and Wright, *Stuart Archive*, 4:300. Pregnancy hastening marriage: Testimony, Chief Nyoniyezwe (13 April 1907, 854) and Nkantolo (15 Feb. 1907, 774–75), *Evidence, Native Affairs Commission, 1906–7*, COM/GR. Unmarried couples eloping: Case 30, Nov. 1892, Melmoth Criminal Record Book, Native Law, 1887–97, Entonjaneni/MR/GR. See also Letter Books, Eshowe/MR/GR. *Isibongo* and a child's "legitimacy": Testimony, Ndukwana, 14 Oct. 1900, 13 Feb. 1903, Webb and Wright, *Stuart Archive*, 1:297, 177–78. Wrath of *amadlozi* and sexuality: Ndukwana, 18 Oct. 1900, ibid., 4:310.

10. "When a husband desires": Testimony, Ndukwana, 15 Oct. 1900, Webb and Wright, *Stuart Archive*, 4:299. Healthy baby and rich harvest: Testimony, Mpatshana, 31 May 1912, ibid., 3:324.

11. Girls choosing the refuge of mission stations: Minute Book 1893, 421, American Board Mission Minutes (NAP)/PT. Breaking *ukungena* practice: Clark, missionary, Natal, to Williams, American Board, Boston, 10 Sept. 1903. "Marriage market": Bunker, Amanzimtoti, to American Board, Boston, March 1900, Southern African Women's Board, American Board Mission (Yale Divinity)/PT. "Heathen girls coming": Statement, Fidelia Phelps, 1904, *South African Deputation Papers*, 50, American Board Mission (Yale Divinity)/PT. "Much grumbling . . . in consequence": Rep. Mag. Nkandla, BB Departmental Rep. 1900, B114, GR.

12. Unmarried sons entering field stations and "parents who . . . the dark": Testimony, Ndhlovu, 10 Nov. 1902, Webb and Wright, *Stuart Archive*, 4:210.

13. "Trying to serve . . . but to warn you": Annual Rep. of the Ireland Home, 1899–1900. "Two determined": L. Smith, Natal, to Dr. Smith, Boston, 17 Oct. 1904, Southern African Women's Board, American Board Mission (Yale Divinity)/PT.

14. "Cases where children [fled]": Min. Mag. Mapumulo to Under-SNA, 10 June 1903, 1/1/301 1679/1903, SNA MinP/GR. "A Christian man": Annual Letter, Inanda Mission Station, 1904–05, Phelps, to American Board, Boston, 1905. Section 289 of the Code of Native Law: Frost, Umzumbe Mission, to American Board, Boston, 9 Nov. 1903, Southern African Women's Board of Missions, American Board Mission (Yale Divinity)/PT. Colonial correspondence on invoking the Code of Native Law: Min. Under-SNA to Mag. Mapumulo, 23 May 1903, 1/1/301 1679/1903, SNA MinP/GR. See also, *South African Deputation Papers*, 36, American Board Mission (Yale Divinity)/PT.

15. "Bible culture": Smith, Umzumbe, to American Board, Boston, 20 June 1905. "In rapid succession": Annual Letter, 1907–8, Phelps, to American Board, Boston, Southern African Women's Board, American Board Mission (Yale Divinity)/PT.

16. "Foundation": Annual Letter, Inanda Mission, 1901–1902. "Nakedness of heathenism" and "If you were to spend": Bunker, Amanzimtoti, to American Board, Boston, March 1900, Southern African Women's Board, American Board Mission (Yale Divinity)/PT. Missionary challenge to African perceptions of time: Statement, Rev. Kilbon, 16–17, and Mellon, 58, *South African Deputation Papers*, American Board Mission (Yale Divinity)/PT. Placement agencies: Taylor, *American Board Mission*, 59; *Ilanga Lase Natal*, 11 Nov. 1904, 1/1/314 2426/1904, SNA MinP/GR. Natal colonial challenges to African perceptions of time and work obligations: Keletso Atkins, *The Moon Is Dead!*

17. Testimony, Madama, 21 Feb. 1882, *Evidence, Natal Native Commission, 1881(–2)*, 249, COM/GR.

18. Homestead wives who "claim a divorce": Cases 22, 23 Feb. 1894, *Sivivi* v. *Nyalela*, Cases Adjudicated, Native Civil Record Book, Nquthu MR/GR. Homestead women's increasing legal actions: Testimony, Induna Class (30 Jan. 1882, 333) and Chief Domba (31 Jan. 1882, 335), *Evidence, Natal Native Commission 1881(–2)*, COM/GR; Min. Resident Commissioner, Eshowe, 9 Nov. 1893, 15, Correspondence, "Divorce & Lobola,

1890–96," Commissioner/GR. "Impotence": Min. Mag. Entonjaneni, 5 Oct. 1903, 3/2/10 PB906/1903, Entonjaneni MinP/MR/GR. Failed marriages creating homestead tensions: Min. Mag. Krantzkop, 29 Dec. 1895, 3/1/1 KK/603/1895, Kranskop MinP/MR/GR.

19. "Fornicating": Testimony, *Sobha Duma* v. *Nomafa*, 24 Sept. 1894, SNA MinP/GR; Min. Mag. Umsinga, 24 Sept. 1894, 1/1/193 R403/94, SNA MinP/GR. Divorce law stipulations, *ukulobola* return, and greater numbers seeking divorce: Case 30 (18 March 1896), Case 1 (16 Jan. 1899), and Case 14 (10 March 1899), Civil Record Book, 1894–1900, Nkandla/MR/GR. See also Register of Divorce Law 1/1869, Lower Tugela/MR/GR; Native Civil Record Book, 1899–1904, Mapumulo MR/GR; Matrimonial Matters, Register of Divorces, Mapumulo MR/GR; Native Civil Record Book, 1902–13, Kranskop/MR/GR.

20. "If an altercation": Testimony, Chief Sibindi, 11 April 1907, *Evidence, Native Affairs Commission, 1906–7*, 845, COM/GR. "If a man . . . actually be granted": Chief Mahlube, 11 April 1907, ibid., 848, COM/GR. Women "on the slightest pretext": Headman Xegwana, 11 April 1907, ibid., 847, COM/GR. "Government": Chief Sibindi, 11 April 1907, ibid., 845. COM/GR.

21. "We object": Testimony, Joko, 1 Feb. 1882, *Evidence, Native Affairs Commission, 1881(–2)*, 354–55, COM/GR. "As fathers": Chief Domba, 31 Jan. 1882, ibid., 355–56, COM/GR.

22. "Return to the old": SNA to Attorney General (16 Oct. 1897) and Min. SNA (2 Sept. 1897), 1/1/254 1830/97, SNA MinP/GR. Decline in the practice of polygyny: Rep. Mag. Umsinga, BB Supp. Departmental Rep., 1888, B33, GR.

23. "Disharmony": Testimony, Mabaso, 16 Dec. 1900, Webb and Wright, *Stuart Archive*, 1:237. "Girl defied": Testimony, Chief Mkentengu, 14 Feb. 1907, *Evidence, Native Affairs Commission, 1906–7*, 769, COM/GR. See also Chief Msiyana (3 June 1907, 890) and Chief Mkonto (3 June 1907, 891), ibid., COM/GR. "Parents formerly": Chief Mqolombeni, 14 Feb. 1907, ibid., 768, COM/GR. "Man's child": Chief Nkomo, 3 June 1907, ibid., 888, COM/GR.

24. "The olden days": Testimony, Chief Mkentengu, 14 Feb. 1907, *Evidence, Native Affairs Commission, 1906–7*, 769, COM/GR. See also Chief Msiyana (3 June 1907, 890) and Chief Mkonto (3 June 1907, 891), COM/GR. "The loose morality": Testimony, J. Africa, 16 Dec. 1900, Webb and Wright, *Stuart Archive*, 1:236.

25. "Mischievous rep.": Min. Mag. Weenen, to Under-SNA, 8 Nov. 1900, 3/2/4 117/1900, Weenen MinP/MR/GR. Kranskop magistrate on the "silly rumour": Rep. Mag. Kranskop, 23 Jan. 1902, BB Departmental Rep. Natal, 1899–1901, 33–34, GR.

26. Testimony, Majumba, 14 Feb. 1907, *Evidence, Native Affairs Commission, 1906–7*, 773, COM/GR.

27. "An apparent . . . disinclination": Testimony, Khumalo, 9 Dec. 1900, Webb and Wright, *Stuart Archive*, 1:230. "In these days": Testimony, Mabaso, 16 Dec. 1900, ibid., 237.

28. "Uncontrollable caprice": Testimony, Mabaso and Khumalo, 16 Dec. 1900, Webb and Wright, *Stuart Archive*, 1:237. Elders altering customs to hold onto power: Min. Mag. Weenen to Under-SNA, 4 Oct. 1897, 1/1/257 2159/97, SNA MinP/GR. Min. Mag. Umvoti to SNA, 27 Oct. 1897, 1/1/263 2424/97, SNA MinP/GR. Elders scrutinizing wealth and

suitability of suitors: Testimony, Under-SNA (18 Oct. 1906, 7), Chief Sibindi (11 April 1907, 844), and Chief Zimema (3 June 1907, 892), *Evidence, Native Affairs Commission, 1906–7,* COM/GR. *Ukulobola* modifications: Rep. Mag. Kranskop, BB Departmental Rep., 1899–1901, B33, GR; Rep. Mag. Mapumulo, 18 Feb. 1904; 1/1/308 249/1904, SNA MinP/GR. "Young man who had fallen in love": Testimony, Majumba, 14 Feb. 1907, *Evidence, Native Affairs Commission, 1906–7,* 773, COM/GR.

29. "The present time": Testimony, Dhlozi, 19 Dec. 1906, *Evidence, Native Affairs Commission, 1906–7,* 709, COM/GR; for similar accounts, see Chief Sibindi (11 April 1907, 846), Chief Zimema (3 June 1907, 892), Nkantolo (15 Feb. 1907, 774–75), Chief Swayimana (15 April 1907, 857), and Mnyango (10 Jan. 1907, 713–14), *Evidence, Native Affairs Commission, 1906–7,* COM/GR.

30. Statement, Ziboni, 25 Oct. 1905, 5, 1/1/328 985/1905, SNA MinP/GR.

31. Return of migrants, idleness, and sexual adventuring: Rep. SNA, Aug. 1900, 22, 1/1/290 1430/1900, SNA MinP/GR; Min. Mag. Weenen to Under-SNA, 5 Sept. 1900, 3/2/3 890/1900, Weenen MinP/MR/GR. "Young men coming": Testimony, Mabaso, 15 Dec. 1900, Webb and Wright, *Stuart Archive,* 1:232.

32. "Wandering away" and punishing young women: Case 95, 4 Aug. 1899, and others in Criminal Cases Adjudicated, 1899–1904, Nkandla MR/GR; Case 25, March 1901, and others in Melmoth Criminal Record Book, Native Law, 1901–06, Entonjaneni MR/GR; Case 22, 15 March 1904, and others in Records of Native Proceedings, 1903–31, Eshowe MR/GR; Native Civil Record Book, Kranskop MR/GR. "Parents have practically": Testimony, Khumalo, 8 Dec. 1900, Webb and Wright, *Stuart Archive,* 1:225. "The cause of boys": Ndukwana, 10 Dec. 1900, ibid., 1:231. Increasing numbers of young men prosecuted: Criminal Cases Adjudicated, 1899–1902, Nkandla MR/GR; Criminal Record Book, 1900–02, 1/2/2/1, Kranskop MR/GR; Rep. Mag. Lower Tugela, 2 Jan. 1902, 4/1/7 LTD 453/1902, Lower Tugela MinP/MR/GR.

33. He "found [y]oung wives": Testimony, Nkantolo, 15 Feb. 1907, *Evidence, Native Affairs Commission, 1906–7,* 774, COM/GR. "A very strong law": Testimony, Chief Majozi, 14 Feb. 1907, ibid., 766, COM/GR. "Agreed [about] bringing": Testimony, Chief Mafahleni, 14 Feb. 1907, ibid., 767, COM/GR. "The amount of seduction": Testimony, Khumalo, J. Africa, and Ndukwana, 8 Dec. 1900, Webb and Wright, *Stuart Archive,* 1:225. Stories about Cetshwayo's *iNgcugce* female regiment not in text: Mtshayankomo, 20 Jan. 1922, ibid., 4:132–35.

34. "The girl and the young man": Testimony, Chief Swayimana, 15 April 1907, *Evidence, Native Affairs Commission, 1906–7,* 859, COM/GR. "Man in great distress": Testimony, Khumalo, 9 Dec. 1900, Webb and Wright, *Stuart Archive,* 1:227.

35. "Indecent assault": Min. Acting Mag. Lower Tugela 1896, *Regina* v. *Uzwelinjani,* Stanger Court Depositions, 1893–1896, Lower Tugela MR/GR. "Immorality": Rep. Mag. Mapumulo, 4 Jan. 1904, 1/1/308 249/1904, SNA MinP/GR. "Seduction," "abduction," and "flogging": Rep. Mag. Krantzkop 1901, BB Departmental Rep. 1899–1901, B33, GR; Criminal Cases Adjudicated, 1899–1904, Nkandla MR/GR; Administrator of Native Law Criminal Record Book, 1898–1903, Mahlabathini MR/GR; Rep. Mag. Mapumulo, BB

Departmental Rep. 1904, 9, GR. "Under the British": Testimony, Khumalo, J. Africa, and Ndukwana, 9 Dec. 1900, Webb and Wright, *Stuart Archive*, 1:227. Mkentengu begging "the Government": Testimony, Chief Mkentengu, 14 Feb. 1907, *Evidence, Native Affairs Commission, 1906–7*, 769, COM/GR.

36. "Before . . . getting": Testimony, Nkantolo, 15 Feb. 1907, *Evidence, Native Affairs Commission, 1906–7*, 774–75, COM/GR. See also Chief Nyoniyezwe, 13 April 1907, ibid., 854, COM/GR. Grave consequences for premarital sex: Testimony, Mkando, 10 July 1902, Webb and Wright, *Stuart Archive*, 3:147; Stuart, "Notes on the History of Zululand," Dec. 1901, file 70, notebooks, J. Stuart, Papers of Individuals (KCL)/PT. "Great contempt," *isirobo*, and "people spat": Testimony, Mkando, 10 July 1902, Webb and Wright, *Stuart Archive*, 3:147. "Such a girl": Ndukwana, 6 July 1902, ibid., 4:354.

37. "Weary of waiting": Annual Rep. Mag. Krantzkop, BB Departmental Rep. 1905, 35, GR. Fines in "seduction" cases: Rep. SNA Circular 52, 1894, 18 Sept. 1894, 1/1/270 2951/97, SNA MinP/GR; Statement, Deputation of Chiefs, Headmen, and Homestead Heads, Umlazi, 26 Oct. 1905, 1/SNA 1/1/328, SNA MinP/GR; Administrator of Native Law, Criminal Record Book, 1898–1903, Mahlabathini MR/GR; Criminal Cases Adjudicated, 1892–1895, Nkandla MR/GR. "Are our girls not punished": Statement, Mabele, 25 Oct. 1905, Min. Mag. Pinetown to Under-SNA, 25 Oct. 1905, 1/1/328, SNA MinP/GR.

38. "Infractions" and colonial officials seeking to hear the opinions: Rep. Mag. Umsinga to Under-SNA, 26 Nov. 1902, 1/1/298 3531/1902, SNA MinP/GR; Min. Mag. Umsinga, 1 May 1903, 1/1/301 1442/1903, SNA MinP/GR; Min. Mag. Mahlabathini (27 Oct. 1903) and Mag. Mahlabathini to Civil Commissioner, Eshowe (29 Oct. 1903), 3/2/2 M690/1903, Mahlabathini MR/GR. "Disloyal" action: Rep. Commissioner Native Affairs, Eshowe, BB Departmental Rep. 1905, 90, GR; *Times of Natal*, 2 June 1904, Newspapers.

39. "Boded them ill" and youth suspicion of census: Rep. Mag. Mapumulo, BB Departmental Rep. 1905, 9, GR. "Rumors of Native unrest": Rep. Commissioner Native Affairs, Eshowe, BB Departmental Rep. 1905, 90, GR. Protests of Bhambatha and Njengabantu: Petition of Njengabantu, 3 June 1904, Min. SNA, 6 June 1904, 1/1/311 1149/04, SNA MinP/GR; *Times of Natal*, 20 May 1904, Newspapers. White settlers' fears of African resistance: Min. SNA to Governor, 6 June 1904, 1/1/311 1156/04, SNA MinP/GR.

40. Colonial government as "father": Testimony, Chief Msiyana, 3 June 1907, *Evidence, Native Affairs Commission, 1906–7*, 890, COM/GR.

4. *"Taxing Our Young Men . . . Separating Us from Our Sons"*

1. Legislative history of the poll tax: Stuart, *History of the Zulu Rebellion*, 98–99. See also Poll Tax Act 1905, 1/1/327 2536/1905, SNA MinP/GR.

2. Poll tax receipts for young men: *Rep., Native Affairs Commission 1906–07*, 43, Rep./GR; Min. Under-SNA, 19 Aug. 1905, 1/1/324 2114/05, SNA MinP/GR.

3. "Instead of helping . . . to defy us": Statement, Chief Mafingo, 26 Oct. 1905, 1/1/328 5/1905, SNA MinP/GR. "Headmen are unanimous": Min. Mag. Umvoti to Under-SNA, 23 Sept. 1905, SNA MinP/GR. "The Poll tax will . . . remov[e]": Mag. Eshowe to Commissioner Native Affairs, Eshowe, 5 Oct. 1905; 1/1/327 2612/1905, SNA MinP/GR. "Impos-

ing": Min. Mag. Mahlabathini, 3 Nov. 1905, 1/1/329 2960/05, SNA MinP/GR. Chiefs in Entonjaneni: Rep. Mag. Entonjaneni, 6 Oct. 1905, SNA MinP/GR. "Taxing our young men": Statement, Chief Tulwana, Nkandla, 10 Oct. 1905, 1/1/328 2675/05, SNA MinP/GR.

4. In "kraal-life . . . of assistance": *Rep., Native Affairs Commission, 1906–07,* 43, Rep./GR. "Fresh tax . . . [their] back": Meeting, Chief Ndunge et al., Min. Mag. Umlazi to Under-SNA, 25 Oct. 1905, 1/1/328 2675/05, SNA MinP/GR. "Contemplated a deal": Min. Mag. Umvoti to Under-SNA, 23 Sept. 1905, 1/1/327 2492/1905, SNA MinP/GR. "The imposition": Meeting, Chief Ndunge et al., SNA MinP/GR. "Bad sons": Statement, Chief Faku; Min, 25 Sept. 1905, 1/1/327 2576/05, SNA MinP/GR. "The disappearance": Min. Mag. Umlalazi, 24 Oct. 1905, 1/1/329 2840/05, SNA MinP/GR.

5. "Hot-headed": Min. Mag. Lower Umfolozi to Under-SNA, 26 Sept. 1905, 1/1/327 2826/1905, SNA MinP/GR.

6. "Anything but . . . levelled at [chiefs]": Colenbrander, Bambata Rebellion, Papers of Individuals (KCL)/PT. See also patriarchs' testimony: Rep. Mag. Nkandla, 1908, 1/1/414 3258/08, SNA MinP/GR; Testimony, Socwatsha (Nkandla, 19 Dec. 1906, 709) and Chief Sibindi (Mapumulo, 11 April 1907, 844–45), *Evidence, Native Affairs Commission, 1906–7,* COM/GR. "Returning from Durban": Testimony, Chief Swayimana, 15 April 1907, ibid., 859, COM/GR.

7. Demonstrations and resentment: Testimony, Msime, 26 Dec. 1906, Webb and Wright, *Stuart Archive,* 4:53. "Quiet" and "loyal" responses: Rep. Mag. Ubombo (1905, 105) and Rep. Sub-Inspector Natal Police (Ingwavuma, 1905, 74), BB Departmental Rep. 1905, GR.

8. Xhosa cattle killing: Peires, "'Soft' Believers and 'Hard' Unbelievers."

9. *Umhlola,* "burning" sky, and "loyalists": Testimony, Chief Mpumela, 3 Nov. 1908, *Stuart Archive,* 3:235; Statement, Constable Mayinga, Umvoti, 30 Nov. 1905, 1/1/330 3198/05, SNA MinP/GR; Rep. Mag. Weenen, 16 Dec. 1905, 86/05, SNA Confidential Papers/GR; Deposition, Gwamanda, 18 Dec. 1905, 1/4/14 87/05, SNA Confidential Papers/GR. "People abandon their homes": Testimony, (Nkandla) Chief Mpumela, 3 Nov. 1908, Webb and Wright, *Stuart Archive,* 2:235.

10. Government officials suspecting Dinuzulu: Stuart, *History of the Zulu Rebellion,* 103–7; Statement, Umandhla (30 Nov. 1905), *Rex* v. *Unjana and Ungedhlana,* 1/1/330 3198/05, SNA MinP/GR. Rumor in colonial Africa: Luise White, "Between Gluckman and Foucault." Pig killing in Umlazi, Weenen, and Umvoti: Rep. Mag. Pinetown (10 Dec. 1905, 65/1905), Statement, Ncinyoni kaNvunyela (Weenen, Dec. 1905, 87/1905), and Van Rooyen (Umvoti, 20 Dec. 1905, 78/1905), 1/4/14, SNA Confidential Papers/GR. Lightning hitting Chief Silwane's homestead: Meeting, Minister Native Affairs, Under-SNA, Weenen Mag., and Weenen Chiefs, Min. 9 Jan. 1906, 1/4/14 78/1905, SNA Confidential Papers/GR. December animal slaying and hidden taboo articles: Rep. Mag. Estcourt (20 Dec. 1905, 91/1905), Rep. Mag. Alexandra (27 Dec. 1905, 95/1905, 1/4/14), Rep. Mag. Lower Umzimkhulu (31 Dec. 1905, 1/4/15 5/1906), SNA Confidential Papers/GR. Rep. Mag. Lower Tugela, 3 Feb. 1906, 1/1/335 372/1906, SNA MinP/GR. Rep. Mag. Umlalazi, 11 Jan. 1906, 3/1906, 34, Confidential Correspondence, Commissioner/GR.

11. "Unrest [among] young men": Min. Governor, Pietermaritzburg, to Sec. State,

London, 27 Jan. 1906, 93, BPP/GR. Chiefs north of Thukela River: Stuart, *History of the Zulu Rebellion*, 122. "Poll tax [was] . . . fomenting mischief": *Greytown Gazette*, 17 Feb. 1906, Newspapers. "Hands and the eyes . . . [before] a Magistrate": Min. Meeting, Minister Native Affairs, Under-SNA, Mag. Weenen, and Weenen Chiefs, Min. 9 Jan. 1906, 1/1/333 1241/1906, SNA MinP/GR.

12. "Veiled threats": Colenbrander, Bambata Rebellion, Papers of Individuals (KCL)/PT; List A, "Brief Summary Rebel Prisoners in the Rebellion, 1906, Not Recommended for Release," 1 Nov. 1907, Memoranda, Natal Natives, 1550, GH/GR. "Exceedingly insolent": Sgt. Matthews, Natal Police, to Inspector George, Natal Police, Empangeni (25 Jan. 1906), and Commissioner Native Affairs, Eshowe, to Minister Native Affairs, Pietermaritzburg (15 Feb. 1906), 1/1/335 459/06, SNA MinP/GR. "Over three hundred . . . listen to him": Mag. Umlalazi to Resident Commissioner Eshowe, 24 Jan. 1906, 34, Confidential Correspondence, Commissioner/GR.

13. "The chief got up . . . haven't the money": Statement, Nkomonopondo, Mapumulo, 5 March 1906, Martial Law, Miscellaneous Rep., Mapumulo MR/GR. The statement was given more than a month after Magistrate Dunn's attempt to collect the poll tax. Stuart said 22 January was the date of Dunn's encounter with Gobizembe's men: *History of the Zulu Rebellion*, 121. "300 men . . . had no money": Min. Mag. Mapumulo, 5 Feb. 1906, 1/1/335 400/06, SNA MinP/GR. Swayimana's men "saluted": Statement, Swayimana, *Rex* v. *Umgodi et al.*, 19 March 1906, 1/1/341 1426/1906, SNA MinP/GR. "Put down their sticks": Statement, Swayimana, 8 March 1906, Martial Law Miscellaneous Rep., Mapumulo MR/GR. "Appeared anxious . . . or their Chief:" Min. Mag. Mapumulo, 5 Feb. 1906, 1/1/335 400/06, SNA MinP/GR. Corroborating reports: Statement, Mhlakazana, Police Sgt. 19 March 1906, *Rex* v. *Umgodi et al.*, 1/1/341 1426/1906, SNA MinP/GR.

14. "Not pay this tax . . . had to go": Min. Mag. Mapumulo, 5 Feb. 1906, 1/1/335 400/06, SNA MinP/GR. "Young men of three Chiefs": *Ilanga Lase Natal*, 12 Feb. 1906, in 1/1/335 445/1906, SNA MinP/GR. "For the sake . . . open defiance": Mag. Mapumulo to Under-SNA, 2 Feb. 1906, 1/1/335 400/06, SNA MinP/GR.

15. "Hob-nobbed": Testimony, Makathini, 24 Oct. 1981, tape 444, OHP, Tape Transcripts/PT. See also Colenbrander, Bambata Rebellion, Papers of Individuals (KCL)/PT; Vilakazi, *Zulu Transformations*, 143.

16. "Trouble . . . fierce": Stuart, *History of the Zulu Rebellion*, 123–26, 136–39.

17. "Succeeded . . . turn out": Governor, Pietermaritzburg, to Sec. State, London, 10 March 1906, 93, BPP/GR. "I do not think . . . favours to come": Testimony, Cooper, 27 June 1907, Webb and Wright, *Stuart Archive*, 1:84–85.

18. "There has been no attack": *Natal Mercury*, 19 Feb. 1906. New anti–poll tax protests: Rep. Mag. Alexandra, 20 Feb. 1906, 1/4/16 103/1906, SNA Confidential Papers/GR; Mag. Ixopo to Commandant Militia (Pietermaritzburg, 19 Feb. 1906, 645/1906), Min. Mag. Port Shepstone (24 Feb. 1906, 647/1906), and Rep. Mag. Lower Umzimkulu (24 Feb. 1906, 654/1906), 1/1/337, SNA MinP/GR. McKenzie "cowing": Rep. Mag. Lower Umzimkulu, 24 Feb. 1906, 654/1906, 1/1/337, SNA MinP/GR. "Young men of the tribes": Governor to Secretary of State, 27 Jan. 1906, 93, BPP/GR. "They are now

imprisoning": *Ilanga Lase Natal,* Feb. 1906, 804/1906, 1/1/337, SNA MinP/GR. "Many reports": District Controller, Johannesburg, to Natal Pass Commissioner, 16 Feb. 1906, 611/1906, 1/1/337, SNA MinP/GR.

19. Independent African Christian preachers and "Ethiopian" ideology: Commissioner Native Affairs Circular to Zululand Magistrates, 8 April 1904, 34, Confidential Correspondence, Commissioner/GR; Statement, S. Mnyeza, *Rex* v. *A. Kumalo,* 16 July 1904, 1/4/13 52/1904, SNA Confidential Papers/GR. "Reason to believe . . . native disturbances": Letter, Secretary of State, London, to Natal Governor, Pietermaritzburg, 14 Feb. 1906, 93, BPP/GR; Rep. Minister Native Affairs, 23 Feb. 1906, 1/1/336 568/1906, SNA MinP/GR. "Propagandists": Rep. Inspector Phillips, Dumisa, 22 April 1906, 1/1/339 1051/1906, SNA MinP/GR. "Exponents advocate": *Ilanga Lase Natal,* 2 March 1906, 1/1/337 498/1906, SNA MinP/GR.

20. "The sons . . . no money": Mag. Kranskop to SNA, 12 Feb. 1906, KK56/06, Kranskop MinP/MR/GR. "The young men . . . nonsense": Min. Mag. Umsinga, 12 Feb. 1906, 506/1906, 1/1/336, SNA MinP/GR. "Named Jingi": Min. Mag. Umsinga to Under-SNA, 16 Feb. 1906, 552/06, 1/1/336, SNA MinP/GR. "Malcontents": Memorandum, 4 May 1907, 2, 1041, MinP, GH/GR. Fines levied on three chiefs: Min. Minister Native Affairs, 20 Nov. 1906, 1/1/355 3785/06, SNA MinP/GR. "The Govr. have saved . . . all the tribes": Statement, Chief Swayimana, 9 March 1906, Martial Law Miscellaneous Rep., Mapumulo MR/GR.

21. Artillery storm and subsequent trial: Stuart, *History of the Zulu Rebellion,* 149–50. See also Interview, Colonel Leuchars and Chief Swayimana, 11 March 1906, Martial Law, Miscellaneous Rep., Mapumulo MR/GR. "If the blame . . . their sons": *Ilanga Lase Natal,* 16 March 1906, Newspapers.

22. Chief Mancinza's legacy: Testimony, Mqaikana, 9 May 1916, Webb and Wright, *Stuart Archive,* 4:14. Bhambatha's diminished status: Minister Native Affairs to Governor (23 Feb. 1906, 981/1906) and Order Supreme Chief, Min. SNA (23 Feb. 1906, 78/1906), 1/1/333, SNA MinP/GR. Challenges to Bhambatha from white settlers and rival chiefs: Statement, Chief Sibindi, 13 Feb. 1901, Min. Mag. Umvoti, 52/1901, Umvoti MinP/MR/GR; Min. Mag. New Hanover, 17 July 1903, 1/1/302 1752/1903, SNA MinP/GR; Statement, Chief Swayimana, 17 April 1905, 1/1/320 912/05, SNA MinP/GR. Claims and cases against Bhambatha: "Record of Criminal and Civil Actions against Bambatha," Umvoti (26 Jan. 1906), and Min. Mag. Umvoti to Under-SNA (8 Jan. 1906) 1/1/333 78/1906, SNA MinP/GR.

23. "Unhesitatingly": Letter, Botha, Greytown, to SNA, 5 Feb. 1906, 1/1/333 78/1906, SNA MinP/GR. Faction fights and more "location" land: Min. Mag. Umvoti, 8 Jan. 1906, 1/1/333 481/1906, SNA MinP/GR. "I hope": Memo Under-SNA (3 Nov. 1905) and Min. Mag. Umvoti to Under-SNA (1 Nov. 1905, 1/1/324 1912/1905), SNA MinP/GR. Greytown *indaba:* "Indaba held at Greytown," c. Dec. 1905, 575.57, KwaMuhle Local History, Photographs. "Meetings called at Bambata's": Prosecutor, Martial Law, Umvoti, to Administrator, Martial Law, Umvoti, 26 July 1906, 1/1/414 3263/1908, SNA MinP/GR. See also McCord, *My Patients Were Zulus,* 114. I thank Rob Morrell for the McCord reference.

24. Umvoti magistrate trying to collect tax: Statement, Malamba, 4 July 1906, Native

Rebellion Court Martial Proceedings, 1/6/28, SNA/GR. "They refused point-blank": Stuart, *History of the Zulu Rebellion*, 162–63. "It happened": *Greytown Gazette*, 3 March 1906, Newspapers.

25. "Sound[ed] the alarm": Testimony, Gasa, 15 Feb. 1981, 16 Oct. 1981, tapes GB30 and MAB2, OHP, Tape Transcripts/PT. "After the chiefs": Testimony, Mazibuko, July 1982, tape MAZS85, OHP, Tape Transcripts/PT. Deposing Bhambatha and appointing Magwababa: Telegram, Mag. Greytown to PM, 22 Feb. 1906, 1/6/30, Native Rebellion Court Martial Proceedings, SNA/GR. Transferring Bhambatha's followers to Mveli: Min. Under-SNA to Magistrates, Umgeni, Lions River, New Hanover, and Krantzkop, 27 March 1906, 1/1/333 981/1906, SNA MinP/GR. "Favours": Testimony, Cooper, 27 June 1907, Webb and Wright, *Stuart Archive*, 1:84–85. "The very worst policy": Memo, Governor, Enclosure 2, 2 March 1906, Military Affairs, Bambata Rebellion, 1463, GH/GR.

26. Bhambatha's low status as a chief might have been reinforced by the fact that Zondi followers were considered *amalala* and scorned by *amantungwa* nobility such as the patriarchs in Dinuzulu's uSuthu coterie: Stuart, *History of the Zulu Rebellion*, 499. He "is a Chief": "Address by Attorney General," 24–25 Feb. 1909, *Rex v. Dinuzulu*, High Treason Trial of Dinuzulu, Proceedings/GR. "The disturbed": Governor, Pietermaritzburg, to Secretary of State, London, 24 March 1906, 93, BPP/GR. "Running about": Min. Meeting between Minister Native Affairs and Chief Kula (26 March 1906, 886/1906) and Rep. Mag. Umsinga (15 March 1906, 831/1906), 1/1/338, SNA MinP/GR. "Body of young men": Statement, Mbovu, *Rex v. Ndolomba et al.*, 28 March 1906, Cases Adjudicated, Martial Law, Kranskop MR/GR. "Defiant . . . insurrection": *Rex v. Fokoti and Nqabeni* (10 March 1906), *Rex v. Hlalela and Nyamana* (23 March 1906), and Min. Mag. Eshowe (20 March 1906), 418/1906, Eshowe MinP/MR/GR.

27. "Young fellow": Statement, Mangati kaGodite, 22 Nov. 1907, 12, Nkandla MinP/MR/GR. See also "Address Attorney General," 17 Dec. 1908, *Rex v. Dinuzulu*, 126, H. E. Colenso, Papers of Individuals/PT. "Handle a gun": Statement, Siye Kiwe, 19 July 1907, Pietermaritzburg, *Rex v. Dinuzulu*, Special Courts, 1/7/61, AGO/GR. See also Mag. Ndwandwe to Commissioner Native Affairs, 16 Nov. 1908, 1/1/415 3441/08, SNA MinP/GR. Magwababa's ordeal: Interview between Governor and Envoys of Dinuzulu, 20 June 1906, 1/1/343 1856/1906, SNA MinP/GR.

28. "Skinned and cut": Statement, Vava Pungula (follower of Chief Bhambatha), 7 April 1906, Weenen, 1/1/339 1104/1906, SNA MinP/GR; *Ilanga Lase Natal*, 13 April 1906, Newspapers. "Enemy's flesh . . . forearm . . . diarrhoea": Testimony, Mpatshana, 2 June 1912, Webb and Wright, *Stuart Archive*, 3:327.

29. Bhambatha's magic invincibility: Rep. Mag. Lower Umzimkulu, 28 April 1906, 1/1/340 1235/1906, SNA MinP/GR. Rebel "impi" in Nkandla forests: Statement, Hlangabeza (follower of Chief Bhambatha) (7 April 1906, Weenen) and Rep. of Mag. (7 April 1907), 1/1/339 1071/1906, SNA MinP/GR. See also Stuart, *History of the Zulu Rebellion*, 175–77.

30. Mazibuko's recollections: Testimony, Mazibuko, July 1982, tape MAZS85, OHP, Tape Transcripts/PT.

31. Sigananda offered sanctuary by Zondi chiefs: Statement, Hlangabeza (follower of Chief Bhambatha), 7 April 1907, Umvoti, 1/1/339 1107/1906, SNA MinP/GR; Statement, Mangati kaGodite, 18 Dec. 1907, 1/4/19 305/1907, SNA Confidential Papers/GR. Sigananda about one hundred years old: "Sigananda Sentencing Recommendation," 28 June 1906, 126, H. E. Colenso, Papers of Individuals/PT. Sigananda recognized as "king": Testimony, Manyonyana, 23 Oct. 1921, Webb and Wright, *Stuart Archive*, 2:228. Chube followers living in *amalala* frontier: Mpatshana, 30 May 1912, ibid., 3:322. Qudeni Mountains and blue monkeys: Mandhlakazi, 2 Feb. 1922, ibid., 2:193; Mtshapi, 7 May 1918, ibid., 4:83–84. "Marks of axes": Mageza, 21 Feb. 1909, ibid., 2:77. Cetshwayo's grave: "Address of Attorney General," 24–25 Feb. 1909, High Treason Trial of Dinuzulu, Proceedings/GR.

32. Rumors that Dinuzulu championed rebel cause: Statement, Vava Pungula (follower of Chief Bhambatha) (7 April 1906) and Hlangabeza (follower of Chief Bhambatha) (7 April 1906), 34, Resident Commissioner, Confidential Correspondence, Commissioner/GR; Mangati kaGodite, 23 Nov. 1907, 1/6/29, Native Rebellion Court Martial Proceedings, SNA/GR. USuthu denial of rumor: Interview between Natal Governor, Dinuzulu, and Headmen, 21 May 1907, 1/4/17, SNA Confidential Papers/GR. "When the English": Min. Meeting between Minister of Native Affairs, Under-SNA, Commissioner of Police, and Muziwake, Pietermaritzburg, 20 July 1907, 1/1/344 2051/06, SNA MinP/GR. Drilling to "*uSuthu*" and donning *ubushokobezi* badges: Secret Correspondence, 25 Sept. 1907, Military Affairs, Bambata Rebellion, 1459, GH/GR; Rep. Lt. Hosking, Intelligence Officer, Carbineers, 24 March 1908, Special Courts, 1/7/52 873/1908, AGO/GR; Testimony, Gasa, 15 Feb. 1981, tape GB30, OHP, Tape Transcripts/PT.

33. Military mobilization: Stuart, *History of the Zulu Rebellion,* 63–64, 225–28. Rebels not responding to white settlers: *Ilanga Lase Natal,* 11 May 1906, in 1/1/341 1486/1906, SNA MinP; McCord, *My Patients Were Zulus,* 116–17.

34. "Did not want to fight": Testimony, Manyonyana, 23 Oct. 1921, Webb and Wright, *Stuart Archive,* 2:228. Colonial officials demanding that Sigananda turn over Bhambatha: Statement, Ndabambi kaLurungu (17 Sept. 1908, *Rex v. Dinuzulu,* Evidence, 117) and "Chronology of Rebellion, Siganada" (n.d., 126), H. E. Colenso, Papers of Individuals (NAP)/PT. Siganada's great age made him vulnerable: Statement, Ndabaningi, 14 Feb. 1907, *Rex v. Dinuzulu,* Special Courts, 1/7/55, AGO/GR; Umgoqo (2 Aug. 1906), Ngidi and Ndukuyezulu (9 Aug. 1906, "Case of Ndabaningi and Others"), Ncubana (10 Aug. 1906, "Trial of Yena and Others"), 1/6/26, Native Rebellion Court Martial Proceedings 1906, SNA/GR. Newcomers agitating Chube followers: Statement, Polomba, 25 June 1906, *Rex v. Sigananda,* 126, H. E. Colenso, Papers of Individuals, PT/GR.

35. "After Sigananda": Statement, Polomba, 25 June 1906, *Rex v. Sigananda,* 126, H. E. Colenso, Papers of Individuals (NAP)/PT. See also Mpikwa kaMkomoyi, 17 Sept. 1908, *Rex v. Dinuzulu,* Statements and Evidence, 117, H. E. Colenso, Papers of Individuals (NAP)/PT. Chakijana as courier, as mere "boy," and as intruder: Statement, Mpikwa kaMkomoyi, 9 Dec. 1908, *Rex v. Dinuzulu,* 1908–9, Special Courts, 1/7/55, AGO/GR; Ndambi kaLurungu (17 Sept. 1908) and Mdumbu kaZiningo (17 Sept. 1908), *Rex v.*

Dinuzulu, Evidence, 117, H. E. Colenso, Papers of Individuals (NAP)/PT. "Chakijana" as weasel: Samuelson, "Zululand and Its Traditions, Legends, and Customs," n.d., Faye, Papers of Individuals (NAP)/PT; Marks, "Class, Ideology and the Bambatha Rebellion," 361, 363.

36. Mankulumana as "most astute": Lugg, *Historic Natal and Zululand,* 151. Ndabaningi assuming leadership: Rep. Mag. Nkandla, Circular, 17/1906, Nkandla MinP, Confidential, MR/GR. "I have come here": Statement, Mankulumana, 27 April 1906, 126, H. E. Colenso, Papers of Individuals (NAP)/PT. For other statements by rebels and non-rebels in docket *Rex* v. *Dinuzulu* that confirm Mankulumana's account, see, for example, Mbonambi kaPalo, 17 Sept. 1908, Statements and Evidence, 117, H. E. Colenso, Papers of Individuals (NAP)/PT. Mankulumana resisting the rebellion plotters and protecting Dinuzulu: Statement, Mkobobi (follower of Chief Sigananda), 21 Sept. 1907, 28, Confidential Correspondence, Resident Commissioner/GR; Statement, Mankonkwana, 28 Dec. 1907, *Rex* v. *Dinuzulu,* 1908–9, 5/1908, Special Courts, 1/7/55, AGO/GR.

37. Chiefs had "been asked": *Ilanga Lase Natal,* 13 April 1906, in Memoranda, Natal Natives, 1550, GH/GR. "A very old man" and subsequent quotations: Rep. Mag. Nkandla, Reply, Circular, Commissioner Native Affairs, 17/1906, 1906, Nkandla MinP, Confidential, MR/GR. Other defections: Rep. Mag. Nkandla, 20 Nov. 1907, 235/1907, 104, PM/GR; Statement, Mangati kaGodite, 23 Nov. 1907, 133/1907, 1/6/29, Native Rebellion Court Martial Proceedings, SNA/GR; Testimony, Hayiyana, 8 Aug. 1908, Webb and Wright, *Stuart Archive,* 1:163–64.

38. "The young men will kill us all": Statement, Mkonto, 17 May 1906, Native Rebellion Intelligence Book, Mapumulo MR/GR. Mkhonto may have overstated the threat to elders to get the Mapumulo magistrate to provide police protection; fathers lamenting sons' departure: Statement, Senguka, 22 May 1906, Rep. Intelligence Officer Sgt. Fitzgerald, Native Rebellion Intelligence Book, Mapumulo MR/GR. Gobizembe's headmen arranging departure: Chief Ndhlovu kaTimuni, 17 May 1906, Native Rebellion Intelligence Book, Mapumulo MR/GR.

39. "Where many . . . own account": testimony, Radebe, Estcourt, 15 Jan. 1907, *Evidence, Native Affairs Commission, 1906–7,* COM/GR. Rebels from Thukela basin streaming into Nkandla forest: Cases, Martial Law Greytown, May 1906–Sept. 1906, Umvoti MR/GR; Rep. Mag. Umvoti, 1906, 1/1/414 3263/08, SNA MinP/GR; Case 8, Statement, Induna Madakawana, Nkandla, 9 June 1906, Criminal Note Book, Martial Law, Nkandla MR/GR. Rebels ignoring traditional controls: "Natal Natives, 29 May 1907 to 30 October 1907," Memoranda, Natal Natives, April 1902–May 1910, 1550, GH/GR. Long-standing feud: Statement, Chief Bambatha (22 Aug. 1902), Under-SNA (25 Aug. 1902), and Chief Sibindi (22 Sept. 1902), 1/1/296 2277/1902, SNA MinP/GR. Bomvu youths joining Zondi youths: Chief Intelligence Officer, Kranskop, to Commandant Militia, Pietermaritzburg (27 May 1906, 1/1/342 1084/1906) and Min. Mag. Krantzkop to SNA (11 June 1906, 1/1/341 1511/06) SNA MinP/GR. Despite the defections, Chief Sibindi was still able to mobilize hundreds of "loyal levies," the most of any chief in Natal: Marks, *Reluctant Rebellion,* 318.

40. "Old enemies . . . rebellious feeling:" Rep. Mag. Kranskop, Circular 11, 1/SNA 1/1/414 3263/08, SNA MinP/GR. Gayede's heir-apparent guiding young men to rebel stronghold: Chief Intelligence Officer, Kranskop, to Commandant, Militia, Pietermaritzburg, 27 May 1906, 1/1/342 1084/1906, SNA MinP/GR. Young men joining anti–poll tax movement: Martial Law Note Book, 1/5/1/1, Nquthu MR/GR; Claim 121, Tagate kaShongela (follower of Chief Maweni), 8 Aug. 1906, Compensation Board, 3/2, Nquthu MR/GR. McKenzie and Chief Mehlokazulu: *Rex* v. *Mtshola kaMswaule* (28, 15 Sept. 1906), *Rex* v. *Pugupugu et al.* (41, 17 Sept. 1906), Martial Law Note Book (1/5/1/2), Nquthu MR/GR. Mehlokazulu and looting in Matshana's chiefdom: Intelligence Rep., Nquthu, to Commandant Militia, Pietermaritzburg (12 Oct. 1906), and Rep. Chief Matshana kaMondisa, "Claim for Restoration of Cattle Seized by Colonel Roysten, 1907," 1/1/358 4208/06, SNA MinP/GR.

41. Acquiescent chiefs: Rep. Mag. Nkandla (Sept. 1906, 2262/1906), "Loyalist and Rebel Chiefs 1906," Rep. Mag. Mapumulo (2305/1906, 1/1/345), and "List of Rebel Chiefs and Their Sentences" (Nov. 1906, 1/1/355 3785/1906), SNA MinP/GR; "Native Chiefs, Headmen, and Others Punished by Fine, Deposition, Disratement, or Deportation in Native Disturbances 1906," Annual Rep., BB Departmental Rep. 1906, 44–7. "The word spoken": Testimony, Gasa, 16 Oct. 1981, tape MAB2, OHP, Tape Transcripts/PT. Mtamo "pretend[ed]": Statements, Mzanywa, Kranskop, 5 April 1907 and 15 Feb. 1907, 588A/1907, 3/1/7, Kranskop MinP/MR/GR.

42. Quotations from Mazibuko: Testimony, Mazibuko, July 1982, tape MAZS, OHP, Tape Transcripts/PT.

43. "First heard . . . one to join": Statement, Mzili, 4 June 1906, Native Rebellion, Intelligence Book, Mapumulo MR/GR. Age of rebels: Cases Adjudicated, Martial Law, Kranskop MR/GR; Cases, Martial Law, Greytown, Umvoti MR/GR; Rep. Zama, Noordsberg, Umvoti, 28 Sept. 1906, Papers Relating to the Rebellion, American Board Mission (NAP)/PT; "List of Prisoners over 50 Years of Age," Memoranda, Natal Natives, April 1902–May 1910, 1550, GH/GR.

5. *"The War of the Heads"*

1. Testimony, Gasa, 15 Feb. 1981, tape GB, OHP Tape Transcripts/PT.

2. Restorationist revolt: Marks, *Reluctant Rebellion*, 336–37; Marks, "Class, Ideology and the Bambatha Rebellion," 357, 366–67. "We of Cetshwayo's army": Testimony, Ndabazezwe, 24 June 1921, Webb and Wright, *Stuart Archive*, 4:189.

3. Dinuzulu's rumored call to arms: *Times of Natal*, 24, 27, 28 Jan. 1908, Newspapers; Military Affairs Bambata Rebellion Secret Telegrams, 1475–76, GH/GR. "Paramount of the Zulus": "Terms of Dinuzulu's Repatriation," n.d., 3, BPP/GR. Rebels who believed in Dinuzulu's opposition to colonial rule: Interview between Governor and Dinuzulu, 21 May 1907, 1/4/17 110/1907, SNA Confidential Papers/GR; Deposition, Umbelayana (recorded as twenty-four years old) (23 Sept. 1908, Nkandla) and Deposition, Mangaqaka (recorded as twenty-five years old) (22 Sept. 1908) *Rex* v. *Dinuzulu*, Special Courts,

1/7/53, AGO/GR. Rebels who believed Natal chiefs were too compliant: Statement, Hlangabeza Dhlamini (7 April 1906) and Statement, Vava Pungula (7 April 1906), 1/1/339 1104/1906, SNA MinP/GR. Drilling around the grave: Mag. Nkandla to SNA, 26 May 1906, 2112/1906, Nkandla MinP Confidential/MR/GR; "Address of Attorney General," Feb. 1909, High Treason Trial of Dinuzulu, Proceedings/GR. "When bullets come": Testimony, Mazibuko, July 1982, tape MAZS85, OHP Tape Transcripts/PT. Male elder healers: Testimony, Mpatshana, 25 May 1912, Webb and Wright, *Stuart Archive*, 3:296; Testimony, Lunguza, 11 March 1909, ibid., 1:323.

4. "From the hilltops": Colenbrander, Bambata Rebellion, Papers of Individuals (KCL)/PT; Mag. Nkandla to Commissioner Native Affairs, 6 Feb. 1907, 746, 3/1/1, Confidential Letter Book, Nkandla MR/GR; Statement, Sivela kaMqandi, 6 Sept. 1907, Memoranda Military Affairs, 1458, GH/GR; Testimony, Makathini, 24 Oct. 1981, untitled tape, OHP, Tape Transcripts/PT. Looting livestock: Statement, Lumbe kaNombona, 2 Aug. 1906, *Rex* v. *Manzoba kaMlegela et al.*, 1/5/1/2, Criminal Note Book, Nkandla MR/GR. "Old loyalist[s] by the Rebels": Statement, Lumbe kaNombona, 2 Aug. 1906, *Rex* v. *Manzoba kaMlegela et al.*, Martial Law Note Books, 1/5/1/2, Nkandla MR/GR. "Doctors from foreign parts": Testimony, Mpatshana, 30 May 1912, Webb and Wright, *Stuart Archive*, 3:322–23. "To which group": Testimony, Mazibuko, July 1982, tape MAZS, OHP, Tape Transcripts/PT.

5. Chief Kula and his young male followers joining Mtele in Umsinga: Statement, Umawiza kaGwala, 7 March 1906, Umsinga, 1/8/104 2840/1906, AGO/GR; Rep. Natal Police Sgt. Stringer, Umsinga, to Sub-Inspector Maxwell (8 March 1906, 1/1/337 726/1906), and Rep. Mag. Umsinga (15 March 1906, 1/1/338 831/1906), SNA MinP/GR. Colonial troop manuevers: Stuart, *History of the Zulu Rebellion*, 319–25; Marks, *Reluctant Rebellion*, 217–19. Bhobe battle: Stuart, ibid., 232–35. British newspaper coverage excerpted from *Natal Mercury*, 11 May 1906, Newspapers. San Francisco earthquake: *Ilanga Lase Natal*, 11 May 1906, 1/1/341 1486/1906, SNA MinP/GR.

6. Medicine failing to protect rebels: Min. Mag. Nkandla to Commissioner Native Affairs, Eshowe, 17 Dec. 1907, 1/1/360 112/07, SNA MinP/GR. Young rebels avoiding direct confrontation: Statement, Mzili, 4 June 1906, Native Rebellion Intelligence Book, Mapumulo MR/GR. "Bambatha's warfare": Testimony, Mpatshana, 30 May 1912, Webb and Wright, *Stuart Archive*, 3:320, 296. "Native levies": Stuart, *History of the Zulu Rebellion*, 240–45. "Burnt many kraals": "Synopsis Wires 6 P.M. 14/5/06 to 6 P.M. 15/5/06," Military Affairs, Bambata Rebellion, 1465, GH/GR. Forest fighters driven into bush: Telegram, 18 May 1906, McKay Zululand Field Force, 230/06, 101, PM/GR. Fire around the grave: Rep. T. Dube (21 May 1906) and Min. Minister Native Affairs to Minister of Justice (21 May 1906), 1/1/342, SNA MinP/GR. "Blood being shed": "Mr. Schreiner's Address" (lawyer for Dinuzulu), 25 Feb. 1909, High Treason Trial of Dinuzulu, Proceedings/GR.

7. Statement, Mangati kaGodite, 22 Nov. 1907, MinP, Confidential, Nkandla MR/GR. See also: "Order Supreme Chief to Sibindi" (4 April 1906, 1/1/339 1026/1906), Min. Mag.

Umsinga Circular (31 July 1906), Min. Mag. Umvoti (31 July 1906), 1/1/347 2533/06, SNA MinP/GR.

8. Images of headringed levies: Barry, Bambatha Rebellion, 19, 29, Natal Museum, Photographs. Recruiting African levies to fight rebels: Min. Mag. Umsinga (31 July 1906) and Min. Mag. Umvoti (31 July 1906), 1/1/347 2536/06, SNA MinP/GR; Statement, Chief Mveli, 12 April 1906, 1/1/339 1204/06, SNA MinP/GR; Min. Under-SNA, 19 June 1907, 749/1907, 3/1/8, Kranskop MinP/MR/GR.

9. "Were sniped [at]": "Synopsis Wires 6 P.M. 14/5/06 to 6 P.M. 15/5/06," Military Affairs, Bambata Rebellion, 1465, GH/GR. "The rebels were hiding": Telegram, 31 May 1906, McKay's Zululand Field Force, to Militia Headquarters, Pietermaritzburg, 230/06, 101, PM/GR.

10. Rebel alliance and colonial militia's invasion of Mome: Stuart, *History of the Zulu Rebellion,* 296–315. "Bambata and company": Testimony, Mpatshana, 31 May 1912, Webb and Wright, *Stuart Archive,* 3:324.

11. Women in rebel camps and rebels surrendering: Mag. Nkandla to SNA, 26 May 1906, 2112/1906, MinP, Confidential, Nkandla MR/GR; Barry, Bambatha Rebellion, "Young Women Surrender at Cetshwayo Grave," 8, Natal Museum, Photographs; "Synopsis Wires," 16 June 1906, Military Affairs, Bambata Rebellion, 1465, GH/GR.

12. *London Telegraph* story and "the medical officer": "International Press Notices 1906," 5956/1906, 1817, Miscellaneous, CSO/GR.

13. Mazibuko on his escape and later arrest: Testimony, Mazibuko, July 1982, tape MAZS, OHP, Tape Transcripts/PT.

14. Poll tax fighters distrusting their homestead heads: Mag. Nquthu to Commandant of Militia, Pietermaritzburg, 12 Oct. 1906, 1/1/358, SNA MinP/GR. Patriarchs testifying against their sons: Deposition, Zwezinye Kuzwayo, 6 Sept. 1909, 1/1/441 2889/09, SNA MinP/GR; Statement, Bayelaka (Nquthu, 9 March 1908), and Mganu (Nquthu, 9 March 1908), *Rex* v. *Mankulumana and Mgwaqo,* 115, H. E. Colenso, Papers of Individuals (NAP)/PT. Matshana and his sons: "Rep. on Chief Matshana kaMondisa's Claim for Restoration of Cattle," 1906, 1/1/358 4208/06, SNA MinP/GR. "On the floor . . . roads and bridges": Testimony, Mazibuko, July 1982, tape MAZS85, OHP, Tape Transcripts/PT.

15. Prosecutors and elders' testimony: Statement, Gwazizulu (imprisoned rebel) (2 Aug. 1906), and Yena kaNomaqonqoto (10 Aug. 1906), "Trial of Yena," Native Rebellion Court Martial Proceedings, 1/6/26, SNA/GR; Testimony, Mpatshana, 31 May 1912, Webb and Wright, *Stuart Archive,* 3:324; Min. Mag. Nkandla to Commissioner Native Affairs, Eshowe, 16 Jan. 1907, 1/1/360 28/07, SNA MinP/GR. Number of rebels arrested: Memo, Natal Natives, 117, April 1902–May 1910, 1549, GH/GR; Governor to Secretary of State, 12 July 1906, Enclosure 2, 1471, GH/GR; *Natal Witness,* 15 Nov. 1906, Newspapers; Native Affairs Annual Rep., BB Departmental Rep. 1906, 44–47, GR; "List of Chiefs Punished, Deposed or Reprimanded for Political Offenses," Min. Minister Native Affairs, 20 Nov. 1906, 1/1/355 3785/06, SNA MinP/GR. Convict labor: Secretary, Law Department to Private Secretary, Acting Lieutenant Governor, Pretoria, 101/48, 113, Minutes LTG

(TAP)/GR. "These young men": Testimony, Socwatsha, 19 Dec. 1906, *Evidence, Native Affairs Commission, 1906–7,* 709, COM/GR.

16. "Turbulent": Telegram Mag. Mapumulo, "Synopsis Wires from 6 P.M. 15 May 1906," Military Affairs, Bambata Rebellion, 1465, GH/GR. Rumors of uprising and Thring's Post: Stuart, *History of the Zulu Rebellion,* 344–52.

17. Rebel mobilization: Min. Prime Minister, 17 July 1906, Pietermaritzburg, 842/1906, 61, PM/GR. Meseni convincing Swayimana's young men: Deposition, Macabacaba, July 1906, Martial Law, Miscellaneous Rep., Mapumulo MR/GR. Criminal Record Book, Martial Law 1906, Mapumulo MR/GR. Swayimana's rivalry with Bhambatha: Min. Mag. Umgeni (16 March 1905, 1/1/318 670/1905) and Statement, Swayimana (17 April 1905, 1/1/320 912/05) SNA MinP/GR.

18. "*Usuthu*" cry and *ubushokobezi: Natal Mercury,* 7 July 1906, Military Affairs, Bambata Rebellion, 1471, GH/GR. Veal killing: Testimony, Msime, 12 Dec. 1906, Webb and Wright, *Stuart Archive,* 4:52, 59. *Intelezi* and "were first to pay": Telegram, Mag. Empangeni to Commissioner Native Affairs, Eshowe, 13 June 1906, 34, Confidential Correspondence, Commissioner/GR. Chiefs fleeing Eshowe: "Cases Tried at Mapumulo Martial Law Courts from July 14, 1906 to 24 Aug. 1906," Martial Law Note Books, 1906, 1/4/1/2–3, Mapumulo MR/GR.

19. Military invasion of the coast: Secret Telegrams, Military Affairs, Bambata Rebellion, 1472, GH/GR; Testimony, H. E. Colenso, 5 Dec. 1906, *Evidence, Native Affairs Commission, 1906–7,* 117, COM/GR. "Isolated instances": Rep. Senior Medical Officer McKenzie's Field Force, 26 July 1906, 3, Despatch Military Affairs, Bambata Rebellion, 1472, GH/GR.

20. Testimony, Sibisi, 13 March 1979, tape 207, OHP, Tape Transcripts/PT.

21. Reward for levies: Statement, Mangati kaGodite (22 Nov. 1907, 1/NKA 3/2/2/1), Min. Mag. Eshowe (12 July 1906), and Min. Mag. Eshowe to Commissioner Native Affairs (14 July 1906), 1/ESH 3/2/5 E1035/1906, SNA MinP/GR. Swayimana targeted for revenge: Min. Mag. Mapumulo, 31 Aug. 1906, 1/1/349 2999/06, SNA MinP/GR. Estimates of rebel casualties: Stuart, *History of the Zulu Rebellion,* 374–83. Mopping-up exercises: Marks, *Reluctant Rebellion,* 239. Colonial threat to confiscate possessions: Circular, Under-SNA to Magistrates, 23 July 1906, Rep. Native Affairs, BB Departmental Rep. 1906, 43, GR. "Hard labour": Case 64, 19 May 1908, Stanger Native Criminal Record Book 1908–1912, 1/2/1/2/4. "Turned out": Statement, Macalana, 1908, Esidumbini, 1/1/399 1476/08, SNA MinP/GR. Macalana was a captured rebel. See also Testimony, Mazibuko, July 1982, tape MAZS, OHP, Tape Transcripts/PT. Rebel prisoner estimate: "List of prisoners over 50 years of age, Natal Natives: 29 May 1907 to 30 Oct. 1907," 42–59, 1550, Memoranda, Natal Natives, April 1902–May 1910, GH/GR. Rebel convictions: "Natal Natives General 1907," 117, 1549, Memoranda, Natal Natives, April 1902–May 1910, GH/GR.

22. Scorched earth: *Natal Mercury,* 20 July 1906 and 26 July 1906, in Military Affairs, Bambata Rebellion, 1472, GH/GR. "Thousands of houses": ibid., 4 Oct. 1906. "Bodies [of rebels lay]": *Times of Natal,* 9 Oct. 1906, Newspapers.

23. "Where the Native . . . were removed": *Ilanga Lase Natal,* 12 Oct. 1906, in 1/1/353

3478/06, SNA MinP/GR. "What would": *Ilanga Lase Natal* article, reprinted in *Natal Witness*, 15 Nov. 1906, 1/1/354 3716/06, SNA MinP/GR.

24. "In the Franco-German war": Testimony, H. E. Colenso, 5 Dec. 1906, *Evidence, Native Affairs Commission, 1906–7*, 117, COM/GR. "Large majority . . . Hard Labour": Assistant Commissioner Police and Inspector Prisons, 1907, 117, Memoranda, Natal Natives, April 1902–May 1910, 1549, GH/GR; Marks, *Reluctant Rebellion*, 237–38. One out of three Africans homeless: Rep. Mag. Mapumulo to Minister Native Affairs, 28 June 1907, 1/1/371 1862/1907, SNA MinP/GR. "Destitute women . . . kraalheads": Commandant Militia, Pietermaritzburg, to Mag. Nkandla, 13 July 1906, 3/2/1/1, MinP, Nkandla MR/GR. "Families are at present": Mag. Nkandla to Commissioner Native Affairs, Eshowe, 14 Feb. 1907, Confidential Letter Book, Nkandla MR/GR.

25. Colonial casualties: Stuart, *History of the Zulu Rebellion*, 541–42. "Severe lesson": Letter, Mag. Nkandla to Comm. Native Affairs, Eshowe, 6 Feb. 1907, 747, Confidential Letter Book, Nkandla MR/GR. "Spirit of self-reliance": Rep. Governor, 4 May 1907, 1041, MinP, GH/GR.

26. Departure of imperial troops and colonial fears: Rep. Intelligence Officer, 17 June 1903, 1/4/12 48/1903, Confidential Papers, SNA/GR. Rumors of Britain failing to aid Natal: Statement, Micah Nkwananzi, 27 June 1904, 34, Resident Commissioner, Confidential Correspondence, Commissioner/GR; Stuart, *History of the Zulu Rebellion*, 38. "The King in England": Statement, Daniels, Secretary to Dinuzulu, 21 March 1908, 3, BPP/GR; Min. Mag. Vryheid to SNA, 1 June 1904, 1/4/13 35/1904, SNA Confidential Papers/GR.

27. Rebel bands in "Thorn Country": "Natives convicted and imprisoned for rebellion, 1907," Assistant Commissioner Police and Inspector of Prisons, 109/07, Memoranda, Natal Natives, April 1902–May 1910, 1549, GH/GR. Rebels laboring for Dinuzulu: *Times of Natal*, 24 Jan. 1908, in Military Affairs, Bambata Rebellion, 1475, GH/GR; Statement, Mankokwane (23 Jan. 1908, "Samuelson's Preliminary Notes," 111), and Mazana (rebel) (27 Jan. 1908, 112), H. E. Colenso, Papers of Individuals (NAP)/PT. Sports at Dalala flats: Statement, Mgano, 26 Sept. 1907, 89/1907, 1/6/29, Native Rebellion, Court Martial Proceedings, SNA/GR. USuthu refuge and bridewealth cattle: *Times of Natal*, 27 Jan. 1908, Military Affairs, Bambata Rebellion, 1476, GH/GR; Statements, Mabanjwa, Mabeqemana, Maboka, Maliba, Manza, et al. (rebels) (*Rex* v. *Dinuzulu*, 1908), Deposition, Sifimela (rebel; Nongoma, 9 June 1908), 112, H. E. Colenso, Papers of Individuals/PT.

28. USuthu homestead as rebel command center: Statement, Mangati kaGodite (rebel), 23 Nov. 1907, 1/SNA 1/6/29 Conf. R. 133/1907, SNA/GR; Statement, Rolela kaFokoti (rebel), 2 Jan. 1908, 29, Resident Commissioner, Confidential Correspondence, Commissioner/GR; Statement, Anonymous (rebel in uSuthu homestead), 29 Nov. 1907, 259/1907, 104 PM/GR; Rep. Mag. Umsinga, 7 Oct. 1907, 1/4/18 183/1907, SNA Confidential Papers/GR. Chakijana "required men": *Times of Natal*, 6 March 1908, 1/GH vol. 1472. "When the crops": Mag. Nkandla to Commissioner Native Affairs, Eshowe, 6 Feb. 1907, Confidential Letter Book, Nkandla MR/GR. See also "Statements of Mganu and

Ndodo, alias Nomapekepeana," *Rex* v. *Dinuzulu*, Special Courts, 1/7/51, AGO/GR. "It was often heard": Statement, Mankokowana, 28 Dec. 1907, Nkandla, 92, Confidential Letter Book, Nkandla MR/GR.

29. Rumors of Bhambatha and bewitching potions: *Natal Mercury* (23 Jan. 1907 in 1/1/361 298/07) and Statement, Usotiki (9 Feb. 1907, Kranskop, 1/1/362 440/07), SNA MinP/GR. "As a distinguishable badge": Mag. Nkandla to Commissioner Native Affairs, Eshowe, 6 Feb. 1907, Confidential Letter Book, Nkandla MR/GR.

30. Mag. Nkandla to Commissioner Native Affairs, Eshowe, 14 Feb. 1907, 3/1907, Confidential Letter Book, Nkandla MR/GR.

31. "Diabolical outrage . . . of terror": Population, Zululand Province, 1907, 70, BB Departmental Rep. 1907, GR. "Rebels belonging . . . being murdered": Min. Mag. Umvoti 29 Jan. 1907, 1/1/361 298/07, SNA MinP/GR. "Wandering about": Min. Mag. Mapumulo to Under-SNA, 7 June 1907, 1/1/372 1982/07, SNA MinP/GR. "Two ex-rebels": Min. Mag. Krantzkop to Mag. Nkandla, 13 April 1907, 3/1/7 367/07, Kranskop MinP/MR/GR. Suspected identity of Gence's assailants: Statement, Mayatana kaSintwango, 17 Jan. 1908, Mtunzini, *Rex* v. *Dinuzulu*, Special Courts, 1/7/55, AGO/GR. See also 1/6/29, Native Rebellion, Court Martial Proceedings, SNA/GR. Jealous vengeance: Letter, Commissioner Native Affairs to PM, 12 Aug. 1907, 28, Resident Commissioner, Confidential Correspondence, Commissioner/GR. Gence's pro-government stance: Deposition, "Native Unnamed," 25 Sept. 1907, 159/1907, 1/4/18, Confidential Papers, SNA/GR. "All those of position": Statement, African Policeman, Min. Mag. Nkandla, 11 Nov. 1907, 958/1907 3/2/1/2, MinP, Nkandla MR/GR. Other rebel threats of revenge against *amambuka*: Deposition, Mazawuzela, 11 April 1908, 1/6/29, Native Rebellion, Court Martial Proceedings, SNA/GR; Commissioner Native Affairs to PM, 6 Sept. 1907, 3, BPP/GR.

32. "Entertain[ing] strangers . . . the rectum": Statement, Sivela kaMnqandi (Sitshitshili's brother), 6 Sept. 1907, Military Affairs, Bambata Rebellion, 1458, GH/GR. Young stranger's activities at the "beer drink": Statement, Anonymous (rebel-turned-police-informer), 12 Nov. 1907, Nkandla, 3/2/1/2 958/1907, MinP, Nkandla MR/GR. "Placed confidence . . . small piece of the bone": Rep. Acting Mag. Nkandla, 27 Aug. 1907, "Compiled from Statements of Sitshitshili's Wives, 'Native Constables' and Natal Police Sgt. Wilkinson," 24–28, Confidential Letter Book, Nkandla MR/GR. Stolen gun from Mpanza: Statement, Rolela kaFokoti (2 Jan. 1908, 29) and Colonial Secretary to Commissioner Native Affairs, Eshowe (12 Dec. 1908, 29), Resident Commissioner, Confidential Correspondence, Commissioner/GR. See Enclosure 2, 27 Sept. 1907, Military Affairs, Bambata Rebellion, 1490, GH/GR.

33. "My heart speaks . . . suffer alone": Statement, Sivela kaMnqandi, 6 Sept. 1907, Nkandla, "Enclosure 4 in Despatch Secret 1," 13 Sept. 1907, Military Affairs, Bambata Rebellion, 1458, GH/GR.

34. Shock to basin loyalists: Min. Commissioner Native Affairs to PM, 6 Sept. 1907, Military Affairs, Bambata Rebellion, 1458, GH/GR. "Recent murder": Telegram, Governor to Sec. State, 11 Sept. 1907, Military Affairs, Bambata Rebellion, 1458, GH/GR. "Several chiefs": Memo Mag. Mahlabathini to Commissioner Native Affairs, Eshowe, 17 Sept.

1907, Military Affairs, Bambata Rebellion, 1490, GH/GR. "Hardly a day": "Governor Secret Enclosure no. 3, 12 Oct. 1907," Military Affairs, Bambata Rebellion, 1459, GH/GR. Attempted murder of Mapoyisa: Telegram, Mag. Nkandla to Commissioner Native Affairs, Eshowe, 9 Oct. 1907, Military Affairs, Bambata Rebellion, GH/GR. Attempted murder of Ndlezana: Statement, Mabalengwe kaSifile (8 Oct. 1907, 102/1907), Mapoyisa kaMbuzo (18 Oct. 1907, 118/1907), and Mabalengwe kaSifile (8 Oct. 1907, 102/1907), 28, Resident Commissioner, Confidential Correspondence, Commissioner/GR. "An amnesty": Rep. Native Population, Zululand, 70, BB Departmental Rep. Natal 1907, GR. Mpumela killing: Mag. Nkandla to Commissioner Native Affairs, Eshowe, 28 Nov. 1907, 139/1907, 28, Resident Commissioner, Confidential Correspondence, Commissioner/GR. Chakijana's alleged role: Statement, Mcimezi (1908, *Rex* v. *Dinuzulu*, 1/7/51) and Statement, Nqalamba kaFebana (11 Jan. 1908, *Rex* v. *Dinuzulu*, 1/7/61), Special Courts Zulu, AGO/GR.

35. "Ruffians": *Ilanga Lase Natal,* 6 Dec. 1907, 1/1/387 3705/07, SNA MinP/GR. McKenzie's operations in Zululand: Rep. Mag. Nkandla, BB Departmental Rep. 1907, GR. "Those who are loyal" and Reuters story: *Natal Witness,* 11 Dec. 1907, Military Affairs, Bambata Rebellion, 1461, GH/GR.

36. Rebels surrendering: Statement, Mangati kaGodite, 23 Nov. 1907, 1/6/29, Native Rebellion, Court Martial Proceedings, SNA/GR. Welcome peace: Rep. Native Pop. Zululand, 70, BB Departmental Rep. 1907, GR; Memo. Commissioner Native Affairs, Eshowe, 6 April 1908, 1/6/29, Native Rebellion, Martial Law Proceedings, SNA/GR. "One can eat": Rep. Mag. Ndwandwe, 1 Dec. 1908, 1/7/56, Special Courts, ABO/GR.

37. "Charges Against Dinuzulu 1908," 29, Resident Commissioner, Confidential Correspondence, Commissioner/GR. "It is true": Statement, E. G. Jellicoe (29 Feb. 1908) and Jellicoe to Colonial Office (16 March 1908), 3, BPP/GR; Marks, *Reluctant Rebellion,* 277–79. Dinuzulu's sentence: "Judgment by Judge-President of Special Court," *Rex* v. *Dinuzulu,* 1908, 1/7/51, Special Courts, AGO/GR.

38. Governor to Sec. State, 9 Jan. 1909, 9/1909, Military Affairs, Bambata Rebellion, 1485, GH/GR.

39. Devastation of homestead economy: Min. Mag. Nquthu to Under-SNA (9 May 1908, 1/1/399 1452/1908), Min. Mag. Krantzkop (4 March 1909, 1/1/424 686/09), Min. Acting Mag. Umvoti (19 Oct. 1910, 1/1/474 3291/10), and "Outstanding Squatter Rents by Division" (1909, 1/1/444 2675/09), SNA MinP/GR. Increase of 26 percent: "Chart of Monthly Registration in Labour Districts, . . . Development of Native Labour from the Principal Sources of Supply," Min. SNA, Pretoria, to SNA, Pietermaritzburg, 30 March 1910, 1/1/460 1154/10, SNA MinP (NAP)/GR. Increase of 60 percent: "Statement of Number of Natives and Other Coloured Labourers Employed in Labour Districts of the Transvaal on the 31 May 1907, and 31 March 1909, Natal & Zululand," 3, Min., GNLB/GR. "Increase in the number . . . anticipated": Minister Native Affairs, Pretoria, to President, Transvaal Chamber of Mines, 28 Sept. 1909, 3, Min., GNLB/GR.

40. Sixfold increase in labor migrancy: "Position Native Labour Supply Proclaimed Labour Districts of Transvaal at 31st March 1909," 3, Min., GNLB/GR. Filling the void

of departing Chinese laborers: Rep. Native Labour Agency, Johannesburg, Native Affairs Department, 6 July 1909, 1/1/420 70/09, SNA MinP/GR. See also Richardson, *Chinese Mine Labour in the Transvaal.*

41. African dissatisfaction with conditions: Statement, Duweni (4 Aug. 1909), and Mcitwa (4 Aug. 1909) 1/1/440 2574/09, SNA MinP/GR. "Mines are becoming": Director Government Native Labour Bureau, Johannesburg, December 1908, "Memo. Native Labour Statistics," 2, Minutes, GNLB/GR. Correspondence on passes, tracking of labor migrants, and contracts: Rep. Director GNLB, "Natal Government re: Recruitment of Native Labour for Mines" (21 Aug. 1907), and Assistant Director GNLB, Johannesburg, to Under-SNA, Pietermaritzburg (23 Sept. 1908), 1/1/412 2894/08, SNA MinP/GR; Director GNLB, Johannesburg, to Minister for Native Affairs, Pretoria, 8 Oct. 1908, 417, SNA (TAP)/GR. Employers' rivalry and "touting": *Natal Mercury* (25 Sept. 1909, 1/1/446 3283/1909) and Min. SNA, to District Native Commissioner, Zululand (27 Aug. 1909, 1/1/441 785/09), SNA MinP (NAP)/GR. Siphoning off workers: Agent, Department Native Affairs, Johannesburg, to SNA, Pietermaritzburg (20 Aug. 1909), Native Labour Superintendent, Central African Railways, Johannesburg, to SNA, Pietermaritzburg (5 Aug. 1909, 1/1/443 3092/09), Nicoll & Co., Port Natal, to General Manager Natal Government Railways (15 March 1910, 1/1/445 3183/09) SNA MinP (NAP)/GR.

42. Government correspondence with Natal employers: Rep., "Apprenticing of Native Children," 1 Aug. 1909, 1/1/449 3644/09, SNA MinP/GR. "Conveyance of natives": Min. Natal Government Railways, to Sec. Railways and Harbours (19 July 1909), and Min. Acting General Manager to Secretry, Railways and Harbours (21 Oct. 1909), 1/1/438 2358/09, SNA MinP/GR. "The government . . . the native": *Natal Mercury,* 25 Sept. 1909, 1/1/446 3283/09, SNA MinP/GR. "On the Mines": *Ilanga Lase Natal,* 21 May 1909, 1/1/430 1362/09, SNA MinP/GR.

43. Mine visits by chiefs and headmen: Assistant Director, GNLB, Johannesburg, to Under-SNA, Pietermaritzburg (23 Sept. 1908, 1/1/410 782/08), Min. Mag. Krantzkop (4 March 1909, 1/1/424 686/09), and Secretary, Transvaal Mines Labour Co., Ltd., to Agent, Natal Native Affairs Dept. (28 June 1909, 1/1/438 2232/09), SNA MinP/GR. "To provide employment": Letter, E. P. Robinson, Johannesburg, to SNA, Pietermaritzburg (10 July 1909), Letter, Sec. Transvaal Mines Labour Co., Ltd., Johannesburg, to Agent Natal Native Affairs, Pietermaritzburg (28 June 1909, 1/1/438 2232/09), SNA MinP/GR. Traveling delegations and "observe the manner": Statement, Nongetshe kaMasakisa kaMtetwa (1 Feb. 1910), and Min. SNA (2 Feb. 1910, 1/1/456 443/10), SNA MinP/GR.

44. Marked decrease in recorded generational conflicts: see Min. of SNA, SNA MinP, 1/1/336–478. Sibindi and Qolota: Statement, Chief Sibindi (24 June 1910, Mapumulo), Mpofana kaMhlane (11 Sept. 1909), and Ncwadi kaMatambo (11 Sept. 1909), 1/1/442 3039/09, SNA MinP/GR.

45. "Bambata has said . . . secret with them": Statement, Zwezinye Kuzwayo kaJakobe (deposed in Johannesburg), 6 Sept. 1909, 1/1/441 2889/09, SNA MinP/GR. "Death of the Country": *Ilanga Lase Natal,* 3 Aug. 1906, in 1/1/348 2675/06, SNA MinP/GR.

46. The scholarship on labor migrancy and African urban life is substantial. For recent studies challenging the view that labor migrants in Natal cities were socially conservative, see Paul La Hausse, "Message of the Warriors: The ICU, the Labouring Poor and the Making of a Popular Culture in Durban, 1925–1930," and Iain Edwards, "Swing the Assegai Peacefully? New Africa, Mkhumbane, the Cooperative Movements and Attempts to Transform Durban Society in late 1940s," both in *Holding Their Ground,* ed. Bonner et al. For studies of life in Johannesburg, see Harries, "Symbols and Sexuality"; Coplan, *In the Time of Cannibals.*

47. On these possible connections, see Nicholas Cope, "The Zulu Royal Family," Ph.D., 56–59, 449–50; Shula Marks, "Patriotism, Patriarchy and Purity: Natal and the Politics of Zulu Ethnic Consciousness," in *The Creation of Tribalism in Southern Africa,* ed. Vail, 225–28.

Postscript

1. Eddie Roux's *Time Longer than Rope* explores twentieth-century African protest movements in South Africa; he calls "Bambatha's rebellion" one of the pivotal struggles for "national and democratic rights [in] South Africa," 87. For others who portray that rebellion as a prototype of anticolonial African violence, see Beinart, "Political and Collective Violence," 460; Bozzoli and Delius, "Radical History and South African Society," 20, 37; Helen Bradford, "Lynch Law and Labourers: The ICU in Umvoti, 1927–1928," in *Putting a Plough to the Ground,* ed. Beinart et al., 421; Beinart and Bundy, *Hidden Struggles,* 31–32; Mare and Hamilton, *Appetite for Power,* 18–19; Boahen, *African Perspectives on Colonialism,* 58–65.

2. Quotations from Shula Marks: Marks, "Class, Ideology and the Bambatha Rebellion," 357–61, 367. Marks drew from scholarship on agrarian revolutions: Wolf, *Peasant Wars;* Eric Hobsbawm, "Class Consciousness in History," in *Aspects of History and Class Consciousness,* ed. Meszaros; Rude, *Ideology and Popular Protest;* Skocpol, *States and Revolutions.* Other period translations of *hlanya:* Roberts, *Zulu-Kafir Language,* which defines *ukuhlanya* as "insane," 160. In certain more modern dictionaries, like the *Scholar's Zulu Dictionary* by Dent and Nyembezi, *ukuhlanya* is a verb, to "become mad" or "behave insanely"; the noun *ubuhlanya* describes the state of "insanity" or "madness," 372. Numerous residents of the lower and middle Thukela basin report that *ukuhlanya, uhlanya,* and *ubuhlanya* refer to those people who are "crazy" or "full of roiling energy," sometimes "gasbags." One resident, Mchunu, who worked for a Jewish couple in Johannesburg more than two decades ago, compared *ukuhlanya* to the Yiddish word *meshuggener,* "a crazy and garrulous person": Mchunu, Makhabeleni, 24, 25 Dec. 1997, 27 April 1995, Interviews.

3. "About thirty years old": Marks, "Class, Ideology and the Bambatha's Rebellion," 361. "It is none of your business": Statement, Polomba, 25 June 1906, *Rex* v. *Sigananda,* 126, H. E. Colenso, Papers of Individuals/PT.

4. "Younger generation": Testimony, Mbovu, 16 Sept. 1904, file 41, notebooks, J. Stuart, Papers of Individuals (KCL)/PT. "To which group": Testimony, Mazibuko, July 1982, tape MAZS85, OHP, Tape Transcripts/PT. In 1906 Ndabaningi was about sixty years old.

5. "Hegemonic ideology": Marks, "Class, Ideology and the Bambatha Rebellion," 366. On Dinuzulu's rumored support, see chapter 5. On Zulu regiments killing women, see chapter 1. "Many knowledgeable men": Guy, *Destruction of the Zulu Kingdom,* 203–4.

6. "Revolutionary political party": Marks, "Class, Ideology and the Bambatha Rebellion, 366–67; Marks quotes "willing and able" from Skocpol, "What Makes Peasants Revolutionary?" Marks depicts the poll tax rebels as "peasants," although many spent more of their productive time working for wages on farms and in mines. In *Hidden Struggles,* Beinart and Bundy warn that "the use of the term 'peasantry' to characterize a rural population in this stage of the process of [proletarianization] is a useful shorthand, but not a precise analytical term," 29.

7. Study of British military tactics and changing notions of Kikuyu patriarchal power ("male genders") among Mau Mau fighters: Luise White, "Separating the Men from the Boys." British Carrier Corps and Kikuyu recruits seeking refuge: Kanogo, *Squatters and the Roots of Mau Mau,* 13–23. British colonial politics before World War I: Lonsdale and Berman, "Coping with the Contradictions."

8. Mau Mau rebels on cooperating with the British: White, "Separating the Men from the Boys." On social divisions among Mau Mau supporters: Berman and Lonsdale, *Unhappy Valley,* 363, 450–51; Maloba, *Mau Mau and Kenya,* 12–15. Historical overview: Furedi, *Mau Mau in Perspective;* Throup, "Origins of Mau Mau."

9. For mounting generational conflicts during black protests in the 1980s, see Carter, "We Are the Progressives"; Bundy, "Street Sociology and Pavement Politics." African youths as foot soldiers of the UDF: Debby Bonnin et al., "The Struggle for Natal and KwaZulu," in *Political Economy and Identities,* ed. Morrell.

10. Tetelman, "In Search of Discipline," 192. Studies exploring the autonomy of radical youths: Colin Bundy, "At War with the Future? Black South African Youth in the 1990s," in *South Africa: The Political Economy of Transformation,* ed. Stedman; Everatt and Sisulu, *Black Youth in Crisis;* Peter Delius, *Lion amongst the Cattle.*

11. In conversations with Inkatha Freedom Party members who denounced "people's courts" in Natal, I learned that the accusations of "sellout" or *amambuka,* were used interchangeably by ANC youths condemning Inkatha opponents: Mkhihle (Mpumalanga), Ntombela (Taylor's Halt) Bhengu (Taylor's Halt), 4 July 1991, Interviews. An analysis of "comrade" culture in Natal: Sitas, "Making of the 'Comrades' Movement." Civil war in Natal and KwaZulu: Kentridge, *Unofficial War.*

12. "Bulwark against radical change": Marks, "Patriotism, Patriarchy and Purity," 217. Origins of Inkatha in the early twentieth century: Cope, *To Bind the Nation;* Mare and Hamilton, *Appetite for Power.* Inkatha politics in the 1980s and links to the Pretoria regime: Colleen McCaul, "The Wild Card: Inkatha and Contemporary Black Politics," in *State, Resistance and Change in South Africa,* ed. Frankel et al. For speeches by Chief Minister Gatsha Buthelezi, showing Inkatha's strategy for an incremental, negotiated, and

nonviolent approach to dissolving apartheid, see Buthelezi Speeches, "Deed of Trust and Consitution," Inkatha Manuscripts/PT. "Older men . . . power of older men": Campbell, "Learning to Kill?" 621. Rogue security forces and vigilantes: *New York Times*, 28 April 1991; *Natal Witness*, 24 July 1991; *Star*, 19 July 1991; *Weekly Mail*, Aug. 2–8, 1991; Aitchison, ed., "The Seven Days War"; *Review of International Commission of Jurists*.

13. "Inter-generational tensions . . . bring them back": Campbell, "Learning to Kill?" 620–21. For UDF and ANC youths moving from home and establishing camps: *Weekly Mail*, 30 May to 6 June 1991, Newspapers. I also learned of the youth mobilization in conversations with UDF and ANC activists: Ngwenya, 5 July; Gasa, 6 July; Mkhize, 25 June; Mabasso, 23 June; Interviews, 1991. Another account of African generational struggles in the Natal civil war: Father T. Smith, "They Have Killed My Children," 6. In 1990 a senior ANC official in Natal acknowledged, in an internal ANC memorandum, that "the use of coercion and threats, especially by the youth to force people into political campaigns . . . alienate various sections of the oppressed." Radebe, "Frank and Critical Look," Unpublished Paper.

14. "To destroy . . . power to children: Mfayela, Durban, 22 June 1991, Interviews. Other Inkatha members expressed similar sentiments about recalcitrant ANC youths: Dladla (Inkatha Women's Brigade leader, Table Mountain, Natal, 4 July 1991) and Mkhihle (Inkatha official, Mpumalanga, Natal, 4 July 1991), Interviews.

Glossary

abafokazana: Marginal or poor people; (adult) weaklings.

abashokobezi: The people who wear the *ubushokobezi,* the oxtail badge.

abasha: The new generation.

amabele: Sorghum beer.

amabhinca: African subsistence producer; homestead dweller who only worships ancestral spirits.

amabutho: Military regiments, usually organized by age.

amadlozi: Ancestral spirits.

amadoda: Older men; married men (singular, *indoda*).

amakhehla: "Headringed" men of senior rank.

amakholwa: African Christian converts; "believers" (singular, *ikholwa*).

amalala: Lineage classification of second-class subjects in the Zulu kingdom.

amambuka: Traitors; Africans who "hobnobbed" with and received their authority from whites.

amantungwa: Lineage classification of elite subjects in the Zulu kingdom.

amaviyo: Fighting bands; regimental formations.

askari: African conscripts who served in colonial armies in East Africa; *askari* is now a slur meaning "traitor."

emathanjeni: "Place of the bones."

ibandla: A chief's council of male elders.

imikhovu: Shadowy, ghostlike spirits; mysterious dwarves who haunt forests.

imizi: Homesteads (singular, *umuzi*).

indaba: A large meeting; an affair (the plural, *izindaba,* means news).

indlu: A hut.

inGobamakhosi: The name of a particular army regiment under the command of King Cetshwayo.

inkosana: Son; male heir by main or first-ranking wife.

inkosi: Chief.

intelezi: Protective medicine or charm.

isibhalo: System of compulsory labor for the Natal Colony.

isibongo: Lineage or clan name.

isibuko sikababa: A projected image of the patriarch and his paternal ancestry (the modern phrase is *isithombe sikababa*).

isigodlo: Part of the royal Zulu enclosure reserved for the king's women.

isirobo: Female whore; a wayward girl who engages in premarital sex.

isishimeyane: Highly intoxicating liquor.

isizwe: Chiefdom; country.

izinduna: Headmen or political representatives of chiefs (singular, *induna*).

izinsizwa: Young men (singular, *insizwa*).

laager: A fortified defensive circle of makeshift barriers or wagons.

mfecane: The violent "crushing" of people (identified with the rise of Shaka and the Zulu to power).

ubushokobezi: A bushy cow-tail badge, usually white, worn on the head or neck by Zulu soldiers.

ukugiya: To dance in an aggressive fashion, mirroring warlike movements.

ukuhlanya: To be crazy; insane.

ukuhlobonga: A form of coitus interruptus (also called *ukusoma*).

ukuhlonipha: To practice rituals of "avoidance"; a highly respectful form of personal presentation; a deferential tone of isiZulu language.

ukukhonza: To give allegiance and tribute to a chief.

ukulobola: To give bridewealth cattle (*ilobolo*) for a bride; Thukela valley residents use *ukulobola* as a verb and noun.

ukungena: To "raise seed" (procreate with) a widow; a man who "entered" into the homestead of his deceased brother to impregnate his deceased brother's wife.

ukuphindisela: To retaliate; exact revenge; take back.

umhlola: A portent or omen.

umkhosi: An annual "first-fruits" festival exalting duty and loyalty to the Zulu royal house; the *umkhosi* festival was held in December or January around the royal Zulu enclosure; a prominent chief with a large following also organized an *umkhosi* to celebrate his rule.

umlingo: Magic.

umntwana: Child; prince; male member of the royal family.

umnumzana(e): A homestead head.

uSuthu: Cetshwayo's faction; also name of Dinuzulu's faction; a war cry.

uThulwana: The name of a particular army regiment under the command of Zulu kings Mpande and Cetshwayo.

voortrekkers: Dutch Cape emigrants who promulgated the Great Trek in the mid-1830s.

Bibliography

For a full explanation of abbreviations of principal sources, archival locations, document titles, and publication titles, see the notes (p.143). The numbers in parentheses in the entries that follow refer to the call number for each set of documents. The works in the bibliography are listed in the following order:

Government Records (GR)
Interviews by Author: Natal and KwaZulu, 1991–95, 1997
Newspapers
Papers and Transcripts (PT): Organizations and Individuals
Photographs
Published Articles, Books, and Pamphlets
Unpublished Dissertations, Theses, and Papers

Government Records (GR)

Unless otherwise noted, entries correspond to Natal colonial offices in NAP.

Attorney General's Office (AGO): Special Courts Zulu Rebellion, 1908–9 (1/7/51-80, 1/8/103-124, 1/9/30-35, 1/9/39-42, 2/1/8-10).

Blue Books (BB):
    Natal: 1879–83 (7/1/27-31); 1884–93 (7/2/1/1-9); 1901-3 (7/3/8-10); Departmental Reports, 1893–1900 (7/4/1-7); 1901–8 (8/2/1-9); Supplemental, Departmental Reports, 1884-93 (7/2/2/1-9).
    Zululand: 1889–97 (ZGH 848-856; 1896, microfilmed, ZGH 1/1/2/5/1).

British Parliamentary Papers (BPP): 1888–92 (vols. 3, 27, 40, 93, 95, 101, 107–9, 111).

Census of 1891; Census of the Colony of Natal, April 1904.

"Code of Native Law as at Present (1876–8) Administered."

Colonial Secretary's Office (CSO):
  Natal: Returns "Native Assault and Faction Fighting Cases. Miscellaneous
    Records": 1897, 1904–7 (vols. 1528, 1714, 1769, 1793, 1804–11, 1817–20).
  Transvaal: Correspondence, 1902 (213, TAP).

Commissioner:
  Chief Native, of Natal: Papers 1911–12 (1-53).
  Mines, of Transvaal: Minutes, 1906 (118, TAP).
  Resident, of Zululand: Confidential Correspondence, 1892–96 (ZA 28–35); Cor-
    respondence, "Divorce & Lobola, 1890–96" (ZA 15); Despatches Received
    from Lieutenant Governor, Natal, 1891–95 (ZA 13); Diary, 1895–96 (ZA 46);
    Letters Despatched, 1892–96 (ZA 44–45).

Commissions (COM):
  Land: Evidence given before the Land Commission, 1903.
  Mining: Regulations, 1907–10, 6 vols. (TAP).
  Native Affairs (by chronology): Commission to Inquire into the Past and
    Present State of the Kafirs in the District of Natal, . . . 1852; Evidence taken
    before the Natal Native Commission, 1881(–2) (8/3/20); Natal Native Com-
    mission, 1881–2, Evidence taken before the Sub-Commission Umvoti
    County (8/3/21); South African Native Affairs Commission, 1903–5, 5 vols.
    (SNA 1/521); Evidence, Native Affairs Commission, 1906–7 (8/3/76).

Government House (GH):
  Natal: Memoranda, Natal Natives, April 1902–May 1910 (1547–52); Military
    Affairs, Bambata Rebellion, 1906–9 (1457–90); Minute Papers (MinP),
    1893–1910 (1032–43); Memoranda, Natal Natives Zululand, 1897–1909
    (1562).

Government Native Labour Bureau (GNLB): Minutes (Min,), 1907–9 (1–5, 436, 18,
  TAP).

Legislative Council: Sessions 1872, 1879–80 (1/1/1/1/18, 26–27); Sessional Papers,
  1879–82 (4/1/2/8-11).

Lieutenant Governor (LTG):
  Natal: Despatches Received, 1891–95 (ZA in NAP; 13).
  Transvaal: Minutes (Min.), 1906, (113, TAP).

Magistrates' Records (MR) (by division [i.e., district] and by town, if appropriate):
Entonjaneni Division and Melmoth Court: Civil Record Books, Native Law, 1887–1910 (2/2/1/2/1-2); Letter Books, 1890–1903 3/1/1/1/3-7); Minute Papers (MinP), 1892–1904 (3/2/6-10); Melmoth Criminal Record Books, Native Law, 1887–1912 (1/2/1/2/1-4).
Eshowe Division and Umlalazi: Civil Record Books, 1903–13 (1/2/1/2/1); Civil Record Books, Native Cases, 1892–1920 (2/2/1/2/3-5); Criminal Record Books, 1888–1912 (1/2/1/1/1/1-6); Interdicts, 1899–1918 (2/7/1); Letter Books, 1892–1911 (3/1/3-8); Martial Law Note Book, 1906 (1/4/1/1); Minute Papers (MinP), 1887–1906 (3/2/1-5); Records of Cases Martial Law, 1906 (1/4/2/1); Records of Native Proceedings, 1903–31 (2/1/1/2/1).
Impendhle Division: Minute Papers (MinP), 1890–1906 (4/1/1-6).
Ipolela Division: Minute Papers (MinP), 1894–1901 (3/1/1).
Kranskop (Krantzkop) Division: Administrator of Native Law Tugela Valley, Minute Papers (MinP), 1890–94; Cases Adjudicated, Martial Law, 1906–8 (1/4/1/1); Civil Native Proceedings, 1888–1915 (2/1/1/2/1-2); Criminal Record Books, 1901–4 (1/2/1/2-4); Criminal Record Books, 1900–1910 (1/2/2/1-5); Minute Papers (MinP), 1894–1910 (3/1/1-11); Native Civil Record Book, 1902–13 (2/2/1/2/1).
Lower Tugela Division and Stanger Court: Administrator Native Law, Criminal Record Books, 1892–99 (1/2/2/1); Branch Courts Notebooks, 1889–1912 (A1/1/5-18); Land Sales Register, 1893–1924 (6/2/1); Martial Law Cases, 1906 (1/2/1/3/1); Martial Law Note Books, 1906 (1/4/2/1-5); Minute Papers (MinP), 1891–1904, 1908 (4/1/4-8); Native Civil Record Books, 1905–15 (2/2/1/2/1); Native Proceedings, 1904–25 (2/1/1/2/1); Register of Divorce Law 1/1869, 1870–1919 (7/3/1/1); Return of Registers, Ukungena, 1873–99 (7/2/2/1); Stanger Court Depositions, 1893–1905 (1/5/1/3-8); Stanger Native Criminal Record Books, 1900–1912 (1/2/1/2/1-4).
Mahlabathini Division: Administrator of Native Law Criminal Record Books, 1898–1910 (1/2/1/1-2); Civil Record Books, 1898–1922 (2/2/1/2/1-2); Depositions, 1898–1903 (1/4/1); Minute Papers (MinP), 1901–13, (3/2/2-3).
Mapumulo Division: Administrator of Native Law, Civil Record Books, 1890–99 (2/2/2/1-2); Administrator of Native Law, Proceedings, 1896–99 (2/1/2/5-7); Criminal Record Book, Martial Law, 1906 (1/2/1/3/1); Matrimonial Matters, Register of Divorces, 1901–14 (4/1/1); Martial Law, Miscellaneous Report, 1906 Zulu Rebellion (5/4); Martial Law Note Books, 1906 (1/4/1/1-4); Native Civil Cases, Annexures, 1894–96 (2/1/2/1-4); Native Civil Cases Proceedings, 1899–1900, and Annexures, 1900–1902 (2/1/1/2/1-5);

Native Civil Record Books, 1899–1922 (2/2/1/2/1-2); Native Rebellion Intelligence Book, Natal Mounted Police, 1906 (1/1/1); Ukungena Register, 1894–97 (5/1).

Nkandla Division: Civil Cases, 1890–1902 (2/1/1/1/1); Civil Note Book, 1902 (2/5/1); Civil Record Books and Civil Cases Adjudicated, 1894–1918 (2/2/1/1/3-5); Confidential Letter Book (3/1/1); Criminal Cases Adjudicated, 1892–1910 (1/2/1/3-9); Criminal Note Book, Martial Law (1/5/1/1-2); Minute Papers (MinP), 1895–1912 (3/2/1/1-2); Minute Papers MinP), Confidential, 1907–13 (3/2/2/1); Rebellion Notes, 1906 (7/2).

Nquthu Division: Cases Adjudicated, Native Civil Record Books, 1887–1924 (2/2/1/2/1-4); Civil Records, Proceedings Native, 1903–27 (2/1/1/2/1); Compensation Board, Native Claims 1-247 European and Native, 1906, (3/1-3); Criminal Record Books, March 1891–Nov. 1910 (1/2/1/1/2-7); Depositions, 1888–1901 (1/4/1/1); Martial Law Note Books, June 1906–Oct. 1906 (1/5/1/1-2); Minute Papers (MinP), 1892–1906, 3/3/4-12.

Umsinga Division: Criminal Record Books, 1900–1910 (2-3); Minute Papers (MinP), 1899–1908 (28–33); Native Civil Record Book, 1904–1910 (14); Native Criminal Record Books, 1906–10 (4-5, 11, 11A); Native Record of Proceedings, 1906–10 (13); Records, Proceedings, 1901–9.

Umvoti Division and Greytown Court: Cases, Martial Law Greytown, May 1906–Sept. 1906 (1/3/2/1); Depositions, 1889–1903 (1/4/413); Minute Papers (MinP), 1890–1909 (3/2/5-9); Native Records of Proceedings, 1899–1909 (2/1/1/2/1-18); Quitrent Land Records, 1879–95 (4/1/1).

Upper Tugela Division: Minute Papers (MinP), 1898–1902 (4/1/1-3).

Weenen: Martial Law Notebooks, 1906 (1/4/2/1-2); Minute Papers (MinP), 1890–1908 (3/2/1-5); Native Civil Record Book, 1905–18 (2/2/1/2/1); Native Criminal Note Book, 1896–1900 (1/4/1/2); Native Criminal Record Books (1/2/2/1-5).

Prime Minister (PM): Papers, 1904–7 (48–62, 101–4).

Proceedings: High Treason Trial of Dinuzulu, 1908–9 (8/5/142).

Reports: Zululand-Lands Delimitation Commission, 1902–4 (8/3/65); Forestry in Natal and Zululand, 1902 (8/5/95); First Geological Survey Natal and Zululand, 1901 (8/5/73); Second Geological Survey Natal and Zululand, 1905 (8/5/117); Report of the Lands Commission, Feb. 1902; Report of the Natal Native Commission, 1881–82 (8/3/19); Report of the Native Affairs Commission, 1906–7 (8/3/75); Report on the Native Mission Reserves.

Rules: Magistrates 1902, 1906, 1910 (8/4/47, 60, 70); Regulating Practice and Proceedings Native Cases, 1903 (8/4/47).

Secretary for Native Affairs (SNA):
  Natal: "Brief Sketch of Zulu History and Each Tribe in the Province of Zululand," 1903 (1/9/6-7); Confidential Papers, 1890–1910 (1/4/4-22); Confidential Letters, 1885–1911 (1/8/10A); Correspondence re: Protests and Written Evidence (1913 Land Act), 1917–18 (2/5/4-5); Delimitation of Boundaries of Reserves, Zululand, 1902–4, nos. 1–16 (1/9/7); Minutes of Interviews with Native Chiefs, 1914–25 (1/9/4-5); Minute Papers (MinP), 1892–1915 (1/1/156-481); Native Rebellion Court Martial Proceedings (1/6/26-30); Statistics, Schedules of Farms, etc. 1917–18 (2/5/6).
  Transvaal (TAP): Confidential Minutes, 1906–9 (SNAC 532–39); Minutes (Min.), 1902–3, 1906–7, 1910 (vols. 24, 102, 392, 402–17, 460).

Year Books (YB): Natal Statistical, 1894–1909 (7/3/1-16).

Zululand Government House (ZGH): Correspondence, 1892–98 (vols. 747–79); Annexation, 1897 (vol. 785).

Interviews by Author: Natal and KwaZulu, 1991–95, 1997

1991: A. Bhengu, Taylor's Halt, Mafunze, 4 July; M. Cele, Makhabeleni, Kranskop, 31 July; S. Cube, Makhabeleni, 31 July; P. Dladla, Magqongqo, Table Mountain, 4, 14 July; M. Gasa, Imbali, Pietermaritzburg, 6 July; V. Mabaso, Sweetwaters, Pietermaritzburg, 23 June; S. Mchunu, Makhabeleni, 29, 30 July; S. Mkhihle, Mpumalanga, 4 July; S. Mfayela, Durban, 22 June; R. Mkhize, Sweetwaters, 25 June; S. Ngwenya, Imbali, 5 July; D. Ntombela, Taylor's Halt, 4, 13 July; F. Nzama, Jameson's Drift, Nkandla, 30 July.

1992: Cube (Shezi), Nkandla, 21 Nov.; M. Dube, Thukela River Mouth, Eshowe, 17–19 Sept.; Chief D. Dunn, Gingindhlovu, Eshowe, 18 Sept.; P. Gasa, Makhabeleni, 20 Nov., 14 Dec.; S. Mchunu, Makhabeleni, 19 Nov., 13, 15 Dec.; S. Ntuli, Nkandla, 17 Dec.; R. Nxumalo, Makhabeleni, 19 Nov.; D. Sibisi, Mtunzini, Eshowe, 19, 20 Sept.

1993: Cube (Shezi), Nkandla, 14, 16 Feb.; P. Gasa, Makhabeleni, 24 Jan., 4, 5 April; S. Mchunu, Makhabeleni, 23 Jan., 4, 26 April; S. Ntuli, Nkandla, 20 Feb.; R. Nxumalo, Makhabeleni, 13, 27 April, 1 May; F. Nzama, Jameson's Drift, 24 Jan., 15 March

1994: P. Khumalo, Nkandla, 27 July; S. Mchunu, Makhabeleni, 28 July.

1995: F. Nzama, Jameson's Drift, 27 April.

1997: S. Mchunu, Makhabeleni, 24, 26 Dec.; M. Cele, Makhabeleni, 24 Dec.; F. Nzama, Jameson's Drift, 26 Dec.; Chief Dhlomo, Makhabelini, 24 Dec.

Newspapers

Unless otherwise noted, the following newspapers were located in the Natal Society Library.

Historical Periodicals
    Greytown Gazette, 1903–10
    Ikwezi, 1904–10
    Ilanga Lase Natal, 1903–10
    Natal Advertiser, 1890–1910
    Natal Mercury, 1892–1910
    Natal Witness, 1890–1910
    Net, 1890–1910 (WCL, the Church of the Province of South Africa (CPSA), 5692NZ4)
    Times of Natal, 1893–1910

More Recent Periodicals
    Natal Monitor, 1991
    Natal Witness, May–July 1991, April 1992–Aug. 1993
    New York Times, 28 April 1991
    Weekly Mail, May–Aug. 1991, April 1992–Aug. 1993

Papers and Transcripts (PT): Organizations and Individuals

American Board Mission
    Killie Campbell Library (KCL): Inanda Seminary Papers, 1885–93, 1901–6; Umzumbe Home, Attendance Registers.
    Natal Archives, Pietermaritzburg (NAP): Annual Letters, 1835–1948 (3/46-47); Annual Reports, 1898–1903, 1905–20 (3/42); Biographical Sketches (4/58-61); Committee Reports and Minute Books, 1847–1906 (1/7-9); General Letters and Documents Received, 1835–1920 (2/10-11); Letters and Documents from Government Officials, 1838–1910 (2/22-24); Letters between Missionaries, 1835–1920, (2/27-30); Letters from the Board, 1899–1910 (2/18); Minutes

(Min.), 1883–1912 (1/1-4); Miscellaneous Letters and Reports, 1835–1962 (3/34-41, 49-50); Newspaper Clippings, 1881–1912 (4/56-57); Papers Relating to the Rebellion, 1906–7 (5/65); Records of Imfume (1886–1905), Adams (1844–1904), and Umzumbe (1860–96) Churches (4/55).

Yale School of Divinity: Letters, Goodenough to Taylor, 26–27, microfilm 200–201; Reports of the American Board, 94–95, 1905–9; Reports of the American Board, 100–104, 1910–14; *South African Deputation Papers*, 1904; Southern African Women's Board of Missions, 1900–1908, 3, microfilm 222; Southern African Zulu Mission Documents and Letters, 1890–99, 13–14, microfilm 188–89; South African Zulu Mission Documents and Letters, 1909–28, 48, microfilm 211.

Church of the Province of South Africa (WCL): Zululand Mission Reports 1892–1912 (CPSA 5692NZ4).

Inkatha Manuscripts (WCL): Miscellaneous (A9573E); Buthelezi, M. G., Speeches (A1045).

Papers of Individuals:
Killie Campbell Library (KCL): Archibald Family; S. B. Bourquin; A. T. Bryant; B. Colenbrander: Bambata Rebellion; G. V. Essery; H. C. Lugg; Marwick; J. Stuart Notebooks.
Natal Archives, Pietermaritzburg (NAP): Colenso, H. E. (14, 29–33, 73–76, 101–4, 111–26; 204); Faye, C. (131); Gerbers, W. F. (464); Shepstone, J. W. (66); Titlestad, E. (1690); Wood, A. A. (1474).

Tape Transcripts (KCL): Oral History Project Relating to the Zulu People (OHP), 1979–82: Gasa, M., 15 Feb., 16 Oct. 1981, tapes GB 30 and MAB2; Makathini, K. S., 24 Oct. 1981, tape 444; Mazibuko, M., July 1982, tape MAZS 85; Mthembu, M., 17 Oct. 1981, tape 143; Radebe, 1981, tape 197; Sibisi, H., 13 March 1979, tape 207; Zondi, n.d., tape 230.

Photographs

Killie Campbell Library (KCL): Bambatha Rebellion, 1906 (1-2, 968.4); Albums of Zulu Customs (2-3, 572.9683).

KwaMuhle Local History: "Indaba Held at Greytown by Mr. J. W. Cross to Explain to Bambatha and Other Chiefs the Details of the Tax, c. Dec. 1905" (575.57); "Surrender and Trial of Dinuzulu, 1907" (575.577); "Zulu Rebellion 1906 (Bambatha), c. 1905" (575.57); "Country Districts: Zululand" (473.8); "General Views of Natal" (473.9); "Buildings: Historic and Common in Zululand" (621.12-13).

Natal Archives, Pietermaritzburg (NAP): African culture, c. 1890s and early 1900s: C167/1, C599, C714, C747, C748, C757, C763, C771, C4730, C4731, C4741, C690, C1395, C260. Poll tax revolt, c. 1906–9: C231, C631/1, C3534/42, C3534/47, C3534/15, C3534/25, C3534/29, C566, C629, C727, C3534/52, C569, C634, C3534/39, C562, C601, C607, C744. (The photographs in this book are from the above collection; other collections that I examined were less readily accessible to copy).

Natal Museum: Barry, R. J., Bambatha Rebellion: "Young Women Surrender at Cetshwayo Grave," 8; "'Headringed' African Levies," 9, 19, 29; Francis, C.: Bambatha's Rebellion and Trials of Rebels at Stanger (H74.861a); Ogilvie Collection: Bambatha Rebellion (H74.939).

Published Articles, Books, and Pamphlets (Abridged Listing)

Aguilar, Mario, ed. *The Politics of Age and Gerontocracy*. Trenton NJ, 1998.

Akyeampong, Emmanuel. *Drink, Power and Cultural Change: A Social History of Alcohol in Ghana, c. 1880 to Recent Times*. Portsmouth NH, 1996.

Aitchison, John, ed. "The Seven Days War: 25–31 March 1990, The Victims' Narrative." Pietermaritzburg: Centre for Adult Education, University of Natal, 1991.

Atkins, Keletso. *The Moon Is Dead! Give Us Our Money*. Portsmouth NH, 1994.

Ballard, Charles. *John Dunn: The White Chief of Zululand*. Johannesburg, 1985.

———. "Natal, 1824–44: The Frontier Interregnum." *JNZH* 5 (1982): 49–64.

———. "A Year of Scarcity: The 1896 Locust Plague in Natal and Zululand." *SAHJ* 15 (1983): 34–52.

Becker, Peter. *Rule of Fear*. London, 1964.

Beinart, William. "Joyini Inkomo: Cattle Advances and the Origins of Migrancy from Pondoland." *JSAS* 5 (1979): 199–219.

———. "The Origins of the *Indlavini*: Male Associations and Migrant Labour in the Transkei." *African Studies* 50, no. 1/2 (1991): 103–28.

———. "Political and Collective Violence in Southern African Historiography." *JSAS* 18, no. 3 (1992): 455–86.

———. *The Political Economy of Pondoland, 1860–1930*. Cambridge GB, 1982.

Beinart, William, and Colin Bundy. *Hidden Struggles in Rural South Africa*. Berkeley CA, 1987.

Beinart, William, Peter Delius, and Stanley Trapido, eds. *Putting a Plough to the Ground*. Johannesburg, 1986.

Berglund, Axel-Ivar. *Zulu Thought-Patterns and Symbolism*. Bloomington IN, 1976.

Berman, B., and J. Lonsdale. *Unhappy Valley: Conflict in Kenya and Africa*. London, 1992.

Berry, Sara. *Fathers Work for Their Sons: Accumulation, Mobility and Class Formation in an Extended Yoruba Community*. Berkeley CA, 1985.

———. *No Condition Is Permanent: The Social Dynamics of Agrarian Change in Sub-Saharan Africa*. Madison WI, 1993.

Binns, C. *Dinuzulu: The Death of the House of Shaka*. London, 1968.

Bird, J. *The Annals of Natal: 1495 to 1845*. 2 vols. Cape Town, 1888.

Boahen, A. Adu. *African Perspectives on Colonialism*. Baltimore, 1987.

Bonner, Phillip. *Kings, Commoners and Concessionaires: The Evolution and Dissolution of the Nineteenth-Century Swazi State*. Cambridge GB, 1983.

———, ed. *Working Papers in Southern African Studies*. Vol. 2. Johannesburg, 1981.

Bonner, Phillip, et al., eds. *Holding Their Ground: Locality and Culture in 19th and 20th Century South Africa*. Johannesburg, 1989.

Booth, A., ed. *Journal of the Reverend George Champion*. Cape Town, 1967.

Bosman, W. *The Natal Rebellion of 1906*. London, 1907.

Bourquin, S. B., ed. *Paula Dlamini: Servant of Two Kings*. Pietermaritzburg, 1986.

Bozzoli, Belinda. "Marxism, Feminism and South African Studies." *JSAS* 9, no. 2 (1983): 139–71.

———, ed. *Class, Community and Conflict: South African Perspectives*. Johannesburg, 1987.

Bozzoli, Belinda, and Peter Delius. "Radical History and South African Society." *RHR* 46, no. 7 (1990): 13–45.

Bradford, Helen. *A Taste of Freedom: The ICU in Rural South Africa, 1924–1930*. New Haven, 1987.

Brookes, Edgar. *The History of Native Policy in South Africa, 1830 to the Present Day*. Cape Town, 1924.

Brookes, Edgar, and Colin de B. Webb. *A History of Natal*. Pietermaritzburg, 1965.

Bryant, A. T. *A History of the Zulu and Neighbouring Tribes*. Cape Town, 1964.

———. *Olden Times in Zululand and Natal*. London, 1929.

———. *A Zulu-English Dictionary*. Mariannhill, 1905.

———. *The Zulu People As They Were Before the White Man Came*. Pietermaritzburg, 1949.

Bundy, Colin. *The Rise and Fall of the South African Peasantry*. London, 1979.

———. "Street Sociology and Pavement Politics: Aspects of Youth and Student Resistance in Cape Town, 1985." *JSAS* 13, no. 3 (1987): 303–30.

Campbell, Catherine. "Learning to Kill? Masculinity, the Family and Violence in Natal." *JSAS* 18, no. 3 (1992): 614–28.

Carter, Charles. "'We Are the Progressives': Alexandra Youth Congress Activists and the Freedom Charter, 1983–85." *JSAS* 17, no. 2 (1991): 197–220.

Chanock, Martin. *Law, Custom and Social Order: The Colonial Experience in Malawi and Zambia*. Cambridge GB, 1985.

———. "Writing South African Legal History: A Prospectus." *JAH* 30, no. 2 (1989): 265–88.

Cobbett, W., and R. Cohen, eds. *Popular Struggles in South Africa*. London, 1988.

Cobbing, Julian. "The Mfecane as Alibi: Thoughts on Dithakong and Mbolombo." *JAH* 29 (1988): 487–519.

———. "A Tainted Well: The Objectives, Historical Fantasies, and Working Methods of James Stuart, with Counter-argument." *JNZH* 2 (1988): 115–54.

Colenso, Harriet. *England and the Zulus*. London, 1890.

Colenso, John, and Harriet Colenso. *Zulu-English Dictionary*. Pietermaritzburg, 1905.

Comaroff, J., and J. L. Comaroff. *Ethnography and the Historical Imagination*. Boulder CO, 1992.

Cooper, Fred. "Conflict and Connection: Rethinking Colonial African History." *American Historical Review* 95, no. 4 (1994): 1516–45.

———, ed. *The Struggle for the City*. Beverly Hills CA, 1983.

Cope, Nicholas. *To Bind a Nation: Solomon kaDinuzulu and Zulu Nationalism, 1913–1933*. Pietermaritzburg, 1993.

Cope, Richard. "Political Power within the Zulu Kingdom and the 'Coronation Laws' of 1873." *JNZH* 8 (1985): 11–31.

Cope, Trevor, ed. *Izibongo Zulu Praise Poems*. Oxford, 1968.

Coplan, David. *In the Time of Cannibals: The Word Music of South Africa's Basotho Migrants*. Chicago, 1995.

Crummey, Donald, ed. *Banditry, Rebellion and Social Protest in Africa*. Portsmouth NH, 1986.

De Kiewet, C. W. *The Imperial Factor in South Africa*. Cambridge GB, 1937.

Delius, Peter. *The Land Belongs to Us: The Pedi Polity, the Boers and the British in the Nineteenth-Century Transvaal*. Johannesburg, 1983.

———. *A Lion amongst the Cattle: Reconstruction and Resistance in the Northern Transvaal*. Johannesburg, 1996.

Dent, G., and C. Nyembezi. *Scholar's Zulu Dictionary*. Pietermaritzburg, 1969.

Doke, C., and B. Vilakazi. *Zulu-English Dictionary*. Johannesburg, 1948.

Dominy, Graham. "The New Republicans: A Centennial Reappraisal of the 'Nieuwe Republiek,' 1884–1888." *Natalia* 14 (1984): 87–97.

Dube, John. *The Zulu Appeal for Light*. London, 1909.

Duminy, Andrew, and Charles Ballard, eds. *The Anglo-Zulu War: New Perspectives*. Pietermaritzburg, 1981.

Duminy, Andrew, and Bill Guest, eds. *Natal and Zululand: From Earliest Times to 1910*. Pietermaritzburg, 1989.

Edgecombe, D., et al., eds. *The Debate on Zulu Origins: A Selection of Papers on the Zulu Kingdom and Early Colonial Natal*. Pietermaritzburg, 1992.

Eldredge, Elizabeth. "Sources of Conflict in Southern Africa, c. 1800–1830: The 'Mfecane' Reconsidered." *JAH* 33 (1992): 1–35.

———. *A South African Kingdom: The Pursuit of Security in Nineteenth-Century Lesotho*. Cambridge GB, 1993.

Eldredge, Elizabeth, and Fred Morton, eds. *Slavery in South Africa: Captive Labor on the Dutch Frontier*. Madison WI, 1994.

Elphick, Richard, and Hermann Giliomee, eds. *The Shaping of South African Society*. Cape Town, 1989.

Etherington, Norman."The Great Trek in Relation to the Mfecane: A Reassessment." *SAHJ* 25 (1991): 3–21.

———. *Preachers, Peasants and Politics in South East Africa, 1835–1880: African Christian Communities in Natal, Pondoland and Zululand*. London, 1978.

———. "Why Langalibalele Ran Away." *JNZH* 1 (1978): 1–24.

Everatt, D., and E. Sisulu, eds. *Black Youth in Crisis*. Johannesburg, 1992.

Feierman, Steven. *Peasant Intellectuals: Anthropology and History in Tanzania*. Madison WI, 1990.

Ferguson, James. "The Cultural Topography of Wealth: Commodity Paths and the Structure of Wealth in Rural Lesotho." *American Anthropologist* 94 (1992): 55–73.

Frankel, P., et al., eds. *State, Resistance and Change in South Africa*. Johannesburg, 1988.

Freund, Bill. *Insiders and Outsiders: The Indian Working Class of Durban, 1910–90*. Pietermaritzburg, 1994.

———. *The Making of Contemporary Africa*. London, 1984.

Furedi, Frank. *The Mau Mau in Perspective*. London, 1989.

Galbraith, J. *Reluctant Empire: British Policy on the South African Frontier, 1834–1854*. Berkeley CA, 1963.

Geary, Christaud. "Photographs as Material for African History: Some Methodological Considerations." *History in Africa* 13 (1986): 89–116.

Gibson, J. *The Story of the Zulus*. London, 1911.

Glassman, Jonathon. *Feasts and Riot: Revelry, Rebellion, and Popular Consciousness on the Swahili Coast, 1856–1888*. Portsmouth NH, 1995.

Gluckman, Max. *Custom and Conflict in Africa*. Oxford, 1955.

———. *Order and Rebellion in Tribal Africa*. London, 1963.

———. "The Rise of the Zulu Empire." *Scientific American* 202, no. 4 (1969): 157–68.

———. *Rituals of Rebellion in South-East Africa*. Manchester GB, 1954.

Golan, Daphna. "The Life Story of Shaka and Gender Tensions in the Zulu State." *History in Africa* 17 (1990): 95–111.

Goody, Jack, ed. *The Character of Kinship*. Cambridge GB, 1973.

——, ed. *The Developmental Cycle in Domestic Groups*. Cambridge GB, 1958.

——, ed., *Production and Reproduction: A Comparative Study of the Domestic Domain*. Cambridge GB, 1976.

Greenfield, Haskel, et al. "Preliminary Results of the 1995 Research at the Early Iron Age Site of Ndondondwane, KwaZulu-Natal, South Africa." *Nyame Akuma* 47 (1997): 42–52.

Grout, L. *Zululand: Or, Life among the Zulu-Kafirs of Natal and Zululand*. London, 1863.

Guest, Bill. *Langalibalele: The Crisis in Natal, 1873–75*. Durban, 1976.

Guest, Bill, and J. Sellers, eds. *Enterprise and Exploitation in a Victorian Colony: Aspects of the Economic and Social History of Colonial Natal*. Pietermaritzburg, 1985.

Gump, James. "Ecological Change and Pre-Shakan State Formation." *African Economic History* 18 (1989): 57–71.

Gunner, Elizabeth. "Songs of Innocence and Experience: Women as Composers and Performers of *Izibongo*, Zulu Praise Poetry." *Research in African Literatures* 10, no. 2 (1979): 239–67.

Gunner, Elizabeth, and M. Gwala. *Musho! Zulu Popular Praises*. East Lansing, 1991.

Guy, Jeff. "Analysing Pre-Capitalist Societies in Southern Africa." *JSAS* 14, no. 1 (1987): 18–37.

——. *The Destruction of the Zulu Kingdom*. London, 1979.

——. "Gender Oppression in Southern Africa's Precapitalist Societies." In *Women and Gender in Southern Africa to 1945*, edited by Cherryl Walker. Cape Town, 1990.

——. *The Heretic: A Study of the Life of John William Colenso*. Johannesburg, 1983.

——. "A Note on Firearms in the Zulu Kingdom, with Special Reference to the Anglo-Zulu War, 1879." *JAH* 12 (1971): 557–70.

——. "Production and Exchange in the Zulu Kingdom." *Mohlomi: JSAS* 2 (1978): 96–106.

Guyer, Jane. "Household and Community in African Studies." *African Studies Review* 24, no. 2/3 (1981): 86–137.

——. "Wealth in People, Wealth in Things—Introduction." *JAH* 36 (1995): 83–90.

Hall, Martin. "Archaeology and Modes of Production in Precolonial Southern Africa." *JSAS* 14 (1987): 1–17.

——. "Dendroclimatology, Rainfall and Human Adaptation in the Later Iron Age of Natal and Zululand." *Annals* 22 (1976): 693–703.

——. "Enkwazini, an Iron Age Site on the Zululand Coast." *Annals* 24 (1980): 97–110.

——. "The Myth of the Zulu Homestead: Archaeology and Ethnography." *Africa* 54, no. 1 (1984): 65–80.

Hamilton, Carolyn. *Terrific Majesty: The Powers of Shaka Zulu and the Limits of Historical Invention*. Cape Town, 1998.

——. "'The Character and Objects of Chaka': A Reconsideration of the Making of Shaka as 'Mfecane' Motor." *JAH* 33 (1992): 37–63.

Hamilton, Carolyn, ed. *The Mfecane Aftermath: Reconstructive Debates in Southern African History*. Johannesburg, 1995.

Hamilton, Carolyn, and John Wright. "The Making of the *Amalala*: Ethnicity, Ideology and Relations of Subordination in a Precolonial Context." *SAHJ* 22 (1990): 3–23.

Hammond-Tooke, W. D. "Descent Groups, Chiefdoms and South African Historiography." *JSAS* 11 (1985): 305–19.

——. "In Search of the Lineage: The Cape Nguni Case." *Man* 19 (1984): 77–93.

Harms, Robert. "Oral Tradition and Ethnicity." *Journal of Interdisciplinary History* 10, no. 1 (1979): 61–85.

Harms, Robert, et al., eds. *Paths toward the Past*. Atlanta, 1994.

Harries, Patrick. "Plantations, Passes, and Proletarians: Labour and the Colonial State in Nineteenth-Century Natal." *JSAS* 13, no. 3 (1978): 372–99.

——. "The Roots of Ethnicity: Discourse and the Politics of Language Construction in South-east Africa." *African Affairs* 87, no. 346 (1988): 25–52.

——. "Slavery, Social Incorporation and Surplus Extraction: The Nature of Free and Unfree Labour in South-east Africa." *JAH* 22 (1981): 309–30.

——. "Symbols and Sexuality: Culture and Identity on the Early Witwatersrand Gold Mines." *Gender and History* 2, no. 3 (1990): 318–36.

——. *Work, Culture and Identity: Migrant Laborers in Mozambique and South Africa, c. 1860–1910*. Portsmouth NH, 1994.

Hattersley, A. *The British Settlement of Natal: A Study in Imperial Migration*. Cambridge GB, 1950.

——. *Portrait of a Colony*. Cambridge GB, 1940.

Hay, Margaret, and Marcia Wright, eds. *African Women South of the Sahara*. London, 1984.

Hemson, David. "'For Sure You Are Going to Die!' Political Participation and the Comrade Movement in Inanda, KwaZulu-Natal." *Social Dynamics* 22, no. 2 (1996): 74–104.

Herbert, R. "*Hlonipha* and the Ambiguous Woman." *Anthropos* 85, no. 4/6 (1990): 455–73.

Hobsbawm, Eric. *Primitive Rebels*. New York, 1959.

Hobsbawm, Eric, and Terrence Ranger. *The Invention of Tradition*. New York, 1983.

Holleman, J. "The Structure of the Zulu Ward." *African Studies* 14 (1986): 109–33.

Hughes, Heather. "Violence in Inanda, August 1985." *JSAS* 13, no. 3 (1987): 331–54.

Hunt, Nancy. "Introduction." Special Issue: Gendered Colonialism in African History. *Gender and History*, 8, no. 3 (1996): 323–37.

Hunter, Monica. *Reaction to Conquest*. London, 1936.

Hurwitz, N. *Agriculture in Natal, 1860–1950*. Vol. 12. Cape Town, 1957.

Iliffe, John. *Africans: The History of a Continent*. Cambridge GB, 1995.

Isaacman, Allen. "Peasants and Rural Social Protest in Africa." *African Studies Review* 33, no. 2 (1990): 1–120.

Isaacman, Allen, and Barbara Isaacman. "Resistance and Collaboration in Southern and Central Africa." *IJAHS* 10 (1977): 31–62.

Jeater, Diana. *Marriage, Perversion and Power*. Oxford, 1993.

Jeeves, A. *Migrant Labour in South Africa's Mining Economy: The Struggle for the Gold Mines' Labour Supply, 1890–1920*. Kingston OT, 1985.

Kanogo, Tabitha. *Squatters and the Roots of Mau Mau*. London, 1987.

Keegan, Timothy. *Colonial South Africa and the Origins of the Racial Order*. Charlottesville VA, 1996.

Kennedy, Peter. "Mpande and the Zulu Kingship." *JNZH* 4 (1981): 21–38.

Kentridge, Matthew. *An Unofficial War*. Cape Town, 1991.

Kirby, P. *Andrew Smith and Natal*. Cape Town, 1955.

Klein, Martin. *Peasants in Africa: Historical and Contemporary Perspectives*. Beverly Hills CA, 1980.

Konczacki, Z. *Public Finance and Economic Development of Natal, 1893–1910*. Durham NC, 1967.

Krige, Eileen. *The Social System of the Zulus*. Pietermaritzburg, 1950.

Krige, Eileen, and J. Comaroff, eds. *Essays on African Marriage in Southern Africa*. Cape Town, 1981.

Krikler, Jeremy. *Revolution from Above, Rebellion from Below*. Oxford, 1993.

Kuper, Adam. "The 'House' and Zulu Political Structure in the Nineteenth Century." *JAH* 34 (1993): 469–87.

———. "Lineage Theory: A Critical Retrospect." *Annual Review for Anthropology* 2 (1982): 71–95.

———. *South Africa and the Anthropologist*. London, 1987.

———. "Zulu Kinship Terminology over a Century." *Journal of Anthropological Research* 35, no. 3 (1979): 373–83.

Laband, John. "The Cohesion of the Zulu Polity under the Impact of the Anglo-Zulu War: A Reassessment." *JNZH* 8 (1985): 33–62.

———. "The Establishment of the Zululand Administration in 1887." *JNZH* 4 (1981): 62–73.

———. *Rope of Sand: The Rise and Fall of the Zulu Kingdom in the Nineteenth Century*. Johannesburg, 1995.

———. "The Usuthu-Mandlakazi Conflict in Zululand." *SAHJ* 30 (1994): 33–60.

Laband, John, and P. Thompson. *Kingdom and Colony at War*. Pietermaritzburg, 1990.

La Hausse, Paul. *Brewers, Beerhalls and Boycotts: A History of Liquor in South Africa*. Johannesburg, 1988.

Lamar, Howard, and Leonard Thompson, eds. *The Frontier in History: North America and Southern Africa Compared*. New Haven, 1981.

Lambert, John. *Betrayed Trust: Africans and the State in Colonial Natal*. Pietermaritzburg, 1995.

———. "Chiefship in Early Colonial Natal." *JSAS* 24, no. 2 (1995): 269–85.

Lodge, Tom. *Resistance and Ideology in Settler Societies*. Johannesburg, 1986.

Lonsdale, J., and B. Berman. "Coping with the Contradictions: The Development of the Colonial State in Kenya, 1895–1914." *JAH* 20 (1979): 487–505.

Lugg, H. C. *Historic Natal and Zululand*. Pietermaritzburg, 1948.

MacGaffey, Wyatt. "Oral Tradition in Central Africa." *IJAHS* 7 (1974): 417–26.

Mack, K., et al. "Homesteads in Two Rural Zulu Communities: An Ethno-archaeological Investigation." *Natal Museum Journal of Humanities* 3 (1991): 79–129.

Maggs, Timothy. "The Iron Age Sequence South of the Vaal and Pongola Rivers: Some Historical Implications." *JAH* 21 (1980): 1–15.

———. "Mabhija: Precolonial Industrial Development in the Tugela Basin." *Annals* 25 (1982): 123–41.

———. "Ndondondwane: A Preliminary Report on an Early Iron Age Site on the Lower Tugela River." *Annals* 26 (1984): 71–93.

Maggs, Timothy, et al. "Spatial Parameters of Late Iron Age Settlements in the Upper Thukela Valley." *Annals* 27 (1986): 455–79.

Maloba, Wunyabari. *Mau Mau and Kenya: An Analysis of a Peasant Revolt*. Bloomington IN, 1993.

Mamdani, Mahmood. *Citizen and Subject: Contemporary Africa and the Legacy of Late Colonialism*. Princeton NJ, 1996.

Mandala, Elias. *Work and Control in a Peasant Economy: A History of the Lower Tchiri Valley in Malawi, 1859–1960*. Madison WI, 1990.

Manganyi, N., and A. du Toit, eds. *Political Violence and the Struggle in South Africa*. London, 1990.

Mann, Kristen, and Richard Roberts, eds. *Law in Colonial Africa*. Portsmouth NH, 1991.

Mare, Gerhard. *Brothers Born of Warrior Blood: Politics and Ethnicity in South Africa*. Johannesburg, 1992.

Mare, Gerhard, and Hamilton, Georgina. *An Appetite for Power: Buthelezi's Inkatha and South Africa*. Johannesburg, 1987.

Marks, Shula. *The Ambiguities of Dependence in South Africa*. Johannesburg, 1986.

———. *Reluctant Rebellion: The 1906–08 Disturbances in Natal*. Oxford, 1970.

Marks, Shula, and Anthony Atmore, eds. *Economy and Society in Pre-Industrial South Africa*. London, 1980.

Marks, Shula, and Richard Rathbone, eds. *Industrialisation and Social Change in South Africa: African Class Formation, Culture and Consciousness, 1870–1930*. London, 1982.

Martin, Phyllis, and David Birmingham, eds. *History of Central Africa*. Vol. 1. London, 1983.

Mauss, M. *The Gift: Forms and Functions of Exchange in Archaic Societies*. New York, 1967.

Mayer, Phillip, ed. *Black Villagers in an Industrial Society*. Cape Town, 1980.

Mazel, A. "Mbabane Shelter and eSinhlonhlweni Shelter: The Last Two Thousand Years of Hunter-Gatherer Settlement in the Central Thukela Basin, Natal, South Africa." *Annals* 27 (1986): 389–453.

McClendon, Thomas. "A Dangerous Doctrine: Twins, Ethnography, and Inheritance in Colonial Africa." *Journal of Legal Pluralism* 39 (1997): 121–40.

———. "Tradition and Domestic Struggle in the Courtroom: Customary Law and the Control of Women in Segregation-Era Natal." *IJAHS* 28, no. 3 (1995): 527–61.

McCord, James. *My Patients Were Zulus*. London, 1958.

McKittrick, Meredith. "The Burden of the Young Men: Property and Generational Conflict in Namibia, 1880–1945." *African Economic History* 24 (1996): 115–29.

Meillassoux, Claude. *Maidens, Meal, and Money: Capitalism and the Domestic Community*. New York, 1981.

Meszaros, I., ed. *Aspects of History and Class Consciousness*. London, 1971.

Miers, Suzanne, and Igor Kopytoff, eds. *Slavery in Africa*. Madison WI, 1977.

Minaar, A., ed. *Patterns of Violence: Case Studies of Conflict in Natal*. Pretoria, 1992.

Mofolo, Thomas. *Chaka: An Historical Romance*. London, 1981.

Moller, V. *Lost Generation Found*. Durban, 1991.

Moodie, T. Dunbar. "Ethnic Violence on South African Mines." *JSAS* 18, no. 3 (1992): 584–613.

———. *Going for Gold: Men, Mines and Migration*. Berkeley CA, 1994.

Moore, Barrington. *Social Origins of Dictatorship and Democracy*. Boston, 1966.

Moore, H. L., and M. Vaughan. *Cutting Down Trees: Gender, Nutrition, and Agricultural Change in the Northern Province of Zambia, 1890–1990*. London, 1994.

Morrell, Robert, ed. *Political Economy and Identities in KwaZulu-Natal*. Durban, 1996.

———. "Youth, Masculinity and Education in Sekhukhuneland." *KLEIO* 30 (1998): 143–50.

Murray, Colin. *Families Divided: The Impact of Migrant Labour in Lesotho*. Johannesburg, 1981.

——. "Migrant Labour and Changing Family Structure in the Rural Periphery of Southern Africa." *JSAS* 21 (1980): 139–56.

Ngubane, Harriet. *Body and Mind in Zulu Medicine*. London, 1977.

Okoye, N. "Dingane: A Reappraisal." *JAH* 10, no. 2 (1969): 221–35.

Omer-Cooper, John. "Has the Mfecane a Future? A Response to the Cobbing Critique." *JSAS* 19, no. 2 (1993): 273–94.

——. *The Zulu Aftermath: A Nineteenth-Century Revolution in Bantu Africa*. London, 1966.

Ong, Walter. *Orality and Literacy*. London, 1982.

Peires, Jeff. *The Dead Will Arise*. Johannesburg, 1989.

——. *The House of Phalo*. Berkeley CA, 1981.

——. "Paradigm Deleted: The Materialist Interpretation of the Mfecane." *JSAS* 19, no. 2 (1993): 295–313.

——. "'Soft' Believers and 'Hard' Unbelievers in the Xhosa Cattle-Killing." *JAH* 27 (1986): 443–61.

——, ed. *Before and after Shaka: Papers in Nguni History*. Grahamstown, 1981.

Peters, Pauline. "Gender, Development Cycles and Historical Process: A Critique of Recent Research on Women in Botswana." *JSAS*, 10 (1983): 100–122.

Radcliffe-Brown, A., and D. Forde, eds. *African Systems of Kinship and Marriage*. New York, 1950.

Ranger, Terrence. "Growing from the Roots: Reflections on Peasant Research in Central and Southern Africa." *JSAS* 5 (1978): 99–133.

——. "The People in African Resistance: A Review." *JSAS* 4, no. 1 (1977): 125–46.

——. *Revolt in Southern Rhodesia, 1896–7: A Study in African Resistance*. London, 1967.

Reader, D. *Zulu Tribe in Transition*. Manchester GB, 1966.

Review International Commission of Jurists 45 (1990).

Rey, Pierre Phillipe. "The Lineage Mode of Production." *Critique of Anthropology* 3 (1975).

Richardson, Peter. *Chinese Mine Labour in the Transvaal*. London, 1982.

Ritter, E. *Shaka Zulu: The Rise of the Zulu Empire*. London, 1955.

Roberts, Rev. C. *The Zulu-Kafir Language*. London, 1909.

Robertson, Claire, and Iris Berger, eds. *Women and Class in Africa*. New York, 1986.

Roux, Edward. *Time Longer than Rope*. Madison WI, 1964.

Rude, George. *The Crowd in the French Revolution*. London, 1972.

——. *Ideology and Popular Protest*. London, 1980.

Sahlins, Marshall. *Stone Age Economics*. Chicago, 1972.

Samuel, R., ed. *People's History and Socialist Theory*. London, 1981.

Samuelson, L. *Zululand: Its Traditions, Legends, Customs and Folklore*. Durban, 1974.

Samuelson, R. *The King Cetywayo Zulu Dictionary*. Durban, 1923.

———. *Long, Long Ago*. Durban, 1929.

Sapire, Hilary. "Politics and Protest in Shack Settlements of the Pretoria-Witwaters-rand-Veereniging Region, South Africa, 1980–1990." *JSAS* 18, no. 3 (1992): 670–97.

Saunders, Christopher, ed. *Black Leaders in Southern African History*. London, 1979.

Scheper-Hughes, Nancy. *Death without Weeping: The Violence of Everyday Life in Brazil*. Berkeley CA, 1992.

Schmidt, Elizabeth. *Peasant, Traders, and Wives: Shona Women in the History of Zimbabwe, 1870–1939*. Portsmouth NH, 1992.

Scott, James. *The Moral Economy of the Peasant*. New Haven CT, 1976.

———. *Weapons of the Weak*. New Haven CT, 1985.

Seddon, D., ed. *Relations of Production: Marxist Approaches to Economic Anthropology*. London, 1978.

Seekings, Jeremy. *Heroes or Villians? Youth Politics in the 1980s*. Johannesburg, 1993.

Simons, H. *African Women: Their Legal Status in South Africa*. London, 1968.

Sitas, Ari. "The Making of the 'Comrades' Movement in Natal, 1985–91." *JSAS* 18, no. 3 (1992): 629–41.

Skocpol, Theda. *States and Revolutions*. Cambridge GB, 1981.

———. "What Makes Peasants Revolutionary." *Comparative Politics* 14 (1982): 315–75.

Slater, Henry. "Land, Labour and Capital in Natal: The Natal Land and Colonisation Company, 1860–1948." *JAH* 16 (1975): 257–83.

Smith, Laura. *Africa: A Course of Twelve Lessons*. Boston, 1901.

Smith, Father Tim. "They Have Killed My Children: One Community in Conflict, 1983–1990." Pietermaritzburg: PACSA, 1990.

South African Deputation Papers. Durban, 1904.

Spencer, Paul, ed. *Anthropology and the Riddle of the Sphinx*. London, 1990.

Spiegel, A., and P. McAllister, eds. *Tradition and Transition in Southern Africa*. Johannesburg, 1991.

Stedman, S., ed. *South Africa: The Political Economy of Transformation*. Boulder CO, 1994.

Stichter, Sharon, and Jean Parpart, eds. *Patriarchy and Class: African Women in the Home and the Workforce*. Boulder CO, 1988.

Straker, G., et al., eds. *Faces in the Revolution*. Cape Town, 1992.

Stuart, James. *A History of the Zulu Rebellion*. New York, 1913.

Sullivan, J. *The Native Policy of Sir Theophilus Shepstone*. Johannesburg, 1928.

Switzer, Les. *Power and Resistance in an African Society: The Ciskei Xhosa and the Making of South Africa*. Madison WI, 1993.

Taylor, Rev. James. *The American Board Mission in South Africa: A Sketch of Seventy-five Years*. Durban, 1911.

Theal, G., ed. *Records of South-Eastern Africa*. Cape Town, 1964.

Thomas, Lynn. "'Ngaitana (I Will Circumcise Myself)': The Gender and Generational Politics on the 1956 Ban on Clitoridectomy in Meru, Kenya." *Gender and History* 8, no. 3 (1996): 338–63.

Thompson, Leonard. *A History of South Africa*. New Haven CT, 1990.

——. *The Unification of South Africa, 1902–1910*. Oxford, 1960.

——, ed. *African Societies in Southern Africa*. London, 1969.

Throup, David. "The Origins of Mau Mau." *African Affairs* 84, no. 336 (1985): 399–434.

Tinker, Hugh. *A New System of Slavery: The Export of Indian Labour Overseas, 1830–1920*. Oxford, 1974.

Vail, Leroy, and Landeg White, eds. *Power and Praise Poem: Southern African Voices in History*. Charlottesville VA, 1991.

Van Onselen, Charles. "Reactions to Rinderpest in Southern Africa, 1896–97." *JSAS* 8, no. 3 (1972): 473–88.

——. "The Reconstruction of a Rural Life from Oral Testimony: Critical Notes on the Methodology in the Study of a Black South African Sharecropper." *Journal of Peasant Studies* 20, no. 3 (1993): 494–514.

——. *The Seed Is Mine: The Life of Kas Maine, a South African Sharecropper, 1894–1985*. New York, 1996.

——. *Studies in the Social and Economic History of the Witwatersrand, 1886–1914: New Babylon, New Nineveh*. 2 vols. Johannesburg, 1982.

Vansina, Jan. "Is Elegance Proof?" *History in Africa* 10 (1983): 307–48.

——. *Oral Tradition: A Study in Historical Methodology*. London, 1965.

——. *Oral Tradition as History*. Madison WI, 1985.

Vaughan, M. "Which Family? Problems in the Reconstruction of the History of the Family as an Economic and Cultural Unit." *JAH* 24, no. 2 (1983): 275–83.

Vilakazi, Absolom. *Zulu Transformations: A Study of the Dynamics of Social Change*. Pietermaritzburg, 1962.

Walker, Cherryl. *Women and Resistance in South Africa*. London, 1982.

——, ed. *Women and Gender in Southern Africa to 1945*. Cape Town, 1990.

Walter, E. *Terror and Resistance: A Study of Political Violence, with Case Studies of Some Primitive African Communities*. New York, 1969.

Warwick, Peter. *Black People and the South African War, 1899–1902*. Cambridge GB, 1983.

Webb, Colin de B. *A Guide to the Official Records of the Colony of Natal*. Pietermaritzburg, 1965.

Webb, Colin de B., and John Wright, eds. *The James Stuart Archive of Recorded Oral Evidence Relating to the History of the Zulu and Neighbouring Peoples*. 4 vols. Pietermaritzburg, 1976, 1979, 1982, 1986.

———, eds. *A Zulu King Speaks: Statements Made by Cetshwayo kaMpande on the History and Customs of His People*. Pietermaritzburg, 1978.

Webb, Virginia. "Fact and Fiction: Nineteenth Century Photographs of the Zulu." *African Arts* 25, no. 1 (1992).

Welsh, David. *The Roots of Segregation: Native Policy in Colonial Natal, 1845–1910*. Cape Town, 1971.

Werbner, Richard. *Tears of the Dead: The Social Biography of an African Family*. Edinburgh, 1991.

White, Landeg. *Magomero: Portrait of an African Village*. New York, 1987.

White, Luise. "Between Gluckman and Foucault: Historicizing Rumor and Gossip." *Social Dynamics* 20, no. 1 (1994): 75–92.

———. *The Comforts of Home: Prostitution in Colonial Nairobi*. Chicago, 1990.

———. "Separating the Men from the Boys: Constructions of Sexuality, Gender, and Terrorism in Central Kenya, 1939–1959." *IJAHS* 23, no. 1 (1990): 1–25.

Wilson, Monica. *For Men and Elders: Change in the Relations of Generations and of Men and Women among the Nyakyusa-Ngonde People*. New York, 1977.

Wilson, Monica, and Leonard Thompson, eds. *The Oxford History of South Africa: South Africa to 1870*. Vol. 1. New York, 1969.

Wolf, Eric. *Peasant Wars of the Twentieth Century*. New York, 1969.

Worger, William. "Clothing Dry Bones: The Myth of Shaka in the Late Eighteenth and Early Nineteenth Centuries." *Journal of African Studies* 6, 3 (1979): 144–58.

———. *South Africa's City of Diamonds: Mine Workers and Monopoly Capitalism in Kimberley, 1867–1895*. New Haven CT, 1987.

Wright, John. "A. T. Bryant and 'The Wars of Shaka.'" *History in Africa* 18 (1991): 409–25.

———. *Bushman Raiders of the Drakensberg, 1840–1870*. Pietermaritzburg, 1971.

———. "Political Mythology and the Making of Natal's Mfecane." *Canadian Journal of African Studies* 23, no. 2 (1989): 272–91.

———. "Pre-Shakan Age-Group Formation among the Northern Nguni." *Natalia* 8 (1978): 22–30.

Wright, John, and Carolyn Hamilton. "The Making of the *Amalala*: Ethnicity, Ideology and Relations of Subordination in a Precolonial Context." *SAHJ* 22 (1990): 3–23.

Wright, John, and Andrew Manson. *The Hlubi Chiefdom in Zululand-Natal: A History*. Ladysmith SA, 1983.

Unpublished Dissertations, Theses, and Papers

Unless otherwise noted, sources are Ph.D. dissertations.

Atkins, Keletso. "The Cultural Origins of an African Work Ethic and Practices: Natal, South Africa, 1843–1875." University of Wisconsin–Madison, 1986.

Cope, Nicholas. "The Zulu Royal Family under the South African Government, 1910–1933: Solomon KaDinuzulu, Inkatha and Zulu Nationalism." University of Natal, Durban, 1985.

Cubbin, A. "Origins of the British Settlement at Port Natal, May 1824–July 1842." University of the Orange Free State, 1983.

Edwards, Iain. "'Mkhumbane Our Home': African Shanty Town Society in Cato Manor Farm, 1946–60." University of Natal, Durban, 1989.

Golan, Daphna. "Construction and Reconstruction of Zulu History." Hebrew University, 1988.

Guy, Jeff. "An Accommodation of Patriarchs: Theophilus Shepstone and the Foundations of the System of Native Administration in Natal." Paper, International Colloquium on Masculinities, University of Natal, Durban, 1997.

Hamilton, Carolyn. "James Stuart and 'the Establishment of a Living Source of Tradition.'" Paper, Institute for Advanced Social Research, University of Witwatersrand, August 1994.

——. "Ideology, Oral Tradition and the Struggle for Power in the Early Zulu Kingdom." M.A., University of Witwatersrand, 1985.

Hedges, David. "Trade and Politics in Southern Mozambique and Zululand, c. 1750–1830." University of London, 1978.

Hemson, David. "Class Consciousness and Migrant Workers: Dock Workers of Durban." University of Warwick, 1979.

Kennedy, C. "Art, Architecture and Material Culture of the Zulu Kingdom." University of California, Los Angeles, 1993.

Kennedy, Peter. "The Fatal Diplomacy: Sir Theophilus Shepstone and the Zulu Kings, 1839–1879." University of California, Los Angeles, 1976.

Klopper, Sandra. "The Art of Zulu-Speakers in Northern Natal-Zululand: An Investigation of the History of Beadwork, Carving and Dress from Shaka to Inkatha." University of Witwatersrand, 1992.

Laband, John. "Dick Addison: The Role of a British Official during the Disturbances in the Ndwandwe District in Zululand, 1887–1889." M.A., University of Natal, 1980.

La Hausse, Paul. "The Struggle for the City: Alcohol, the Ematsheni and Popular Culture in Durban, 1902–1936." M.A., University of Cape Town, 1984.

Lambert, John. "Africans in Natal, 1880–1899: Continuity, Change and Crisis in Rural Society." University of South Africa, 1986.

Mael, R. "The Problem of Political Integration in the Zulu Empire." University of California, Los Angeles, 1974.

McClendon, Thomas. "Genders and Generations Apart: Labor Tenants, Law, and Domestic Struggle in Natal, South Africa, 1918–44." Stanford University, 1995.

Radebe, Jeff. "A Frank and Critical Look at the Situation in Natal." Paper, ANC Conference, 1990.

Slater, Henry. "Transitions in the Political Economy of South-east Africa before 1840." University of Sussex, 1976.

Smith, Alan. "The Struggle for Control of Southern Mozambique, 1720–1835." University of California, Los Angeles, 1970.

Wright, John. "The Dynamics of Power and Conflict in the Thukela-Mzimkhulu Region in the Late 18th and Early 19th Centuries: A Critical Reconstruction." University of Witwatersrand, 1989.

Index

Reconsiderations in Southern African History